CLASSIC H

CLASSIC HURLING MATCHES 1956–75

NORMAN FREEMAN

Gill & Macmillan

Published in Ireland by
Gill & Macmillan Ltd
Goldenbridge
Dublin 8
with associated companies throughout the world
© Norman Freeman 1993
0 7171 2030 9
Index compiled by Helen Litton
Print origination by Seton Music Graphics Ltd, Bantry, Co. Cork
Printed by ColourBooks Ltd, Dublin

A catalogue record is available for this book from the British Library.

1   3   5   4   2

To my wife Bernie,
for all her help and support

CONTENTS

	Acknowledgments	
1956	Wexford v Cork	1
1959	Waterford v Kilkenny	18
1961	Tipperary v Dublin	37
1962	Tipperary v Wexford	53
1966	Cork v Kilkenny	69
1968	Wexford v Tipperary	90
1972	Kilkenny v Cork	106
1971–73	Limerick v Tipperary Saga	126
1974	Kilkenny v Wexford	151
1975	Galway v Cork	172
	Index	192

ACKNOWLEDGMENTS

One of the great pleasures of writing these books has lain in meeting and talking to some of the men who played in these great games of hurling. They gave me the benefit of their time, their recollections, their insights into particular games and into hurling. The hurling community sees it not just as a sport but as an expression of skill, courage and endurance, something that strikes joyfully resounding chords deep within the human personality.

My thanks to those great exponents of the game. Invariably they were generous to their former opponents and modest about their own attributes — the characteristic of true sportsmen. They include John Henderson and Eddie Keher of Kilkenny and Diarmuid Healy who straddles both Kilkenny and Offaly; Damien Martin of Offaly; Jimmy Barry Murphy, Gerald Mc Carthy and Willie John Daly of Cork; Donie Nealon, Michael Keating and Nicholas English of Tipperary; Jimmy Gray and Larry Shannon of Dublin; Seumas Power of Waterford; Jimmy Smyth of Clare; Eamonn Cregan of Limerick; Ciaran Barr of Antrim; Joe Mc Donagh and Peter Finnerty of Galway; and Ned Wheeler, Billy Rackard, Ned Buggy and Phil Wilson of Wexford.

With so much detail in terms of names and events to be included and checked for accuracy, I was fortunate to get the help of Tom Ryall of Kilkenny, Tommy Barrett of Tipperary, Gerry Holohan of Cork, Seamus Grant and his colleagues in Waterford, Brendan Furlong of Wexford, John Murphy of Limerick and Michael Connolly of Offaly. Some fine journalists gave me sound advice and assistance and these included Seamus Hayes of the *Clare Champion*, Cormac Liddy of the *Limerick Leader*, Michael Dundon of the *Tipperary Star*, John Knox of Kilkenny and Sean Og O Ceallachain of RTE.

I owe a special word of thanks to the doyen of hurling writers, Paddy Downey of the *Irish Times*, for the benefit of his advice in identifying some of the outstanding games described in these volumes.

The fountainhead of hurling writing is Raymond Smith and during the course of work I turned to his many fine books about hurling, particularly the painstaking record book compiled by himself and Donal Keenan of the *Irish Independent*.

There were other people who gave me help and encouragement and these include Pat Quigley, former PRO at Croke Park and his successor Danny Lynch as well as Fionnbarr Breathnach of Cork and Dalkey and, not least, my colleague Pat Heneghan.

I want to thank Fergal Tobin of Gill & Macmillan for his guidance and support, and his able assistants, Jillian Tynan and her successor, Clare Connolly, who did so much research work for these books. A special word of thanks has to go to Jonathan Williams, literary agent exemplaire, for his role in the commissioning and publication of these volumes.

Jim Connolly, the official GAA photographer, provided many of the photos for these books and was very helpful generally.

I willingly share any credit these books may engender with those mentioned above. At the same time I must take full responsibility for the content and the details.

My attitude to the players mentioned in these books is essentially one of gratitude for the great entertainment they gave to hurling lovers. They, and the great games of which they were part, provided marvellous material for a writer. I hope I have done them justice.

Cover Photograph

Unfortunately, no colour photographs are available for the period covered by this book. The cover photograph features Tony Doran of Wexford, one of the stars of the great Leinster final of 1974, still hurling against Kilkenny nearly ten years later.

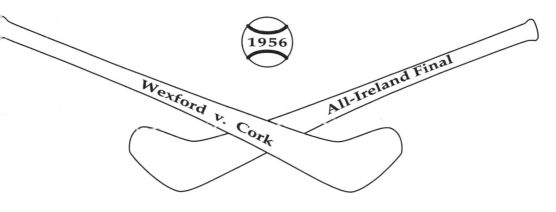

1956
Wexford v. Cork
All-Ireland Final

REMATCH OF THE TITANS

Three minutes to go. The torrential roar of 83,000 spectators, frenzied with excitement, could be heard two miles away across the city roof-tops on a still afternoon. A Cork team which had some of the most skilful hurlers ever to play the game were two points down to the reigning All-Ireland champions, Wexford, whose appearance in this final gave it a special glamour and sense of joy.

Then the fiercest competitor and the most accomplished player on the field, the stocky, balding Christy Ring raced over to the right wing. His tall limpet-like marker, who wore a tweed cap, Bobby Rackard, was at his elbow. But the Corkman, face shiny with perspiration, eluded him and gathered the ball to a huge explosion of cheering from the Cork supporters. Holding the ball on his stick, he began a jinking sprint towards the Wexford goal.

Alarm on the faces of the Wexford backs. They knew how dangerous this hurling firebrand was, how powerfully he could hit the ball. They closed on him but he unleashed a missile-like shot from 25 yards out. It was no more than a brief blur to most spectators. Then, a few inches below the wooden crossbar, it met the grasping left hand of the smallest man on the pitch, Artie Foley. Few goalkeepers ever made this kind of save from Ring.

Protected by his full-back, the ever reliable Nick O'Donnell, Foley cleared the ball away. Ring, the unrelenting attacker, always followed the ball in, hoping for a rebound or fumbled ball. He did so this time. To the amazement of Foley and O'Donnell, and perhaps to himself, this man, who hated to be thwarted, ran in and briefly shook the goalkeeper's hand.

Perhaps it was that Ring, who had developed an acute sense of the ebb and flow of games over the years, sensed now that the tide had finally gone out for the battling Cork side. He was right. The ball came in again and another dangerous Cork forward, Paddy Barry, had another shot at goal. But Foley, in unbeatable mood, saved it and sent it down the field.

The Wexford captain, Jim English, playing in the half back line, sent a long ball up into the right corner of the Wexford attack. There one of the corner forwards, Tom Ryan, got the ball, escaped the attentions of the lanky Vin Twomey and came tearing across towards the Cork goalmouth.

Clinching Goal

In the scramble, the redoubtable Nick Rackard was left unmarked. The big full forward, who had had a frustrating hour under the elbow to elbow marking of the Cork full back, John Lyons, gladly accepted the pass from Ryan. He put his fourteen stone into the swing and the ball stretched the netting at the back of the goal. The explosion of sound from the massed audience reverberated round the stadium.

Shortly afterwards, the other Wexford corner forward, Tom Dixon, who had got little change out of Jimmy Brohan during most of the game, flicked the ball over the bar to put the seal on a memorable 6-point victory and bring the curtain down on one of the greatest finals in the annals of the game.

Few other All-Irelands had been looked forward to so much by supporters of both sides and hurling lovers everywhere. It was a rematch between virtually the same two teams which had met two years before and had provided an enthralling battle before an even bigger crowd.

In 1954 Wexford had also been two points up with four minutes to play. They had played marvellously well against the vastly experienced Cork side, All-Ireland champions for the previous two years. It seemed like the big men in purple and gold, the most popular team ever to play in a final, were about to take their first title since 1910, despite the handicap of having lost their full back, Nick O'Donnell. Then the ball came into the Wexford goal area. It broke behind Ring, the Cork captain, and two of the Wexford backs and was going out over the end line when Johnny Clifford of Cork ran to it. With a left-handed swing he whipped the ball off the grass and it flew past Foley, who had partly advanced, and across and into the goal from the narrowest of angles.

This score clinched the game for Cork. It left Wexford feeling that they had the game for the taking but had let it slip. They wished for nothing more than to meet the men in the red jerseys in another final. They wanted to win an All-Ireland to crown all the efforts the team had made for the previous five years.

Emergence of Wexford

At the end of the 1940s the Wexford side had emerged fresh onto a hurling scene gone stale from the continuous dominance of the three giants of the game — Tipperary, Cork and Kilkenny. These three were sharing most of the All-Irelands between them and indulging in an incestuous rivalry to see who could win the most titles. Wexford was one of the seven or eight counties who challenged the dominant ones year after year but were inevitably beaten, often badly.

Then a team of great power began to make their presence felt. They were led and inspired by a player whose outstanding qualities in the '40s had led to his being picked for the Leinster side in the Railway Cup competition, Nick Rackard. This man was one of the strongest and most determined men ever to play the game. Under his leadership and that of players like Martin Byrne and Wilkie Thorpe they began to get the better of the craft and artistry of the game-wise Kilkenny teams in league and challenge matches and then in the championship.

Many of the Wexford side were six foot and over. They were broad shouldered, barrel-chested warriors, six or seven near the 14 stone in weight. They went against the conventional wisdom which said that the way to win games was not to stop the ball but pull on it first time and send it on its way. These men in gold and purple were expert at catching the ball in the air or lifting it off the sod. They were able to do this because they were big enough and strong enough to hold off their opponents. And when they had grabbed the ball amid flailing hurleys they had the shoulder-power to burst past their adversaries and send the ball soaring away in lengthy pucks.

'And they worked on their game. They were improving all the time. That team was getting better every time we played them', says Willie John Daly, who played centre half back for Cork in the 1956 final.

Genial Sportsmen

But what endeared this team to hurling followers and indeed to their opponents was their good-natured sporting attitude. They knew how to use their weight but they did so fairly and without enmity. They often laughed and joked on the field, even in the heat of intense battle. They seemed to play primarily because they loved the sport.

However, their popularity and fair-play approach did not yield results. They were beaten by Tipperary in their first final in 1951, when they were easily the equal of their rivals but were beaten by lack of experience, missed chances and the fact that the selectors could not make up their minds about a regular goalkeeper.

Unlike the big counties, Wexford did not have a heritage of team management or of team training because they were so new to the All-Ireland scene.

The Great 1954 Final

'After the defeat of 1951 it took us an awful lot of effort and training to try to keep going, determined and all as we were to win an All-Ireland.

Those were hard years', recalls Ned Wheeler, the big Wexford midfielder who was born in Rathdowney in Co. Laois.

The team, driven by the need to vindicate themselves, were back again in 1954. They faced the All-Ireland champions Cork who were now going for their third title in a row. This was one of the most powerful Cork teams ever to emerge from that rich hinterland of hurling talent. From 1949 on they had plunged into enthralling and legendary battles for hurling supremacy with a great Tipperary side. They were beaten narrowly in '49, '50, and '51 by a team that went on to win the All-Ireland. It was Cork who hurled their way ahead in '52, '53 and '54, overcoming their tough rivals in knuckle-scarring encounters at Limerick.

The dominant figure was Ring, a man who had dedicated his whole being to hurling. He was obsessive about achieving perfection in all the skills of the game, and practised endlessly. There were stories of Christmas days when other players were at home in the warmth of family while Ring was out in the field in the wan light of the winter evening, hitting the ball into the air and meeting it coming down, sending it back up again and again, a lone figure in a Munster twilight.

So great was the interest in the meeting of these contrasting sides, the newcomers versus the established, the clash of personalities and styles, that the biggest crowd ever seen at an All-Ireland — 84,000 — packed into Croke Park for the 1954 game.

It was a pulsating contest. Both sides threw everything they had into the game from the start. There was nothing between them. They matched one another point for point. It was a game full of thrilling incidents and marvellous displays of stickwork, courage and endurance.

It was level pegging most of the time. Then, midway into the second half came a pivotal incident. Ring came charging in towards the Wexford square, where the big full back, Nick O'Donnell, moved out to block him. There was a collision of muscle and bone and O'Donnell was carried off with a broken collarbone. He had been the sheet-anchor of the defence and it was a serious blow for Wexford.

Bobby Rackard, who had been playing a storming game at centre back, moved into O'Donnell's berth. There he gave one of the most memorable exhibitions of catching the high balls as they came in and clearing them downfield. He saved the Wexford goal time and again to the thunderous applause of the attendance. But the rearranged Wexford defence was less effective and near the end of the game Cork found a gap and Johnny Clifford scored that narrow angle goal just on the end line.

It was a galling experiece for the Slaneysiders. But this indomitable team was back the following year to beat a very good Limerick team in the semi-final and then went on to win the county's first senior championship in 45 years, and second in all, by beating Galway.

The Westerners were not the power that they had been earlier in the decade or were to become some twenty years later. So when Wexford beat them fairly comfortably, after a very competitive first half, their satisfaction was diminished by a feeling that they would have to beat one of the Munster giants, Cork or Tipperary, before they could count themselves real All-Ireland champions.

Great Expectations

Now, in the August days of 1956, with Cork having beaten a good Limerick side in the Munster final at Thurles, and Wexford having taken care of Kilkenny and then Galway, a great sense of anticipation began to buzz in all the hurling counties and amongst hurling lovers everywhere.

'This is one match I'm going to see at all costs', was the oft-repeated phrase as hurling followers besieged county chairmen and Croke Park for tickets weeks in advance and began to save the fare to Dublin.

The teams began their training. They began to work out their strategies to make the most of their advantages, to seek out weak points in the other side and lay plans to exploit them. Each evening crowds of spectators turned up to watch the teams and substitutes being put through their paces.

Sean Browne, the chairman of the Wexford county board and Kevin Sheehan were in charge at Enniscorthy. At the old Athletic Grounds in Cork, the veteran trainer and manager of so many teams, Jim 'Tough' Barry, watched his charges through narrow, thoughtful eyes.

When the teams were selected and the eager followers could see who was going to mark who, see which player was being called upon to play a vital role, there were endless discussions and arguments.

'Bobby Rackard won't show Ring much of the ball.'

'That's what happened against Limerick — Ring was marked out of it except for a few minutes near the end, when Limerick were coasting to a win. Then he escaped his marker for a few minutes and got three goals and put Cork into the All-Ireland.'

Ring and Rackard

Ring was at left corner forward, a wily campaigner who changed his tactics with every ball that came his way. He was capable of accurate first-time pulling on the ground or in the air, left or right, scoring with stick or with palm, dodging and darting. He was low-slung, had heavy thighs, and was hard to knock off the ball. He had the thickest, strongest wrists that most people had ever seen. But they were supple and he used his heavy hurley like a magic wand to control the ball. Nobody who had ever played the game had the same range of diligently honed skills.

But there was more to Ring than skill. On the field of play he radiated a startling competitive fervour. His blue eyes had a feverish lustre. He was so utterly determined to win the ball that he risked injury without hesitation. His hands and face were wound-scarred. His front teeth had long since been knocked out in ferocious and sometimes dangerous clashes; when he took out his false teeth his mouth became a grim, sunken slot, tight with resolution. His presence had an electrifying effect on his team and on all the spectators. People came from near and far to see this phenomenon, a man unlike the rest of men. At 36 he was the oldest man on the field. He had won his first All-Ireland medal in 1941 and had gone on to collect another seven.

Bobby Rackard, who would be marking him, was a skilful, intelligent hurler who would give careful thought as to how the difficult task could be best accomplished. He and his brothers Nick and Billy, playing at full forward and centre back respectively, came from farming country under the slopes of the Blackstairs mountains. They were horsemen as well as hurlers, hunting on big animals, galloping across fields at full tilt, clearing high ditches and dusting themselves off with a laugh and a quip whenever they came a cropper. Sportsmanship, giving and taking knocks without rancour was an endearing trait in these men from Rathnure as it was for the Wexford team as a whole.

Wexford Leader

Nick, the eldest, was the veteran of the side and a father figure of the team. Weighing 14 stones and strong as a bull, his shoulder power was awesome when he made a burst towards the goal. He was the most feared and effective full forward in the game. He had skill too, developed over the years, was reliable with frees and had a lethal shot when he got the chance. He led the attack and he led the team too.

'He was 35 at the time and he was a father figure to us all. He was full of encouragement to less experienced or confident players', recalls Ned Wheeler.

The crowd loved this genial sportsman, sharpshooter and battering ram combined.

But nobody who knew the state of play imagined that the Cork full back, John Lyons of Glen Rovers, was going to be in any way overawed by Rackard. Lyons was almost as weighty; a calm, stocky man who went about his task without much ado. Lyons did not intend to let his big blond opponent go charging in on the goalkeeper, a ploy allowed in those days. They had met before, shouldering and jostling, each trying to outwit and out-muscle the other in front of goal.

Opponents

The third and youngest of the Rackard brothers, the red haired Billy, had become one of the outstanding centre backs since he had moved into that position. He had worked at catching the ball, protecting his hand with the hurley as he did so. His clearances were prodigious. But he would be marking one of the hardest-working centre forwards, the tough Josie Hartnett. This man from the Glen Rovers club had a bustling, energetic style. He sprayed the ball to colleagues unselfishly, carried it in when he could. He had a stout shoulder which he used to effect; he was able to take a lot of physical bumping and boring. The Cork followers loved this unassuming, workhorse who gave his all in every game, who never minded being overshadowed by players like Ring or Paddy Barry, the other most dangerous of the Cork forwards.

Barry, whose stickwork and accuracy had produced many memorable goals and points, was going to be marked by the Wexford captain, Jim English, now one of the most effective right half backs in the game.

All of the other Cork forwards were accomplished players from a county with the greatest reservoir of talent. Terry Kelly would be battling it out with the acknowledged prince of full backs, Nick O'Donnell, a native of Kilkenny now playing with St Aidan's, the Enniscorthy club. Some commentators wondered if the youngest player on the Wexford side, 23-year-old Mick Morrissey, would be able to hold the fair-haired Christy O'Shea, who had given good displays for club and county over the previous year. In front of them Jim Morrissey and Mick O'Regan would be fighting for supremacy. Morrissey was one of the key figures on the team, had been an outstanding midfield player and much was expected of him.

Most commentators inclined to the forecast that Wexford's Seamus Hearne and Ned Wheeler would get the upper hand of Pat Dowling and Eamon Goulding. But both Cork players were vigorous men who had played well in recent games. At centrefield, as elsewhere on the field, there was going to be no easy possession, no unhurried strokes.

When followers and the newspaper commentators got round to summing up the Cork half back line and the Wexford half forwards whom they were going to have to contain, two facets were remarked upon. First of all they wondered if Cork was wise in asking a young player like Paddy Philpott to try to mark the wily, battle hardened 30-year-old Padge Kehoe, a star of the Wexford side since it came into prominence eight years before.

The other subject of discussion was whether the tall farmer from Rathnure, Martin Codd, would make any impression on one of the foremost of the Cork hurlers, Willie John Daly. The Carrigtwohill man was so skilled and adept a hurler that Cork had asked him to man the centre half back berth, even though he had gained fame as a steely, hard-driving wing forward.

'Codd is a soft kind of a player — you need to match steel with steel when you are on Willie John', said one of the commentators.

Another player from Carrigtwohill, who like Daly had tempered his skills in the great battles with Tipperary since 1949, Matt Fouhy was marking the fast, ball-juggling Tim Flood on Wexford's left wing.

Either side of the 35-year-old Rackard in the Wexford full forward line were Tom Ryan and Tom Dixon. Both could expect to get little leeway from two of the most renowned corner backs playing at that time, Tony O'Shaughnessy, who was captaining Cork, and the highly reliable Blackrock player, Jimmy Brohan.

The Cork goalkeeper, Mick Cashman, also came from the Blackrock club. He did not like playing in goal but he had emerged as an utterly reliable minder of the net. His opposite number, Artie Foley, had established himself as the first choice goalkeeper after several years in and out of favour and had minded a good net, especially during the Leinster final against Kilkenny.

Both sides had outstanding sets of substitutes, men of experience who had played in crucial matches and had trained just as hard as the fifteen taking the field. Cork had Vincent Twomey, Jackie Daly, Pat Healy, Gerry Murphy, Willie Walsh.

In the Wexford substitutes were two players, now veterans, Mick Hanlon and Paddy Kehoe who had helped bring the county to the fore. The other subs were Ted Bolger, Pat Nolan, Ted Morrissey and Oliver Gough.

Polio Scare

All was ready for the big game. But there was an unexpected delay. There was a polio scare in Cork and the authorities felt that until they could be sure it was fully under control it would be taking risks to allow a vast crowd to assemble in one place. This All-Ireland would not be played until 23 September. On the Saturday and Sunday morning tens of thousands of fans streamed into the city along the narrow roadway and along railway lines on special trains. Every means of travel was used — vans and lorries and even tractors. In Wexford town two funerals had to be postponed until the Monday as the hearses were being used to take supporters to the capital city.

In that era there was standing room beneath the Cusack stand, as well as the Canal and Railway ends. For most spectators it was a matter of getting to Croke Park early, queuing patiently and getting as good a vantage point as possible — and holding on to it at all costs as the incoming crowd packed tighter and tighter together.

The Game Under Way

The teams took the field to a tumultuous roar on a calm, sunny interval in a period of unsettled weather. Many people were aware that these were two of the best teams ever to contest a final and that they would both fight it out until the final whistle of the referee, Tom O'Sullivan, an army sergeant from Limerick.

There had been some rain on Saturday and the ground was slightly soft and damp. These were ideal conditions for the Wexford style of lifting the ball at every opportunity. It put Cork at some disadvantage in that most of the players favoured whipping the ball fast along the ground.

The teams as they lined out were:

CORK

Mick Cashman
(Blackrock)

Jimmy Brohan
(Blackrock)

John Lyons
(Glen Rovers)

Tony O'Shaughnessy, capt
(St Finbarr's)

Matt Fouhy
(Carrigtwohill)

Willie John Daly
(Carrigtwohill)

Paddy Philpott
(Blackrock)

Eamonn Goulding
(Glen Rovers)

Pat Dowling
(Castlemartyr)

Mick O'Regan
(Doneraile)

Josie Hartnett
(Glen Rovers)

Paddy Barry
(Sarsfields)

Christy O'Shea
(St Vincent's)

Terry Kelly
(Tracton)

Christy Ring
(Glen Rovers)

Substitutes: Vincie Twomey (Glen Rovers); Gerry Murphy (Midleton); Willie Walsh (St Finbarr's); Pat Healy (Glen Rovers); Jackie Daly (Glen Rovers). *Trainer*: Jim Barry. *Selectors/mentors:* Jack Barrett (Kinsale); Andy Scannell (Fermoy); Dinny Barry Murphy (St Finbarr's/Cloughduv); Paddy 'Fox' Collins (Glen Rovers); Sean Og Murphy (Blackrock) who died in July of that year. *First aid*: Sergeant Denis Healy; Jimmy Buckley.

WEXFORD

Artie Foley
(St Aidan's, Enniscorthy)

Bobby Rackard
(Rathnure)

Nick O'Donnell
(St Aidans)

Mick Morrissey
(New Ross)

Jim English, capt
(Rathnure)

Billy Rackard
(Rathnure)

Jim Morrissey
(Camross)

Seamus Hearne
(Blackrock, Cork)

Ned Wheeler
(St Martin's)

Padge Kehoe
(St Aidan's)

Martin Codd
(Rathnure)

Tim Flood
(Cloughbawn)

Tom Ryan
(St Aidan's)

Nick Rackard
(Rathnure)

Tom Dixon
(St Aidan's)

Substitutes: Mick Hanlon (Horeswood); Ted Morrissey (St Aidan's); Paddy Kehoe (Cushinstown); Ted Bolger (St Aidan's); Pat Nolan (Oylegate); Oliver Gough (St Aidan's). *Trainer*: Kevin Sheehan. *Manager*: Sean Browne. *Team doctor*: Dr Pat Daly. *Masseur*: Billy Esmonde.

The referee was Tom O'Sullivan of Limerick.

Cork won the toss and Tony O'Shaughnessy elected to play against the slight breeze, into the Railway end goal. The Artane Boys band and a pipe band paraded the teams about the field. Years later Ned Wheeler recalled the feeling of being totally enclosed by the immense walls of faces, the noise of over 80,000 thousand voices so great that it was impossible to hear an opponent coming up from behind or calls between the players, let alone shouted instructions from the sideline.

Michael O'Hehir, in the Radio Eireann radio commentary box, described the scene to the thousands listening at home. This game was to be rebroadcast through the powerful short wave station at Brazzaville, in the then French Congo. It was heard by missionaries in Nigeria and Tanganyika, by men on tea plantations in Travancore, by exiles and people of Irish ancestry in Buenos Aires and Rio Grande do Sul and on board at least one passenger ship, bound for Mombasa, Dar es Salaam and Zanzibar from Bombay.

There was a great explosion of sound at the end of the national anthem. Then the game everybody had been waiting for got under way with the static of excitement crackling and rippling in the air.

The patron of the GAA, Archbishop Jeremiah Kinane, who came from Upperchurch in Co. Tipperary and had been a hurler in his seminary days, threw in the ball and the game was on.

Right from the start the play swept back and forward from one end of the field to the other. Billy Rackard fielded the ball and sent Wexford on the attack, but his opposite number, Willie John Daly, a dark frown of concentration on his face, sent it back. Again Rackard caught the high dropping ball under great bustling by Josie Hartnett and sent a long clearance into the Cork half. Martin Codd tipped it on to the quick-running Tim Flood who flicked it over the bar for the first score of the game after 30 seconds play. The Wexford flags waved exultantly all round the stadium.

Wexford Goal

After the puck out there were tremendous clashes at midfield where the rivals were trying to get the measure of one another. Both sides went on the attack but so fast was the play and so determined the marking that players had to get rid of the ball quickly before they were bottled up. Then Seamus Hearne, winning the first of many balls at midfield, sent it in to Codd, whose height put Willie John Daly at a disadvantage in the aerial duel. The big man lost but retrieved the ball and sent it across to where he saw Padge Kehoe racing along the right wing. From 30 yards out the powerful Enniscorthy player sent a piledriver through a ruck of players and into the net. Only three minutes had elapsed. On the radio the roar of the crowd drowned out the high-pitched voice of Micheal O'Hehir.

'Philpott — will you mark your man, for God's sake', roared an irate Cork supporter.

There was no question that any player could completely subdue a player of the calibre of Padge Kehoe but the fair-haired Blackrock player was to give an exhibition of hurling that day. He covered acres of ground, went to the help of Daly, raced into midfield. He was everywhere. But what delighted the crowd was the cool and stylish way he struck the ball whenever it came his way. He and his colleague behind him, Tony O'Shaughnessy were to take the brunt of the thrusting Wexford attack. Without the ability of both these players Wexford might have put the match out of sight in the first half.

But in the Cork attack a player of Paddy Barry's experience was not going to be marked out of any game, not even by Jim English. He was adept at flicking the ball out to better placed opponents. He raced into open spaces, waiting for a chance to strike. He sent a pinpoint ball to Mick O'Regan who struck it swiftly towards the goal. The way Foley saved this dangerous ball, with great authority and calm, gave great reassurance to the Wexford team and supporters.

A Score for Cork

Wexford were playing very well but the resourceful Matt Fouhy got great length into his clearances. From one of these Terry Kelly got a shot in but it was blocked down by Mick Morrissey. There was a melee. Cork were awarded a 21 yard free. Over came the low-slung, muscular Ring and, to the cheers of the Cork followers, unerringly sent the ball over the centre of the crossbar for the Munster champions' first score. Five minutes had gone by.

Wexford Pressure

All the Wexford forwards combined in dangerous attacks. Ryan was narrowly wide, Dixon swept several balls across to Nick Rackard, Flood went on jinking runs, Codd's overhead striking was being cheered wildly and Kehoe, despite the efforts of Philpott, was always foraging with great determination. Only the tenacity and game-wiliness of the Cork backs prevented the scores from piling up. Rackard was being so tightly marked that he had only split seconds to part with the ball before the grappling presence of John Lyons was upon him. The other big factor at that period and throughout the game was the great goalkeeping of Mick Cashman. He was sharp and swift and had an astute sense of danger.

Hearne on Top

Seamus Hearne became unbeatable at centre field, full of endless energy, collecting balls, tussling for them, stopping attacking Cork movements, starting Wexford ones. His performance was all the greater in that he and Wheeler were pitted against two enterprising players in Goulding and Dowling. In the second half Cork were to put the heroic Philpott to the centre of the field but even he was unable to break the dominance of the man with whom he played on the Blackrock team.

In the left corner of the Cork attack the battle royal between Ring and Bobby Rackard was intense. The Rathnure man was glued to Ring's side. His plan was to get to the ball first or to be so close to Ring on all occasions that the maestro could find little room to swing the hurley. It was a battle of attrition that sprung to life whenever the ball came their way. Ring was at least able to send passes out to Terry Kelly, Christy O'Shea and Mick O'Regan or, as he did on several occasions, send it low along the ground to Hartnett, whom he knew was very powerful on ground strokes.

Billy Rackard Dominant

But the Wexford full back line was very sound. O'Donnell enhanced his already great reputation and Mick Morrissey allayed any fears about his youth and suitability. It was from the half back line that many of the Wexford attacks began. Billy Rackard kept his mastery of the high balls. On one memorable occasion he held off Josie Hartnett and, bending backwards, reached for the ball and caught it way behind his head. Jim Morrissey was playing soundly on O'Regan while Jim English was able to clear the ball down the field whenever he could take his eye of his dangerous opponent, Paddy Barry.

A tough, skilful battler like Daly was going to keep going despite the height advantage of Codd. But to make up for height he often resorted to one-handed hurling and rarely got in any long clearances. His predicament epitomised one of the factors which helped give Wexford the upper hand: the Slaneysiders had worked out a plan to gain the maximum benefit from their advantage in height and weight. They were a stone a man heavier and taller too. Their keeping the ball in the air and their ability to catch it or double on it paid dividends. Cork were faster and crisper on the ground balls but much of the time the ball was well off the sod. Codd and Wheeler did some great overhead doubling which delighted the crowd.

Daly, not a man to make excuses, said that he just could not get into the game. 'The day you're playing bad is the hardest game of all. You are trying so hard but the ball is always a few inches away. You know the balls you should be winning but it's just not there with you.'

Cork Captain Goes Off

In another Wexford attack Tim Flood parted to Codd at the last minute for the big man to score a point. In the tussle around the goalmouth the Cork captain and inspirational corner back, Tony O'Shaughnessy, toppled over after an accidental stroke to the head. As he was helped to the line many Cork followers shook their heads in dismay. But his replacement, the lanky Vin Twomey, was an experienced performer. Cap jammed tight on his head, he got into the game straight away. In possession of the ball under pressure he used do an amazing backward leap to give himself time and space to clear.

Seventeen minutes into the game Cork got their second point from Mick O'Regan after a pass from Ring. Four minutes later Nick Rackard for once got clear of his burly opponent and hit a point over the bar. It raised a great cheer of applause for the indomitable leader of the attack. Shortly afterwards Tim Flood went on one of his dazzling, ball-juggling runs and put over another point for Wexford. The same player shortly whipped over another to leave the score Wexford 1–5 to Cork 0–2. Wexford were thundering along at this stage. Tom Dixon gained control, passed to Tom Ryan, and ran out to take the pass back and flash over another point.

Cork All-Out Effort

But in the last five minutes of the half Cork, fearing the game might go away from them, made a supreme effort. They attacked with great vigour. Wexford conceded a free forty yards out. Ring trotted out, stood calmly over the ball and put it over the bar. Ring and O'Shea were at the centre of another attack. Billy Rackard once more cleared but Eamon Goulding gathered the ball and from centrefield rifled a great long-distance point over the bar. Right on the call of half time Cork pressure resulted in another 21-yard free which Ring pointed.

When the whistle blew with the score at 1–6 to 0–5 in favour of Wexford many people felt that Cork had done fairly well after being almost steamrolled by the powerful Wexford attack during the second period.

'Come on Cashman', a Cork-accented voice shouted as the teams made their way to the dressing-rooms. Cashman, beefy but fast, waved back. The Wexford supporters were also pleased with their man, Artie Foley, for his sharpness and the confident way he caught balls and cleared them.

Second Half

When Cork lined up for the second half, Kelly and Hartnett had exchanged places, as they were to do during the game. Paddy Barry had moved into the right corner and Christy O' Shea came out to right half forward. Tony O'Shaughnessy, head heavily bandaged, sat disconsolately on the sideline. His was a painful and disappointing experience amid all the exultation of a great game.

A delighted crowd cheered as the referee threw in the ball and the great surges of attack and defence began again. There were near misses and great saves at both ends. The marking was man to man but both sides played an open game that gave enough room for players to display their skills. There were thrills and spills each moment, with great clashes of bodies, tearaway play, courageous blocking-down, whirling tussles for the ball between utterly determined players.

The game saw a number of the great sideline cuts by one of the experts at the art, Ned Wheeler, distinguished by his bleached blond hair and his giant stature. He cut under the ball and it took off in a long, soaring flight, travelling fifty or sixty yards, while the crowd marvelled, before dropping down into the goal area.

'The heel of my hurley was nearly an inch and a half thick. You need that to get under the ball', he said. His hurley and that of many of his team-mates had been tailor-made by John Randall of Killurin, whose saw-mill still stands in the heavily wooded countryside by the Slaney to the north of Wexford town. Willie John Daly's most cherished hurley had come from the same source. 'It was perfectly balanced, with a thick heel for ground play. When you got possession you knew exactly where you were going to land the ball', he said.

Wheeler joined in a Wexford attack and placed Tom Ryan who was fouled. Nick Rackard took the free and sent it over the bar.

Another Wexford attack ended in a 70. Billy Rackard stood over the ball, lifted it carefully and flighted it between the posts with a powerful swing.

Wexford seemed about to begin coasting to victory. But Philpott and Fouhy had other ideas and they began to clear balls down into the Wexford half. A player like Daly would never say die and he now began to win more of the ball and on one occasion instigated a dangerous Cork attack with a long clearance.

Significant Moment

Then came one of the pivotal moments of the game. Eamon Goulding, getting possession at midfield sent a ball sailing into the Wexford square. Foley got it in his hand and ran out to clear it. He was buffetted about. The referee's whistle blew. It was expected to be a free out by many spectators. They had seen Foley's hurley being held by a Cork player. But the referee maintained that Foley had held on to the ball too long. He awarded Cork a 21-yard free.

The Wexford backs lined the goalmouth. Ring, flexing his shoulders, swinging his heavy stick got ready to take the free. This was one of the great set-pieces of Ring's game. He had practised it again and again. He would run up to the ball, lift it up and throw it forward in an arc. As it came down, now only 16 or 17 yards from the goal-line, Ring in forward flight would meet it on the upswing. This was a hundred miles an hour missile, capable of serious facial injury. Ring could direct the ball wherever he liked. He usually kept it away from the range of the goalkeeper. Many spectators could never claim to have seen him score one of his many goals in this way simply because the ball went too fast to see unless you were right behind the flight of the ball.

Ring ran up to the ball. He belted it low and it hit the ground about two yards from the line. The spectators saw the umpire raise the green flag and Foley turn to retrieve the ball from the back of the net. Cork were back in the game. Not long afterwards Ring managed to escape the shackles of Bobby Rackard and shot a point to leave only two points separating them.

Increasing Tempo

The tempo of play and effort began to rise and so did the volume of sound from the massed spectators. The clashes got fiercer. Wexford kept their composure. One of the best points ever scored by Padge Kehoe, a long ball from out near the sideline put them three points ahead again. But Cork were pulling out all the stops. A Wexford attack was broken up by the lithe Jimmy Brohan who came racing out, gathered the ball and sent a long clearance down the field. Paddy Barry, running out from the corner, got the ball inside the 40 yard line and went racing in on a solo run that only ended when he shot the ball into the net.

The sides were level. The final dramatic quarter was under way. Cork began to get the upper hand and launched a series of thundering attacks. Often only split seconds and inches as well as desperate defending stopped them going ahead. But go ahead they did shortly afterwards. Ring got the ball. Bobby Rackard was glued to his side, matching him stride for stride. There was no room to swing his hurley but Ring's big hand slapped the ball over the bar to put Cork into the lead. All round the ground the red and white flags created a dazzling scene. Their hero had done it again.

Fateful Juncture

At this juncture the game teetered on a knife-edge. A lesser team than Wexford might have felt dispirited at this reversal of fortunes when so much had gone so well for them. But they were made of courageous fibre and they held their heads. Their attacks were not quite as fluid as they had been but attack they did. And the Wexford hero, Nick Rackard, thundered out to grab a ball sent in by Seamus Hearne and helped on its way by Martin Codd. Rackard put it over the bar, turned and waved his hurley at his colleagues. He had taken a blow to the head but he did not even bother to wipe away the blood that ran down his face.

Goulding and Dowling both sent Cork into the attack but the backs of the Slaneysiders held out. The ball went narrowly wide on two occasions. Then the Wexford puck out was met in mid air by Codd. Flood got it and was about to set off on a run when he was fouled.

Nick Rackard came trotting out to take the free. It was fifty yards out. This was going to be a crucial effort. There was tremendous relief among the Wexford supporters when the big man hit it dead centre on the boss of his hurley and it went straight as a die between the uprights.

Wexford were now two points ahead with only four minutes remaining. Then came Ring's last gasp effort and Foley's courageous and magnificent save, followed by Rackard's clinching goal and the point by Tom Dixon as the curtain came down on this marvellous contest.

When the whistle went some of the most extraordinary scenes ever seen in Croke Park took place. As the crowds of spectators charged on to the field, Nick O'Donnell and Bobby Rackard ran to Ring. O'Donnell put his arms around him and gave the ironhard competitor a peck on the cheek.

Then they lifted Ring on their shoulders as a sporting tribute from generous hearted players to the man they knew was the most accomplished player of all. This was a unique gesture, typical of Wexford, who had been gallant in defeat two years previously and, in all the subsequent celebrations, were full of praise for their adversaries.

Jim English took the Liam McCarthy cup on the presentation stand and held it high. There was a resounding cheer from the faithful followers who had come in their thousands to support their heroes. When he called for three sporting cheers for the Cork team they responded lustily and so did the Wexford players.

Proud Participation

The Cork team and supporters were not dispirited. They had taken part in a great game and a great occasion. The players had shown tremendous courage and grit, displayed marvellous resilience and skill against one of the most powerful teams ever to contest an All Ireland. And they had come close enough to winning. They were not very disappointed. They had won before and they would win again. In the previous thirty years they had contested fifteen All-Irelands and won all but three.

Ring Plays On

Nobody could have imagined that Cork, one of the bedrocks of the hurling tradition, would not be seen in an All-Ireland again for a full ten years. In that long interval they would be beaten, sometimes resoundingly, by Tipperary and Waterford.

Ring continued on hurling, getting weightier and slowing as he got into his forties, but still so accomplished that he could get vital scores. He loathed to retire from the game to which he had given his all. But he drifted out of the Cork team in 1964 when he was forty-four.

He had married late and was the father of two children. He began to mellow as a person. For all his fierce pride and competitiveness he had a great loyalty to the hurling community in the country. He valued the friendships of both past opponents and team-mates. He became a selector for the county team in the mid-'70s, putting all his astute observation about players and the game to good use.

He rejoiced in Cork's All-Ireland victories in 1976, '77 and '78. Sometimes he could not contain his excitement during a big game, but rushed out of the dugout and went racing up and down the sideline as if he were playing a kind of supportive game. One of the last photographs of him is his holding the McCarthy Cup aloft in a massive hand, radiant with joy, to a vast celebratory crowd after the three-in-a-row triumph of 1978. Six months later this charismatic, complex man died of a heart attack in the street in Cork city. Nobody before or since had mastered all the facets of hurling or provided exhilarating extertainment to so many people over so long a period of time.

Rackard's Triumph and Tragedy

The winning of the 1956 All-Ireland was a triumph for the great personality of the Wexford team, Nick Rackard. It crowned years of flamboyant sporting endeavour to put Wexford on the hurling map. After that game, the hurling community, including Cork, was warm in its congratulations to the Wexford team and to Rackard.

There was a sad side to all the boisterous, bibulous celebrations that followed. This genial, outgoing personality, who loved company, was constantly plied with drink. To buy him a drink was seen as a way of saying thanks for all the joy he had brought to Wexford and to the world of hurling. Already a prodigious drinker, he went further down a dark alcoholic road, caused pain and sadness to those he loved and who loved him. His story is an uneasy reminder that the uproarious, after-match celebrations sometimes carry a cost in family relationships and happiness.

Those very close to him were full of admiration at the way he had been able to shake off the effects of all-night drinking bouts, pull himself together after nights without sleep and go out on a field of play and score goals in vigorous matches. He played his last championship game the following year when Wexford went out to Kilkenny in the Leinster final.

Rackard was made of stern stuff. After he had retired from the game he fought a rearguard battle against alcoholism. With great effort and will-power he contained it. He then became a generous and encouraging friend and mentor to the many who were also battling with this all too common affliction in Irish life. He was an inspirational figure in this as he had been on the field of play. His time of regeneration was comparatively short. He died of cancer in 1976.

The funerals of Ring and Rackard were crowded and emotional events. The hurling community converged on the burial grounds to pay tribute to these great warriors. On each of these occasions the great All-Ireland of 1956 was recalled and the incidents that had made it memorable related. These two, with all the other players, had made that final a legendary one.

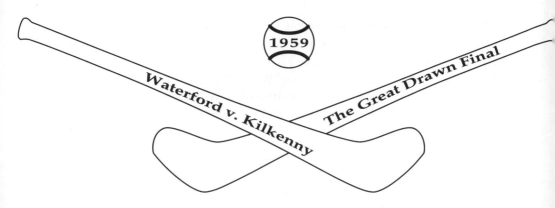

THE GREAT DRAWN FINAL

When the referee blew the long final whistle at about 4.45 on 6 September 1959 it was the signal for the start of a prolonged surge of applause from the 74,000 spectators that lasted for a full ten minutes. Hundreds of people jumped over the wire and raced over the grass to surround the players who had given such an exhibition of skilful and competitive hurling that made this match one of the top five games of the modern era.

This was different to the usual All-Ireland scene after the final whistle has gone. This time there were no jubilant shouts of exultant victory, no sad and disappointed shaking of heads. The great contest between near neighbours and proud rivals, Waterford and Kilkenny, had ended in a dramatic draw — the first since 1934.

Along with the grateful applause from the spectators at being given a feast of excitement and delightful stickwork was a huge collective sigh of relief. The legions of Waterford followers with their blue and white flags and rosettes were limp with joy that their great team had lived to fight another day, after being on the very brink of defeat two minutes from the end of play. The Kilkenny supporters could hardly believe that their stalwarts had escaped defeat by the margin of about three feet only seconds before full time.

All the neutral followers in the great crowd were happy that there were no losers that day. Such was the minute by minute excitement, the thrills and spills, the bodily clashes, the touches of stickwork, that they felt nobody deserved to lose such a marvellous game.

At the end of that memorable game there were less neutral supporters than there had been at the beginning. First one side and then the other fought their way back with such tenacity and resolution that they aroused the sympathy of hundreds who had no county affiliations.

False Impression

One of the great ironies of that game was that the man who had saved the day for Waterford with his last-minute goal and almost won it for them with a long-range effort at a point, was under the impression that his side had actually won.

'I thought we had won — there were so many scores on the board that day', recalled Seumas Power, one of the giants of the Waterford side. 'With all the cheering and backslapping and everything I was inside in the dressing-room before I realised that it was only a draw.'

He had scored the dramatic goal which gave Waterford a scoreline of 1-17 to Kilkenny's 5-5 almost on the call of time. Then Ollie Walsh, who was virtually unbeatable in the Kilkenny goal that day, retrieved the ball from the back of the net, made his familiar prancing run, took a wide swing on the ball and sent it way out the field.

'I was about 75 yards out and I was left all on my own. Like us in 1957 when we thought we had it won, Kilkenny had dropped their defences completely. The ball came straight into my hand. I made ground, five or six yards, with no one at all to challenge me, over towards the Cusack stand side. I thought we were a point ahead. The referee had nodded to indicate that time was just up. I hit it an almighty flake, not too concerned about accuracy. It went a yard or so wide. If I had known we were level I had all the time in the world — all the time in the world — to steady myself and score a point', said the midfielder from the Mount Sion club.

However, the hurling exhibition given that day, the man to man duels all over the field, the differing styles of the rivals, the performances of some of the players, were so splendid that many were delighted with a draw. They looked forward to more of the same.

Traditional Rivalry

The great rivalry between these two counties at the end of the 1950s and early '60 was one of the showpieces of the hurling scene. There was always a competitive edge between these neighbours. Along the banks of the river Suir, lush grassy country with a good deal of ash growing in the ditches and in copses, the fishermen and farmers from around Mooncoin and their opposite numbers on the southern bank of the river had played against one another going back over the decades.

A repository of rivalry and great games went into the folk memory of the area. But this rivalry, which sometimes had an intensity engendered by neighbourhood pride, was given a special dimension by the fact that many players from the Slieverue and Glenmore districts of south Kilkenny went to school in Waterford. Paddy Buggy from Slieverue, who played in the

Kilkenny half back line that day in 1959, had gone to school to the Christian Brothers in Mount Sion, the nursery for the Waterford side.

Players like Buggy and Power played together and played against one another. Many of the rivals got to know one another and to respect one another. This was a factor in ensuring that the clashes between the two sides were usually sporting, without the ferocious rancour that had sometimes soured Tipperary-Cork clashes at the start of that decade.

Kilkenny Hurling Culture

Since the foundation of the GAA Kilkenny had developed a strong hurling ethos. Teams largely powered by players from the south Kilkenny area, and from Tullaroan and Kilkenny city, began to be serious contenders for the All-Ireland title at the start of the century. Between 1904, when the county won its first All-Ireland, and 1913, the county took seven titles and laid the foundation for a tradition that bred confidence and style in Kilkenny hurling.

Over the following decades the county, along with Cork and Tipperary, formed a triumvirate of dominance in the game. Year after year they produced an endless stream of top-class hurlers. They won the minor and senior All-Irelands regularly. It was considered almost tragic in the county if the team went without winning the All Ireland for any longer than four years. In 1959 they were going for their fifteenth title.

Waterford Background

Waterford, on the other hand, were nothing as successful in winning championship titles. Each year in the Munster championship they had to contend with Tipperary and Cork and, during the '30s and early '40s, with a powerful Limerick side as well. Anything Waterford gained they earned the hard way. They reached their first senior final in 1938, when they were beaten by Dublin, despite the presence of legendary hurlers like John Keane, Christy Moylan, and Mick Hickey.

These three were still playing when Waterford won its first title in 1948, to universal rejoicing in the county and among those delighted to see one of the 'outsiders' get to the top after years of effort and great entertainment for hurling followers.

The 1957 Final

Waterford and Kilkenny had played one another in league and tournament games over the years, but it was not until 1957 that a Waterford side won the Munster title again while once more Kilkenny took the Leinster crown. Their meeting in the All-Ireland of that year produced a classic encounter which many would place alongside the final of 1959 in terms of excitement and quality of play.

1957 was the start of a great era in Waterford hurling. A group of outstanding players emerged from the county championships over the previous few years. Now under the tutelage of John Keane, who was a loved and respected figure on the hurling scene, the team took shape. The great characteristic of the team was its speed, with players racing into the attack, whipping balls along the ground, using the wings.

'We were all fairly light and many were small — so we had to rely on speed and skill in playing fast balls into the forwards', said Seumas Power. 'When light forwards are up against big heavyweight backs — as many back lines were in those days — you have to whip the ball in quickly to give advantage to speed.'

Waterford Speed

Players like Power and his Mount Sion team mates, Frankie Walsh and Mick Flannelly, could race at full speed onto a flying ground ball, judge precisely where to meet it, pull quickly on it and send it accurately goal-wards low along the ground.

The Waterford full backs contrasted with the normal last line of defence. Before the rules to protect goalkeepers were introduced at the start of the 1970s the full backs were usually rugged stalwarts whose job was to mind their goalkeeper by holding off inrushing forwards and allowing him to clear the ball. The Waterford full back line hurled the ball, relying on skill rather than weight. The six backs were delightful to watch as they swept the ball out of defence.

'We were basically an attacking side — all players felt they were part of the attack', explained Seumas Power who, with his clubmate Phil Grimes, made up one of the most effective and celebrated midfield partnerships in the history of the game.

When the men in white went racing down the pitch, the ball often flying from wing to wing as they converged on the opposing goal, a great cheer went up not just from their own followers but from all spectators, including the opposition. 'That's how to hurl — they are like lightening', people shouted.

Tom Cheasty

The light, fleet-footed forwards needed a ball-fetcher, a ball carrier, a strong centre player to complement their attributes. In Tom Cheasty of Ballyduff they had one of the most unorthodox but effective centre forwards in the land. Muscular and heavy shouldered, he competed fiercely for every ball that came his way. He was able to jostle opponents off their stride. When he gathered the ball he crouched over it, holding it on his hurley as he bobbed and weaved forwards, usually in a direct line for the goal. It was almost impossible to dispossess him. He was frequently fouled. He took a great deal of sharp pulling and shouldering and his big farm-hardened hands were scarred. He was once likened to a charging rhinocerous as he knocked opponents off their feet.

Cheasty attracted so much attention from the opposing backs that forwards like Walsh and Guinan were able to feed off his efforts, when he broke up the play and got the ball out to them on the wing.

Vulnerability

But Waterford attacking spirit, so exhilarating to watch, made them vulnerable to snap goals. They allowed forwards to play the game. Their attacking instincts made their backs reluctant to close down a game, to mark opponents so tightly that they could barely hit the ball.

This vulnerability cost the Decies men dearly in the All Ireland final of 1957. They met a Kilkenny team that had some of the very best exponents of Kilkenny hurling. Players like Denis Heaslip, Sean Clohosey, Billy Dwyer and their colleagues had all the Noresiders' range of sharp skills. They had a highly developed sense of position and anticipation which made it seem as if the ball sought them out, often when they were completely on their own. They liked to take the ball in the hand but they lifted it with apparent ease, could tap it, twist with it, strike it quickly and accurately. Many used light sticks and were great exponents of the one-handed flick which took the ball off an opponent's stick or knocked it away.

Kilkenny Tradition

These stick artists were part of a great tradition where ball control, fast wristy striking, and body swerves to avoid the tackle were revered. But there was more to Kilkenny hurling than skill. Tradition, the winning of All-Irelands decade after decade, has given Kilkenny hurlers a supreme self-confidence that almost seems like arrogance. They expect to win. They don't collapse when the game is going against them because they have a deep game-memory of great recoveries, of thundering back into games.

One of the most potent hurling memories is the number of times that Kilkenny teams seemed beaten, on the very brink of defeat as the final whistle drew, near only to make one supreme effort. Such efforts were always allied with an incomparable cuteness both by players and mentors. They knew how to compensate for their own weakness and to exploit the weakness of their opponents.

The number of games, of All-Irelands, won by late Kilkenny surges is astonishing. The number of All-Irelands that they won by a single point is unusual. It is a tribute to their skill and their indomitable will to persist and to win.

The 1957 Final

These characteristics came to the fore in the 1957 final. Waterford looked by far the better side. They won the individual duels in many positions round the field. With ten minutes to go most people in the huge crowd of 75,000 accepted that the flying speedsters in white were going to take their second title. They led by six points.

Then, seemingly against the run of play, Kilkenny struck back. Billy Dwyer, the stocky Kilkenny full forward, scored a goal. But Grimes, with two points, put Waterford five points ahead with full time nearing. Then the Kilkenny half forward Mick Kenny scored a point and followed it with a superb goal. While the bewildered Waterford side, who had been anticipating accepting the McCarthy Cup, seemed mesmerised by how suddenly the game had changed, the red-headed Sean Clohosey from Tullaroan levelled. Mickey Kelly, the Kilkenny captain, got the winning point three minutes from the end.

Waterford had one last chance to save the game. A free was awarded. Phil Grimes wanted to ensure that his shot for a point went safely over the bar; he struck the ball carefully but it landed short. Ollie Walsh, the Kilkenny goalkeeper, giving an astonishing display of skill and anticipation in his first All-Ireland, stopped it and it was cleared. The whistle went. The game's master poachers had lifted the prize from under the noses of the stunned Waterford players, who almost seemed like spectators in the last crucial five minutes.

This was a devastating defeat for the Waterford team. The following year they reached the Munster final but were overwhelmed by Tipperary on a scoreline of 4–12 to 1–5. Tipp went on to beat Kilkenny in the semi-final and overcome Galway in a one-sided All-Ireland.

Year of Recovery

Waterford took a full year to recover, to regain a steely determination to win the prize they felt they well deserved. Under the eye of John Keane they trained and practised their skills. Some of the old traditionalists had already written them off as a team who had missed their chance.

They were drawn against Galway in the first round. After the All-Ireland drubbing Galway joined Munster in an attempt to build up game experience. Waterford met them in the first round at Limerick. The scoreline of 7–11 to 0–8 suggested that the Decies were regaining their rhythm and morale.

The All-Ireland champions, Tipperary, were next. Waterford went to play them in Cork in the Munster semi-final on 12 July 1959 before an attendance of 27,000. Many Tipperary followers did not bother to travel, expecting an easy win.

The hurling world was in for a shock. So fast were the Waterford men, their combination so instinctive in attack, that they kept the ball in their possession until they parted with it — to the Tipperary net. The final score was an astonishing 9–3 to 3–4 in favour of John Keane's men. It was not just the forwards like Guinan, Kiely, Ware and Cheasty that pulverized the champions. Joe Harney of Ballydurn, Austin Flynn of Abbeyside and John Barron of the De La Salle club in the city hurled the Tipperary forwards away from the goal area. Martin Og Morrissey mastered his opponents in hip-to-hip duels and sent the team into the attack again and again.

In the Munster final Cork tried to counter the Waterford style and partially succeeded in doing so in a thrilling game in sweltering conditions at Thurles. Waterford won on a scoreline of 3–9 to 2–9. John Kiely, the grey-haired veteran of the side in the full forward line, made a powerful contribution to the victory. They had reached the All-Ireland.

Kilkenny's Progress

Meanwhile in Leinster Kilkenny had progressed on a somewhat more subdued level. They were not extended in beating Offaly. Their opponents in the Leinster final were a fine Dublin side who had beaten Wexford in the other semi-final. Dublin were leading up until the last minute when a goal from the immensely skilful Sean Clohosey gave the Noresiders a somewhat lucky win.

The prospect of another great contest between the neighbouring counties created a great hum of excitement in the hurling world. People began to sum up the strengths of the sides. Ollie Walsh had emerged as the outstanding goalkeeper of the day, who had lightning-fast reflexes and a huge puck out. His opposite number, Ned Power of Tallow, had made some marvellous saves in the Munster final and had gained the confidence of the Waterford followers.

Kilkenny Last Line

In front of Ollie Walsh was a sturdy full back line. Tom Walsh of Dunamaggin was in the right corner while his brother Jim, known as 'The Link', was at full back. These two hardy farmers made sure nobody came charging in on top of the goalkeeper. 'The Link' was a 14-stone, square-jawed man who shouldered hard and pulled hard when the ball came into the square. Tom was an unobtrusive player, very adept at tipping the ball out of danger in front of goals. On the left was John Maher, who played for Kilmacud Crokes in Dublin. He was a fast, stylish hurler, a great man to cover off. Full backs and goalkeeper had developed a remarkable level of understanding that stood them well in tight situations.

Tom Walsh was going to have to contain the bustling, barrel-chested John Kiely from Dungarvan, who had been playing a long time, knew all the tricks, rarely went through a game without a score. Donal Whelan of Abbeyside had been moved into the full forward position and adapted well to it. People wondered how he and 'The Link' would measure up against one another. In the other corner it was Maher versus Charlie Ware of Erin's Own, son of a man who had played in Waterford's first All-Ireland appearance in 1938.

It was reckoned that the players in the Kilkenny half back line were going to have the making or breaking of Waterford in their hands and hurls. They had to contain three of the best forwards of the decade in hurling, including the exceptionally fast Frankie Walsh, captain of the side, who could whip on the moving ball with uncanny accuracy.

Centre of the forward line was the powerhouse of the attack, Tom Cheasty, who needed not one but several backs to stop him when he went on a run, heavy legs holding the ground, shouldering opponents out of the way. On the other side was a man who combined some of the characteristics of both Cheasty and Walsh — Larry Guinan. He was often described as the 'terrier' of the team. He raced to every ball, he took his man on, he twisted and turned, he could strike the ball sharply. Guinan never gave up; there was an admirable persistence about him that was inspirational for the team and supporters.

Backs and Forwards

Paddy Buggy of Kilkenny had marked the Waterford captain before. The Slieverue man was fast and nippy and skilful. Many half backs who could not keep up with Walsh fouled him and gave away frees that were invariably pointed. Buggy's innate sense of sportsmanship would ensure that Walsh would get few frees off him.

The Kilkenny centre back, Mick Walsh, also from Slieverue, had had many tussles with Cheasty both in county and tournament games. It was going to take him all his time to contain him and nobody expected him to deliver long clearances down the field. On the left hand side of the line was the stocky Johnny McGovern of Bennetsbridge. He was one of the best players on the side, now pitted against Guinan.

How would midfield fare? Here were four accomplished hurlers — Paddy Kelly of Thomastown — playing in his first final — and Mick Brophy, who played for Danesfort, against the redoubtable Power and Grimes. Spectators expected to see some of the best and most skilful hurling when these four battled it out.

Kilkenny's right half forward, Denis Heaslip of Knocktopher, was as fast as Frankie Walsh and had played well in the 1957 game. He was lithe and light, always ran into the open spaces in front of goal to score. He would be marked by one of the newcomers to the Waterford side, Jackie Condon of Erin's Own, who had played very well in the Munster campaign.

Dick Carroll, the Kilkenny centre forward, had been off the county team for some years, but his displays of skill and craftiness with Bennettsbridge brought him back. Keeping watch on him was the strong, sturdy Martin Og Morrissey. It was said of him that year that he got better in every game, almost unbeatable in hip-to-hip pulling, capable of sending long clearances to get the forwards moving.

Mick Lacey of Cappoquin, Waterford's right half back, had been left out of the 1957 side, much to the annoyance of many followers who saw him as a tireless and reliable player. His opponent was Mick Fleming who played for Kilmacow, also in his first All-Ireland. He had come to the fore in the National League campaign of the previous year and had kept his place.

All the commentators said it was going to be a battle royal between the Kilkenny full forwards and their markers. Right corner forward was Sean Clohosey, one of the great sylists on the team, a dashing opportunist whom the crowd loved. He was being marked by the unassuming but workmanlike John Barron of De La Salle who had invariably played a sound game. Austin Flynn of Abbeyside had been an automatic choice as Waterford full back since 1954. He had never played better than in the 1959 championship. He was ranged against a very hard hurler in Billy Dwyer, a bustling, burly player who was at his most dangerous when low balls came into the square. Dwyer, from Foulkstown, rarely had a bad game and had been selected on the Leinster Railway Cup team in 1957.

Tommy O'Connell of the Kilkenny city side Eire Og was at left corner forward for the Noresiders. He was light, not much over ten stone. He was the youngest man on the field at 21, playing in his first All-Ireland but he was proving to be a prolific scorer, with quick touches and deft strokes around the goal area. Marking him was Joe Harney of Ballydurn, also playing in his first All-Ireland. He was one of the heroes of the Munster final, with blocking and interceptions which saved the day at crucial moments in a neck-and-neck race.

Waterford Favourites

Coming up to the day itself the newspaper commentators made Waterford favourites, based on their forward power and the way they had used it in the campaign so far. Yet there was a feeling that Kilkenny were always a different team in a final, extremely hard to beat, with a glistening treasure of medals and prizes giving them a comfortable feeling going into an All-Ireland. Waterford had never beaten them in a big game.

That weekend of the All-Ireland the modest cars, many bursting at the seams, stuffed with heavy men and boys, trundled up the roads from Tallow and Kilamery, from pasturelands, from the valleys of the Nore and Suir, from the Comeragh mountain area and the high ground near Thomastown. Many ramshackle buses, roaring under the weight of bodies, gears grinding at corners and the start of slopes, joined the long line of vehicles. From little railway stations, now overgrown with grass, Kilmacow, Ballyragget and Tallow, crowds waited for the special trains.

People brought their own food because the special trains never had any dining facilities. Apart from that most people had no intention of paying money for food when they could leave their own home with a parcel of carefully made sandwiches, wrapped in brown paper.

First TV Coverage

74,000 spectators crammed into Croke Park that day, a record for the reduced capacity of the ground. For the first time, television cameras were seen there. The BBC had decided to cover it and transmit an edited version on a sports programme some days later. Their star commentator, Kenneth Wolstenholme, was perched on the upper deck of the Hogan Stand.

The teams as they lined out were:

WATERFORD

Ned Power
(Tallow)

Joe Harney	Austin Flynn	John Barron
(Ballydurn)	(Abbeyside)	(De La Salle)

Mick Lacey	Martin Og Morrissey	Jackie Condon
(Cappoquin)	(Mount Sion)	(Erin's Own)

Seumas Power   Phil Grimes
(Mount Sion)   (Mount Sion)

Larry Guinan	Tom Cheasty	Frankie Walsh, capt
(Mount Sion)	(Ballyduff)	(Mount Sion)

Charlie Ware	Donal Whelan	John Kiely
(Erin's Own)	(Abbeyside)	(Dungarvan)

Substitutes: Tom Cunningham (Dungarvan); Mick Flannelly (Mount Sion); Freddie O'Brien (Mount Sion); Paudie Casey (Ballygunner); Michael O'Connor (Cappoquin); Tom Coffey (Tourin); Joe Coady (Erin's Own). *Trainer*: John Keane. *Mentors/selectors*: Pat Fanning (Mount Sion); Declan Goode (Dungarvan); Jim Ware (Erin's Own); Terry Dalton (Dungarvan); Paddy Joe O'Sullivan (Clonea). *Medical officer*: Dr Milo Shelley. *Physiotherapist*: Jack Furlong (Erin's Own).

KILKENNY

Ollie Walsh
(Thomastown)

Tom Walsh	Jim 'Link' Walsh	John Maher
(Dunamaggin)	(Dunamaggin)	(Freshford/Crokes)

Paddy Buggy	Mick Walsh	Johnny McGovern
(Slieverue)	(Slieverue)	(Bennettsbridge)

Paddy Kelly   Mick Brophy
(Thomastown)   (Danesfort)

Denis Heaslip	Dick Carroll	Mick Fleming
(Knocktopher)	(Bennettsbridge)	(Kilmacow)

Sean Clohosey, capt	Billy Dwyer	Tommy O'Connell
(Tullaroan/New Ireland)	(Faughs)	(Eire Og)

Substitutes: John Sutton (Glenmore); Timmie Kelly (Bennettsbridge); Mickie Kelly (Bennettsbridge); Liam Cleere (Bennettsbridge); Martin Treacy (Bennettsbridge); Jim Hennessy (Tullaroan) and Eddie Keher (Rower-Inistioge) were added to the panel for the replay. *Trainer/coach*: Rev Tommy Maher. *Mentors/selectors*: Tom Hogan; Nicholas Purcell. *Team doctor*: Dr Kieran Cuddihy.

The referee was Gerry Fitzgerald from Limerick.

All eyes were on the referee, Gerry Fitzgerald from Limerick, when he called Clohosey and Walsh together for the toss. They shook hands briefly. The coin was flipped. Frankie Walsh won and indicated that Waterford would play into the Railway goal, with a breeze at their backs.

Then the Artane Boys Band struck up the national anthem. Just as it ended a great roar of encouragement, anticipation and delight burst out and drowned the final notes. The referee threw in the ball at twelve minutes past the hour of three to a chorus of yells. The long awaited game was under way.

Right from the first seconds it became apparent that this was going to be a cracker of a game. Both teams were galvanised by a fierce determination that aroused something deeply, even savagely competitive in the spectators. The clenched jaws, the tense frowns of concentration, the thunderous bodily clashes, the stinging smack of hurleys pulling against one another created an excitement that lasted until the final whistle.

At the throw-in there was a collision of bodies and hurleys. Out of this scramble Mick Brophy snatched at the ball. He tried to burst his way to open space to hit it but the referee said he was charging with the ball and awarded a free to Waterford.

Phil Grimes came over to take it. It was said of him that he could land the ball on a cow's nose at sixty yards' range, such was his precision and control. He sent it into the centre in front of the goal. Larry Guinan, gaunt-faced with zealotry, snapped it up and sent it over the bar for the first score of the game.

Ollie Walsh Pucks Out

One of the great delights of this game, as in 1957, was to watch the way Ollie Walsh took the ball in hand well behind the goal-line, then leaped forward in a series of balletic prances, swung the hurley way back above his head, threw the ball forward and then met it with a full flamboyant swing. This was an act of hurling showmanship that people loved. More importantly for Kilkenny, the puck outs reached the maximum distance that it was possible for a man to hit a ball.

As it came down well past centrefield, despite the moderate breeze, a whirling pyramid of arms and hurleys rose to meet it. The centrefield battle was under way, a place of split-second advantage, of inches separating the opponents. The ball went over the sideline off a Waterford hurley.

Mick Brophy went over and clipped a good ball into the danger area. But the energetic Grimes had run into the back area. He cleared the ball with a stylish stroke. It went towards Kilkenny's left corner but John Maher came racing to it, got possession and hit it a long way down the field. It was a sign that the Waterford full forward line were going to find little room for the kind of hammer blows they had delivered to Galway and Tipperary on the way to the final.

The dark haired, heavily built Martin Og Morrissey, whipped the ball off the ground after a frenetic bout of play on the 40 yards mark and sent it off down the field. This got a resounding cheer, gave the Waterford supporters a comfortable feeling that this rock-like player was on his game. The ball ended up in front of Charlie Ware but his marker, Maher, barely gave him room for a hurried stroke and the ball went wide.

When the ball went out to Kilkenny's right wing, the speedy Heaslip managed to elude Jackie Condon. As Flynn and Dwyer grappled in front of the goal, the ball came flying in while the massed crowd behind the goal swayed like a field of wheat in a gale. Ned Power in the goal saved with a show of confidence and sent the ball off down the field. It was his first touch of the ball. Again Heaslip, light and full of skilful feints and swerves, got possession. But he over-carried the ball and with Condon glued to his elbow he sent the shot wide.

Waterford Attack

Now Waterford began to get into their attacking style. They whipped the ball low along the ground, raced onto it, sent it zipping goalwards. The Waterford supporters yelled when they saw the jinking, crouching Cheasty had got possession near the goal-line. His hurried shot was parried at the expense of a 70 by Ollie Walsh. Grimes stood over the ball, looked at the goal, raised the sliotar perfectly and sent a long shot high between the posts. Waterford were two points ahead after six minutes.

Seconds later the ball was down at the other end of the field and the youthful Tommy O'Connell pulled on a loose ball and sent it flying goalwards. Ned Power saved it. But it was a sign that the corner forward could be lethal if he got the opportunity.

Gradually, after the frantic first minutes, Waterford began to get a slight edge at midfield. This helped the forwards go into racing gear and take the game to Kilkenny. Seumas Power hit a drop shot off his left which landed near John Kiely. He snapped it up, raced out to make space for himself, with Tom Walsh in hot pursuit and sent it over the bar.

The fastest man on the field, the greyhound-slim Frankie Walsh, tore down the field and centred the ball. There was a fierce tussle between 'The Link' Walsh and Donal Whelan. The Waterford man whipped quickly and the ball shot goalwards. It looked a certain goal but Ollie Walsh, with millisecond reflexes, made what seemed like a miraculous save. It was the first of many that day, when he gave one of the most memorable displays of goal-saving ever seen before or since.

After twelve minutes Kilkenny got their first score when Denis Heaslip controlled a difficult ball out on the wing, twisted and turned and sent it in. Billy Dwyer doubled on it and it flew over the bar to a great cheer from the heartened Kilkenny followers.

Kilkenny Goal

This was the start of a period of Kilkenny pressure. Heaslip and Fleming both had wides but like all players that day, there was hardly more than two seconds to swing on a ball, before being shouldered or hooked by an opponent. Billy Dwyer and Austin Flynn played out a battle of wits and brawn and skill, with Dwyer using all his experience to open up the Waterford defence.

The Kilkenny mentors decided to take the talented Clohosey out from the corner to the half forward line in an exchange with Dick Carroll. Not long after this change both players combined to outmanoeuvre the Waterford backs, giving Flynn little option but to rush out to stop the inrushing Carroll who, at the last second, dropped the ball at the feet of the unmarked Dwyer. He slammed the ball into the net from just outside the square. The roar of delight which rose upwards from the Kilkenny supporters caused a flock of pigeons tearing through the sky above to veer away in some fright. Kilkenny were now in front.

Not long afterwards there was almost another goal when Heaslip's fast shot hit the upright, riccocheted outwards where Billy Dwyer met it and sent it goalwards again. It went wide off Dick Carroll's hurley.

Waterford came thundering back, with Frankie Walsh and Guinan racing along the sideline, pulling fast on ground balls that came in low and made it difficult for the Kilkenny backs. John Kiely got the ball from a maul and was dangerously poised in front of the goal when he was pulled down. From the free Walsh sent over the bar to level the scores. Soon he was tearing along the sideline once again until he got near enough to sent the ball over the bar.

Great Goalkeeping

Just then there were two great saves, first by Power and then at the other end when Walsh smothered a cracking shot from the muscular Kiely. It was as if there was also a duel between the goalkeepers to see who could bring off the most spectacular and inspirational saves.

In front of each goalkeeper franctic wrestling, bumping and boring took place whenever the ball came into the square. These were the days when the goalkeeper could be buffeted and bundled into the net, ball and all. Backs grappled with forwards, heaving and grunting. Obscene abuse, elbowing and digging the hurley into an opponent's ribs were part of the tribal battles which roused primitive instincts in the crowd.

This game was tough too, and tempers were roused by skinned knuckles and smarting ankles, but only once or twice did it risk spilling over into real violence. It was played within the rules of rough sportsmanship.

The speedy Waterford forwards kept coming in waves. Frankie Walsh again went haring up the wing and hardly changed stride before clipping another point over. Someone among the Kilkenny supporters roared at Paddy Buggy as he raced desperately after Walsh, 'Hit him will you.'

Buggy ignored all such advice. He was a sporting player. It would have taken a world-class sprinter to keep up with Walsh once he got away.

Going for Points

'We went for points, as we were told to do by John Keane', said Seumas Power. 'We knew how good Ollie Walsh was and that we had to take our points when we got the chance. As well as that, in an All-Ireland, if you are scoring points you feel that you are in there, that you are doing what you are supposed to do. It gives a team great confidence.'

When the ball came whistling into the Kilkenny square, Kiely, full of guile and tireless foraging, managed to get clear of the quietly effective Tom Walsh, made room for a hard shot at the goal. The fair-haired Kilkenny goalkeeper got his stick to it. When the ball came back out Cheasty caught it and sent it over the bar. In another Waterford attack Kiely this time raced across the goal and lofted a point over the bar.

At this time Kilkenny suffered a loss when the determined Johnny McGovern, who was playing well, suffered a serious shoulder injury and had to retire. He was replaced by Timmie Kelly. On the Waterford side, Charlie Ware, hampered by old injuries, was not playing to form. John Keane sent in Tom Cunningham of Dungarvan in his place.

Just before half-time Cheasty, the workhorse of the Waterford side, surrounded by Kilkenny backs, sent the ball out to Frankie Walsh, who ran forward along the left touchline and sent the ball over the bar. When the whistle went Waterford were leading by 9 points to Kilkenny's 1–1. The game was going well for the men in white.

Both teams got an ovation from the huge crowd as they walked across the field to the dressing-rooms. Many neutrals had the feeling that Waterford were going to win this great trial of skill and stamina.

Second Half

Waterford did indeed get off to a good start when Tom Cheasty got possession. All the power of his muscular shoulders were behind the shot which was skimming over the bar when the super-confident Ollie Walsh leapt up with outstretched hurley to try to save it. But the ball hit the upright and riccocheted over for another point.

Paddy Kelly of Thomastown, whose athletic training gave him a store of tireless energy, got the ball at centrefield and sent over a long-range point, aided by the breeze. The game swept back and forwards and then in a Kilkenny attack the Waterford backs conceded a 70. Mick Walsh, the centre half back, rose the ball carefully and sent it sailing beautifully between the posts.

Kilkenny were now about to come to terms with this quicksilver Waterford side, and to fight their way into the game. A minute later, the ball came into the Kilkenny forwards, Clohosey managed a powerful, stylish stroke which sent it hurtling goalwards. It hit off the upright, flew back out. It was sent back into the net by Tommy O'Connell, whose supple wrists enabled him to flick his light hurley like a rapier, to make scores out of nothing. A huge cheer went up from the Kilkenny followers. Their team was now only a point behind and looking extremely danger-ous when they went on the attack.

But the Waterford players kept up their relentless play. They attacked and the Kilkenny backs gave away a free. Grimes, whose tussles with Brophy at centrefield were ending in stalemate for both players, came up and, with his fluid swing, sent the ball over the bar.

Great Cheasty Point

Then came one of the most memorable scores ever seen in any All-Ireland final. The redoubtable Cheasty got the ball, shouldered his way past one back, crouched low over the ball, took a charge from a second back, kept the ball in his possession, shuffled and sidestepped another assault, charged straight into the next man and bowled him over, took on a fifth tackle, got clear and lofted the ball over the bar to a resounding cheer from the spectators. In an exaggerated description of this great run, one com-mentator said that he had left the ground behind him strewn with Kilkenny backs, like crumpled wasps.

O'Connell Again

The Waterford cheers had hardly subsided than Paddy Kelly got control of the ball at centrefield and sent a long centre into the Waterford goal area. Before anyone knew what was happening Tommy O'Connell had tipped it into the net. This was the kind of goal, coming at the time it did, that raised the spirits of the Kilkenny team and supporters. It seemed to say that, despite all their dash and power play, the Waterford backs were vulnerable to balls flying and skidding about in the goalmouth, where Dwyer and O'Connell were particularly dangerous. It looked like Waterford might be losing their grip on the game.

The goal however only increased the determination of the men in white. They came roaring back and only a goalkeeper of the genius of Ollie Walsh could have stopped a ball screaming into the net. He caught it in his hand, dodged two incoming forwards, went dancing out 25 yards and then took an almighty swipe at it which sent it into the Waterford square. Clearly there were going to be no goals to be had from him.

Cheasty was fighting like a lion for every ball that came his way. He shouldered his way onto the next one, lifted the ball, bent almost double and went off on a swerving, bursting run. He was almost impossible to dispossess or knock off his feet on runs like these. He finished the run with a point.

Not long after the Waterford backs conceded a free about 30 yards out. Dick Carroll went for a goal but the men on the line stopped it and cleared it away. Carroll was then unlucky with another free which just went wide.

Waterford went on the attack and once again Frankie Walsh went sprinting along the left wing with the ball and swung it over bar to make the score Waterford 0–14 to 3–3 for Kilkenny.

By this stage supporters of both sides and indeed all spectators were red-faced with the excitement evoked by the succession of thrills and spills, the bodily clashes, the marvellous skills on display, the courage and grit of the two sides locked in unrelenting combat. In every part of the field there were fierce duels, hectic races for the ball, blocking and hooking, and sweet striking.

Right-Hand Point

A long ball from Martin Og Morrissey, one of his many fine clearances under pressure, went flying onto the forwards. It ended up with a free to Waterford. There was no designated free-taker because there were so many sure strikers. Seumas Power was nearest. A left handed player, he had worked endlessly to perfect his striking from the right. Now, hardly giving it a thought, he hit the free off his right and sent it over the bar.

Waterford seemed to have regained control and kept up their attacking play. Frankie Walsh put another free over the bar to leave the score 0-16 to 3-3 with twelve minutes remaining. Then disaster struck Waterford. Paddy Kelly, endlessly energetic, sent in a long floating ball. Backs and forwards converged on it almost on the goal line with Ned Power trying to get sight of the ball as sticks — including Tommy O'Connell's — reached for it. The ball ended in the back of the net. The Noresiders were only a point behind.

This was a great boost to Kilkenny and they hurled with additional fire, began to win more of the ball in more positions. The whole team stretched every limb and sinew to get to ball faster, to strike quicker than their opponents.

To a team of lesser determination and grit than Waterford this fourth goal could have had a deeply demoralising effect. It seemed that all the attacking flair, all the speed, the swinging of play from wing to wing, the string of hard-earned points were being negatived by snap goals from Kilkenny. Half a minute after Kilkenny's goal Larry Guinan won the ball on the right wing, sped along the touchline and then closed in to score a fine point. Waterford were now two points to the good with ten minutes to go.

Kilkenny's Fifth Goal

Now Kilkenny, playing outfield with greater assurance, sent the ball low into Billy Dwyer. There was a desperate scramble with the ball skittering off hurleys and bodies before it went out off a Waterford player for a 70. Mick Walsh sent the ball into the goalmouth. Dick Carroll pulled on it and sent it into the Waterford net for Kilkenny's fifth goal and one which put them a point ahead. The black and amber flags waved all over the terraces and stands. Waterford followers looked at one another in dismay. It seemed as if the game they had dominated for so long was going away from them.

Now the whole Kilkenny team came on top note together. Carroll, who had been outhurled for much of the game by Morrissey, led another sortie. He got the ball in his hand and raced across the field to send over a splendid point. Kilkenny kept up the pressure — Heaslip and Clohosey coming into it more and more. John Sutton, master of the aerial ball with his crisp overhead striking, had come on for the injured Mick Fleming and added his experience to the final surge. Waterford gave away a free under the onslaught. Carroll went over and took it and sent it over the bar to a tremendous cheer. This seemed the clinching score to give yet another All-Ireland title to Kilkenny. The Kilkenny followers, certain of victory, were ready to come racing onto the field from the sidelines.

Desperate Attack by Waterford

With two minutes to go Waterford went on a desperate all out assault. A Kilkenny back touched the ball over the sideline, 55 yards out from the Kilkenny goal. There was so little time left that Frankie Walsh ran over and prepared to take it without waiting for a half back or midfielder to come up, as would normally be the case. Seumas Power, who had tirelessly covered acres of ground during the game, ran in to the 40 yard line, hoping to pick up a breaking ball. He knew that Walsh was very skilful on sideline cuts and that the ball was likely to come floating into the goalmouth. He positioned himself for a run from about 35 yards out.

To Power's dismay — and the dismay of the Waterford supporters — Walsh's cut went straight to Paddy Buggy, who nonchalantly gathered the ball and drove it down the field. Waterford had lost their attacking position and it seemed that they had lost the game also.

Saving Goal

But all was not lost yet. Mick Flannelly of Mount Sion, who had come on for Jackie Condon in the half back line, raced to the ball, won it, dodged his way past two tackles and sent a long raking puck forward and across the field towards the right-hand side under the Hogan Stand, catching Kilkenny somewhat unawares. The ball was heading for the sideline when Larry Guinan came racing across for it. His leg had been injured and he was exhausted after the killing pace of the game. Panting heavily he just made it front of his opponent and before the ball went over. He let fly on it. Seumas Power, who had stayed forward, found himself loose about 45 yards out and came running in. The ball from Guinan went straight in front of him. He gathered it on his right.

'The ball came up beautifully. I went practically unchallenged for almost twenty yards with the ball on my stick. I was on the 21-yard line and was aiming to strike the ball off my stronger left-hand side. But the Kilkenny backs were beginning to wake up and were converging on my left. I pretended to be going to hit it left-handed but at the last second I swung back and let fly from the right for all I was worth', recalls Power.

'The Link' Walsh and Ollie Walsh were in the goalmouth. The goal-keeper seemed to have it covered but the ball was deflected off the stick of the full back and shot into the net.

In the deserted little streets and roadways near the GAA grounds on the heights of Waterford city — an area referred to as 'Up the roads' — a spontaneous chorus of cheers rang out from all the houses where people sat tense and, up to now, distraught around their radios. One of their own, one of the seven Mount Sion men who backboned the team and became known later as 'The Magnificent Seven', had pulled the fat out of the fire for Waterford in the very last minute.

Then Power caught the puck out unchallenged and but for his belief that Waterford were ahead could have steadied himself and sent it over the bar.

When the whistle went the supporters of both sides rushed out onto the field to surround their heroes. Spectators, drained of all emotion and energy by the gripping, non-stop battle, stood limp but happy. No spectator had any doubt but that they had seen one of the great finals. All the newspaper reporters, making final jottings in their notebooks in the press section, were to offer their opinion that this was one of the very best. The BBC's man said that he was utterly astounded at the skill and endurance of these amateur players.

It took a long time for the people to leave the scene of this memorable encounter. As they walked back along the seedy, littered streets they began to talk of the replay.

It was fixed for the 4 October. It too proved to be another spine-tingling contest. It attracted a crowd of 77,825, the largest to see a Kilkenny or Waterford side play. The replay had, however, a different pattern. Waterford burst into the attack from the throw in, again and again, but could not score. They had several agonising misses. Then Kilkenny took up the running and scored 1–4 to Waterford's solitary point.

It looked as if the Decies were going to be well beaten. Then Mick Flannelly, who had held his place for the replay, sent a goal crashing into the net. This seemed to lift the binding tension off the Waterford side and to release their immense power and thrust. Cheasty got two great goals and they led by 3–5 to 1–8 at half-time.

Waterford Learned Lessons

Waterford were that few inches ahead to every ball, that split second faster in striking. They seemed brimful of a desperate hunger for success. Kilkenny, although still full of skill and hurling guile, had not quite the same white-hot urgency as they had shown in the first game.

Waterford had learned lessons. Their backs were much tighter now. They marked in the accepted style of the time, did less open hurling in the back line. Joe Harney, who had been criticised for letting Tommy O'Connell score three goals in the drawn game, now effectively policed the Eire Og man out of the game. The other full backs, Austin Flynn and John Barron, did the same.

Kilkenny scored only two points in the second half, both by Eddie Keher, who came on as a substitute at the age of 18. There was always a possibility that the black and amber clad men would snatch a goal or two but with ten minutes to go it was apparent that they had run out of steam while the men in white kept running and chasing as if their lives depended on winning every ball.

The final score was Waterford 3–12 to 1–10 for Kilkenny. After the near run thing of the drawn game the Decies men had proved that, along with providing the most entertaining hurling seen for years, they could also win an All-Ireland.

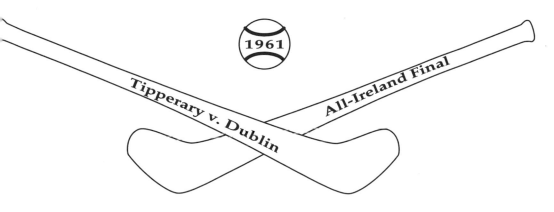

1961
Tipperary v. Dublin
All-Ireland Final

A THRILLING WIN AND COSTLY LOSS

Predictions about the attractiveness of the All-Ireland final of 1961 between Tipperary and Dublin were far from favourable. All the commentators gave it to Tipperary. Some were expressing the fear that this would be a disappointingly one-sided final. The feeling among many hurling followers was that Dublin, perennial outsiders, would be easy meat for Tipperary, one of the Big Three of the hurling world.

In Tipperary itself there was less interest than usual in the All-Ireland. They were used to winning. And they were discerning about games. They wanted to see Tipp win but they wanted to see a good match as well and they were not at all sure that it would be worth their while to travel to Croke Park on the first Sunday in September.

Yet, against all the odds this turned out to be a thrilling encounter with a neck-and-neck finish that made it one of the most memorable finals of the sixties.

Significance

This game had a greater significance. It marked the last appearance of Dublin in a final. It also marked the decline of Dublin as a major hurling power and the decline of the quality of the game in the metropolis.

'The game in Dublin badly needed local, city-grown heroes. And it needed those heroes to be honoured and feted because of winning the All-Ireland. The game needed the spotlight to be on some of the great Dublin players who could match any of the better-known hurlers.'

So says Jimmy Gray, the goalkeeper on the Dublin side that day and since then a leading administrator with the GAA and a hurling lover of proven record.

His assessment of the outcome of the game is that Dublin's losing of the All-Ireland did a great deal of harm to the promotion of hurling in the capital. It is one of the great regrets of his life.

Dublin-Born Only

But this All-Ireland also served to bring attention to a controversial practice which had been introduced for the very purpose of promoting the game in the capital — having a Dublin-born team to represent the county with very few exceptions.

On the team which took the field for the All-Ireland of 1961 only one was from outside Dublin, Paddy Croke from Ballinure in Co. Tipperary, who had won Harty Cup medals with Thurles CBS ten years previously.

The history of hurling in Dublin is inextricably linked with the growth of the city and the influx of people from the hurling counties who brought their love of the game and their skills with them. In the 1920s and '30s there were top-class sides representing the county, largely composed of country players resident in the city. Dublin won its last All-Ireland in 1938 with a team composed predominantly of country players. The same went for the teams that contested the finals '41, '42, '44 and 1948. The 1952 side that had met Cork in their last All-Ireland appearance was about half and half.

But by the time a Dublin team again came on the scene to vie for national honours in 1961, there had been a marked change of policy on the part of hurling's administrators.

'It all sprang from the fact that many country players were playing with Dublin and most of them were top-class hurlers. It would have been all right if they had given their allegiance to the county and helped us create a new tradition. However, the better they were the more their own counties were anxious to claim them. Quite a number of non-Dublin players were on the team as it played through the year and in the League, but when the time of year came for players to declare their allegiance many opted out and reverted to their native counties', explains Jimmy Gray.

These players were quite entitled to do that but they disrupted the team-building efforts of the Dublin mentors. Some undoubtedly used the Dublin team as a springboard to prominence and a career with their own counties. As well as that there was now a new crop of native Dublin players, very talented and skilled, who found it difficult to get a place or even a trial with the Dublin side because of the presence of country players of doubtful allegiance.

The hurling authorities decided on native teams only, with a few exceptions from those who proved their total commitment to the Dublin side. The players were coming from clubs like St Vincent's, Eoghan Rua and Crumlin whose membership was largely made up of Dublin people.

Emergent Dublin

The first real evidence of a strong Dublin side under the new regime was in 1957. Then Dublin drew with Kilkenny in the first round of the Leinster championship. They lost the replay to the team that went on to take the All-Ireland. The following year Dublin almost dethroned the champions when they met in Wexford. They were seven points ahead with seven minutes to go but Kilkenny levelled the match on the call of time and won the replay by a single point in one of the best games seen in the Leinster championship for many years.

The following year Dublin reached the Leinster final against Kilkenny, the first time the sides met at this level since 1947. Dublin went ahead in the fourth minute of the second half when their towering blond player, Des Foley, scored a goal. Kilkenny were lucky to score a winning goal with virtually the last puck of the game when Sean Clohosey turned a sideline cut by Johnny McGovern to the net. The following year Dublin went out after a close match with Wexford, the side that went on to beat Tipperary and win the All-Ireland crown.

Then in 1961 Dublin again found themselves up against Wexford in the Leinster final. The champions had some of the greatest hurlers of all time on their side — players like Billy Rackard, Ned Wheeler, Nick O'Donnell, Padge Kehoe and Tim Flood. Yet Dublin's lesser known players beat them on a score of 7–5 to 4–8.

Despite this well merited but unexpected win the hurling followers outside of the city made Tipperary odds-on favourites to win the final. The reason was partly out of tradition — giving the nod to one of the giants of the hurling scene that was only occasionally beaten. Another reason was because the Dublin players were largely unknown.

The Dublin Side

The best-known, because he had played for Leinster several times was a thick-haired player from the stronghold of Dublin hurling and football, St Vincent's, Dessie 'Snitchie' Ferguson. Now at right corner back he was a fearless tackler, covering the back line with fire and zest.

The other player who had won a place on the provincial side was the Dublin full back and captain of the '61 side, Noel Drumgoole. He was a forceful leader of the side, never took his eye off the ball but was always aware of the play around him and often came out with the ball for a long clearance downfield.

In the left corner was the burly Lar Foley, a man of great spirit and determination. He had a great eye for the ball and it rarely passed him — nor did any ball-carrying forwards either. In the right half back position was Liam Ferguson, brother of Dessie. This left-hander was a solid player with a good sense of positional play. Whenever goal-keeper Jimmy Gray wanted to hit the ball to safety he looked for Ferguson, who always moved into position to receive it. Centreback was Christy Hayes, a sound player who covered the line well, could hit left and right. On his left was one of the least demonstrative of the Dublin side, Shay Lynch. In an unobtrusive way he marked good forwards out of the game.

Des Foley

Paddy Grace, former Kilkenny player and county secretary of many years' standing, used say of Des Foley that he was the best midfield player he had ever seen apart from the legendary Lory Meagher of Tullaroan. The fair-haired St Vincent's man, brother of Lar, was clever, athletic, skilful and courageous. He was all over the field during a game, helping the attack and the defence, usually dominating midfield, with a great pair of hands to catch a ball. Foley's midfield partner was Fran Whelan of the Eoghan Rua club, a skilful player who held the fort at midfield to allow Foley greater freedom of movement.

On the Dublin forward line-up for the All-Ireland in 1961 were three converted backs. But all three were skilful enough and versatile enough to be able to play in the forward line. At right corner forward was Bernard Boothman, from the Crumlin club St Columba's, who was normally a half back. He was one of the first hurlers who sported an ear-ring.

At full forward was Paddy Croke who played full back on the Young Ireland's team and at centre forward was Mick Bohan, an Army man who usually played centreback or at midfield with Scoil Ui Conaill. He had come back from the Congo where he had served with the UN forces and had fitted in well to the centre forward position.

Left half forward on the side was Larry Shannon, one of the most accurate and skilful forwards on the Dublin scene. On the other side of the half line was Achill Boothman, brother of Bernard. He had great skill and used the ball intelligently. The fact that he was prematurely bald was deceptive — he was the fastest player on the Dublin side with a subtle body swerve to go past opponents.

In the left corner of the attack was Billy Jackson of New Ireland's. He was the goal-getter of the side. Once he rounded his man the goalkeeper could expect to see him racing forward to let fly a hard ball, often across the goal and into the netting on the far side.

Dublin's own goalkeeper was the small, wiry Gray. He was an eagle-eyed player, with fast footwork back and forth and across the goal. He had built up a great relationship with his three backmen and they worked as a cohesive unit.

Tipperary Side

Tipperary had won the All-Ireland in '49, '50 and '51. They even had a survivor of that side, John Doyle, still on their team. They had won in '58 with many of the present side playing. The only slight feeling of discomfiture in Tipperary was the memory of the previous year, 1960, when they were red-hot favourites to beat Wexford. Instead they were comprehensively and decisively beaten, out of the game well before the final whistle blew.

That defeat, for a county used to winning, punctured Tipperary pride and they now intended to reinforce their traditional dominance on the All-Ireland scene.

Tipperary in 1961 had a fine combination of both strong and skilled players that knitted well together under the astute eye of Paddy Leahy, long-time selector and leading team mentor. They were experienced on the All-Ireland scene, both players and sideline people.

That year they had overwhelmed Cork in a torrid Munster final in Limerick before over 60,000 people. They had shown that they were the strongest team in the southern province and they had some of the best players ever to grace the hurling scene.

Jimmy Doyle

In Jimmy Doyle they had a man who could do just about anything with the ball, such was his skill. One of his great feats was to hold the hurley delicately and loosely and reach out and cushion and trap balls coming at speed from all angles. He would hold the ball for a second on the boss and then double it away. He developed a special attribute — he could slice the ball when he hit it so that it went away in a curve. These curved balls were most dangerous when he sent them towards the goal, pinpointing them to land two feet in front of the goalkeeper, where they spun to one side, often into the goal over the goalkeeper's deceived hurley. There was a story of him sending such a curved ball at head height towards the goal in a championship game. The goalkeeper saw it coming and shifted his stance slightly to the right. He put up his hand but did not make enough allowance for the curved flight. It hit off his outstretched fingers and went into the net for what looked like a lucky goal.

The full back shouted at the goalkeeper 'You should have got that.' When the puck out was taken the goalkeeper charged out and grabbed the full back by the arm. 'Should have got it? Did you see the spin on it? Why can't that fucker hit the ball like everyone else?'

For all his accomplishments Doyle was a team player, sending out passes to his colleagues, beautifully weighted balls that landed in a way that gave them advantage over their markers. He himself could side step, almost fade away so that markers found themselves shouldering the air and Doyle was racing goalwards. This natural left hander rarely missed frees; he was like clockwork the way he lifted and struck the ball over the bar, even from acute angles.

The Rearguard

Tipperary's goalkeeper was the ginger-haired Donie O'Brien. His exceptional alertness had come to the fore in the Munster final. He often raced out to collect incoming balls while the full backs held off the forwards and sent long relieving clearances down the field. One man whom few forwards passed on way to goal was the indestructible Kieran Carey. Stories about his endurance abounded — about the time in a full speed collision a shoulder bone was knocked out of joint with an audible 'click' and how he had slapped it back into place with his free hand and continued playing.

Before the goal was Michael Maher of Holycross, a good hurler as well as a strong resolute full back. Reliability and cool temperament characterised the way he went about his task. In the other corner was a strong, totally reliable player, Matt Hassett. From Toomevara, he was the captain of the side. He had endeared himself to Tipperary followers by the modest and self-effacing manner he accepted cups and praise.

Mick Burns at right half back was a speedy, wiry player. He was a tenacious tackler, a curber of wing forwards who also sent the forwards good balls. In the centre was one of the most controlled and dedicated of Tipperary half backs, Tony Wall. He had the discipline and emphasis on training and practice of the Army man that he was. Wall could hit the ball off the ground or in the air, left or right. There were few centre forwards who got the better of him.

On his left was the tall, teak-hard figure of the durable John Doyle. He had been playing with Tipperary since 1949, a swashbuckling figure, hair falling over eye as he brought the ball out of danger, tipping it along the ground in front of him, holding off opponents, sometimes taking blows to lower legs and ankles but keeping going until the ball was safely away.

At centre field was Matt O'Gara whose commitment to the game and whose courage was emphasised by the fact that he took the risk of wearing glasses. Without them he found it difficult to see the ball. Wear them he did and in addition was a good hurler, a hardy player who was in the thick of things. His partner was a man who had come late to the Tipperary team but who proved to be a centrefield man of exceptional stature — Theo English. He covered an enormous amount of ground during a game, was strongly built and had a great stroke on the ball, especially on the ground.

Tipp Forwards

At centre forward was Liam Devaney of Borrisoleigh who was so good a player that, like Jackie Power of Limerick before him, he was asked to play in all sorts of positions. He could handle balls coming from all directions, control them, sweep them away out of his hand, on the ground, left or right. Like his colleagues, he was a team player and worked hard for the side. The other half forward, on the opposite side to Jimmy Doyle was Donie Nealon, from Burgess in north Tipperary. Apart from being a hard-working team player, Nealon had exceptional skill with hurley and ball. He slid away from his marker into advantageous positions because he was a great reader of the game, an astute assessor of who was going to get the ball, how it might break. Nealon has been described as the most influential member of the side because of his strong character and his ability to express himself well.

The Tipperary full forward line had three fine players in John 'Mackey' McKenna, Billy Moloughney and Tom Moloughney. McKenna, from Borrisokane, was a low-slung, hard running player with great deftness in tight tussles round the square. Billy Moloughney was wiry and strong. He was much more active than the traditional full forwards of that era, making space for other players, slipping the ball to them. In the other corner was a very strong player Tom Moloughney of Kilruane. He was a wholehearted player who had recovered from a foul blow struck in the torrid Munster final.

Dublin Support

However about the reluctance of some Tipperary folk to risk travelling to a one-sided game, there was no shortage of Dublin support. Indeed there was a majority of Dublin followers in the crowd of 68,000 thousand who saw this game — the largest crowd to see Dublin play.

It was hard for the Tipperary players to cope with the tag of red-hot favourites. 'I was hurling with UCD at the time and had played against all the Dublin fellows and I knew how good they were', said Donie Nealon, 'but it is difficult to get away from all the supporters and commentators who tell you that you are going to win easily. If you let it get to you then you won't bring out that extra willpower that you need to win an All-Ireland. When you are favourites you know you will get no credit for winning and get a lot of blame for losing.'

Tipperary did have a disadvantage — three of them, in fact. Jimmy Doyle, Tony Wall and Kieran Carey were all carrying injuries into this final. The mentors were hoping that these three key players could last the game.

Dublin too had a disadvantage. None of them had ever experienced what it was like to play before such an immense crowd.

The dressing-rooms before All-Irelands are places where the air crackles with nerves and tension, with players lacing and re-lacing their boots, having another pee, somebody occasionally retching in the toilet. Not all players feel such nervous pressure but many of the best do.

In those days the dressing-rooms were under the Cusack Stand, at the end of the tunnel. The tunnel acted as a channel and an echo chamber for the sounds made by tens of thousands of excited and expectant human beings. The air in that narrow space trembled with the clamour and noise of voices and footsteps and the muffled thump of the base drum in the band on the field outside.

When the door of the dressing-room opened to let the teams out this sound met the players as they emerged into the long concrete passageway. It could be a frightening introduction for a newcomer. Players were glad to get the feel of grass beneath their feet and to have room to swing their hurleys and puck a ball about.

It was a humid, overcast day with no more than a light breeze blowing from the Canal end. When referee Gerry Fitzgerald of Limerick called the captains together, Noel Drumgoole won the toss and elected to play into the Canal goal.

The teams as they lined out were:

DUBLIN

Jimmy Gray
(Na Fianna)

Des Ferguson	Noel Drumgoole, capt	Lar Foley
(St Vincent's)	(St Vincent's)	(St Vincent's)
Liam Ferguson	Christy Hayes	Shay Lynch
(St Vincent's)	(New Ireland's)	(St Vincent's)

Fran Whelan   Des Foley
(Eoghan Rua)   (St Vincent's)

Achill Boothman	Mick Bohan	Larry Shannon
(Crumlin)	(Scoil Ui Conaill)	(Scoil Ui Conaill)
Bernard Boothman	Paddy Croke	Billy Jackson
(Crumlin)	(Young Ireland's)	(New Ireland's)

Substitutes: Eamonn Malone (St Vincent's); Joe Lenihan (St Vincent's); Mick Kennedy (Faughs); Paddy Maycock (Crumlin); Seamus 'Sob' O'Brien (Eoghan Rua). *Trainer*: Mick Ryan (St Vincent's). *Mentors*: Joe Drumgoole (St Vincent's); Paddy Lillis (St Vincent's); Christy O'Driscoll (Crumlin); Dominic Bohan (Scoil Ui Conaill); Mick Leahy (Eoghan Rua).

The referee was Gerry Fitzgerald of Limerick.

Tipperary

Donal O'Brien
(Knockavilla)

Matt Hassett, capt	Michael Maher	Kieran Carey
(Toomevara)	(Holycross)	(Roscrea)

Mick Burns	Tony Wall	John Doyle
(Nenagh)	(Sarsfields)	(Holycross)

Matt O'Gara   Theo English
(Toomevara)   (Marlfield)

Jimmy Doyle	Liam Devaney	Donie Nealon
(Sarsfields)	(Borrisoleigh)	(Burgess)

John McKenna	Billy Moloughney	Tom Moloughney
(Borrisokane)	(Kiladangan)	(Kilruane)

Substitutes: Tom Ryan (Toomevara); John Hough (Toomevara); Sean McLoughlin (Sarsfields); Roger Mounsey (Toomevara); Pat Ryan (Moycarkey). *Mentors/selectors*: Paddy Leahy (Boherlahan); Jim Stapleton (Solohead); Philly Dwyer (Boherlahan); Martin Kennedy (Kiladangan); Sean Ryan (Toomevara). *Assistant trainer*: Gerry Doyle. *Masseur*: Ossie Bennett. *Team doctor*: Dr Paddy Moloney.

The Game Begins

As the teams took their places the Tipperary players exuded a certain confidence and ease. Many of the Dublin players were visibly discomfited by the eyes of 68,000 people directed at them.

Almost from the throw in, Liam Devaney got possession and tried for a long range point. It went just wide. From the puck out Tipperary again got in control. A ball went in to the right corner of the attack where Mackey McKenna got to it before Lar Foley. From close range he belted a pile-driver that was going for goal until it met the stick of Jimmy Gray and was deflected over the bar for Tipperary's first point. This was an important save by Gray. A goal at this early stage might have undermined his side badly. Even so, it was an ominous start by Tipperary, with a player of McKenna's striking power having the freedom to shoot for goal.

From the puck out Tipperary again attacked. In desperation Shay Lynch fouled Jimmy Doyle to stop him racing goalwards. Doyle stood over the placed ball, lifted it with style and struck it over from his left with grace and accuracy. There was a reassuring cheer from the Tipperary followers, who rarely saw the small, dark-haired man miss frees.

Only a minute later the Sarsfields player raced through for a spectacular point that put Tipperary three points ahead. To foul him meant a point and to let him though meant a point or even a goal — a frustrating dilemma for any defender.

Tense and Tentative

While Tipperary were playing comfortably, hurling well in a relaxed way, Dublin were tense and tentative. They struck the ball badly, as if afraid of making mistakes. There was a ray of light at midfield where the tall Des Foley was getting a fair amount of ball and coming into the game.

The Dublin full forward line kept running out, as if to draw their heavier, heftier markers with them and try to make space behind, where their speed might give them an advantage in a race for or with the ball.

'There was no point in trying to slog it out, toe to toe, with those backs', reflects Larry Shannon.

The problem was that the players needed to be striking well to make this ploy work. From the first Dublin attack Paddy Croke, running out and turning to strike the ball, sent it well wide. Then Bernie Boothman sent in a hard shot across the goal to Billy Jackson. There were groans from the massed Dublin followers on Hill 16 when he failed to connect and a real chance was lost. However Jackson made up for this miss shortly afterwards with a well-taken point for his side's first score.

From the puck out Des Foley sent his side on the attack again. It was becoming apparent that one thing Dublin did have on their side was speed — especially in the forward line. They went on the attack and won a free. Shannon, who took the close-in frees, sent it over the bar.

As if to show who was in control Tipperary moved the ball down field soon afterwards and the strong Tom Moloughney eluded Dessie Ferguson and shot over a good point. Both corner men had now scored and it seemed as if Dublin might be vulnerable in their full back line. This was not to be. From then on the Dublin full back line took full control and were impregnable, sending back ball after ball in the first half, when many of their colleagues were being outplayed further out.

Tipp Control

At his side of the field the bespectacled O'Gara was winning a lot of ball and starting the attacks that washed against the Dublin full back line. At centre back Tony Wall dominated; but it was noticed that his injury hampered his covering back and forth across the line as he did when fully fit. Burns and John Doyle had not the kind of back-up that Wall usually provided.

In the next Dublin attack the speed advantage of Achill Boothman over John Doyle became apparent when he and his brother combined in an attack that ended with Achill sending over another point for Dublin.

Yet by this stage Tipperary were having the better of matters almost everywhere, surer in their striking, much more astute in the way they used the ball, sending good passes to one another. Devaney and Nealon were using all their wiles and experience to create chances, to try to get scores themselves or get in good passes to the full forward line. Dublin kept giving away frees trying to stop these attacks. In the twelfth and fifteenth minutes Jimmy Doyle stretched Tipperary's lead with points off frees.

Dublin replied when a long distance free was sent over the bar by Des Foley, who was carrying the midfield standard for the metropolitans. Fran Whelan was playing far below his best and was giving his opponent, Matt O'Gara the freedom to shine.

Meanwhile Dublin's attack was unable to finish with scores some promising moves begun from the half forward line. Croke and the Boothmans missed good opportunities for points. Some attacks did get through and Jackson and Boothman both shot for goal. Donie O'Brien handled these well. He was fast on his feet and on several occasions he was to run out to collect balls that had come into the goal area while the full forwards and their markers were well out.

The Difference

The next score came from O'Gara who gathered the ball at midfield, made space and sent a long ball that sailed between the uprights for a fine point. The following score was made by that tireless forager, Theo English, who flicked a weighted pass for Nealon to strike it over a neat point. This score seemed to epitomize the difference between the composed, skilful Tipperary men and the earnest but tension-stifled Dubliners.

Yet Dublin kept trying. Bernie Boothman picked off a good point from an angle to keep his side in the chase. Then once again Tipperary attacked. It was left to the full back line of Ferguson, Drumgoole and Foley to handle the brunt of these assaults and they performed well. But Dessie Ferguson picked the ball off the ground in one scramble and from the resulting free Jimmy Doyle once more sent the ball over the bar. A minute later, he faded away from his marker, and hit over another point to leave his side leading by 0–10 to 0–5.

Disallowed Goal

Dublin came back to the attack and were awarded a free which Shannon pointed. Then came one of the controversial moments of this game. In a Tipperary attack, almost on the call of half-time Jimmy Doyle sent a slow, lobbing ball into the Dublin square — the kind that allowed the forwards to charge in.

'We all pulled together. I got a crack on the nose — a sore thing I can tell you — and came to lying just outside the line with someone lying on top of me', recalls Donie Nealon. The ball was beside him. Impishly, he elbowed the ball over the line but the umpire was standing looking down at him. In any case he was adjudged to be in the square before the ball came in. It acually went into the goal and had rolled out to the vicinity of Nealon's elbow.

'A goal at that stage would have been a bad blow for Dublin because they were getting by, holding out until half-time', says the Tipperary forward. In those last few minutes Dublin were coming more into the game. A goal would have damaged their growing morale.

When the referee blew for half time the score stood at Tipperary 10 points to Dublin's 6. It was felt that this hardly reflected the superiority of the Munster side over the underdogs. The Tipperary side went in reasonably pleased with their performance. They felt that they should be more ahead but they had seen nothing about the Dublin side that really troubled them. The only troubled person was O'Gara. In a clash under the Hogan Stand one of the lens had flown out of his spectacle frame. He would be at a serious disadvantage without it. Somebody was given the task of finding the lens in the grass — not quite as bad as looking for a needle in a haystack but certainly in the same category. To everybody's surprise the searcher returned with the lens. It was reinserted in O'Gara's frames and he went out to continue his starring role in the second half.

The atmosphere in the Dublin dressing-room was thoughtful and determined. They knew they had played badly, been affected by nerves, been a bit overawed by the reputation of their rivals. Drumgoole called for attention.

'We know now that there is no need for us to fear Tipperary. We're in this game with a good chance. But we have to get out there and hurl, give it all we have, forget about the tension', he said.

Dublin reappeared on the field determined to throw caution to the winds, open their shoulders and hurl with a sense of freedom. However in the first six minutes of the game the close marking resulted in a lot of missing by both sides. There was a good deal of scrambling about that did not please the hurling purists in the attendance. Tom Moloughney had a miss and, unusually, Jimmy Doyle had a miss with a free. Dublin had three wides by Bernie Boothman, Whelan and Shannon. It did not seem to matter that much because the feeling was that this interesting but ordinary game on this dull day would eventually go Tipperary's way.

Great Enlivening Goal

Then in the sixth minute came the score that set this game alight. Christy Hayes broke up a Tipperary attack, sent the ball to Shannon who noticed Billy Jackson free and flighted the ball into his hand 35 yards out. Jackson, light and fast, left Hassett behind as he raced for the goal. From less than 20 yards he let fly a hard shot that streaked to the net on O'Brien's left.

A huge roar reverberated about the stadium. The light blue and white flags shimmered on Hill 16. There were exultant looks on the faces of the Dublin players. This score seemed finally to lift the yoke of tension and awe from the shoulders of most of their players. Dublin were now only a point in arrears. Des Foley stormed about the midfield area, striking balls right and left, rising to catch balls amid swinging hurleys. Hayes, Ferguson and Lynch in the half back line became much more forceful, and got attacks going.

Fran Whelan, overshadowed by O'Gara for much of the time, set up the next Dublin attack. He passed a great ball to Achill Boothman for the Crumlin man to bring the sides level.

From now on every clash, every challenge for the ball, every block-down, every clearance, every good stroke of the ball brought out a succession of roars from the crowd. There was no question that hardened battlers like Tipperary were going to wilt under the heat of the Dublin surge of zest and power and the thunderous support of their followers and the many others who wanted the underdogs to create the surprise of the decade and actually win. They too fought like tigers and with both sides at it tooth and claw the rest of this match had a level of excitement as intense as in any other final of the period.

Dublin Ahead

The speed of the Dublin attack was now creating more dangerous situations, spreadeagling the Tipperary defence. In one of these the ball came to Larry Shannon in front of the goal. He was about to belt it into the goal when he got a shoulder from John Doyle. The ball skimmed over the bar instead. But Dublin were now ahead for the first time, something that seemed unimaginable at half time.

At this stage Tom Ryan of Toomevara replaced Mackey McKenna in an attempt to shake the rock-like Dublin full back line. It was also clear that Tony Wall's effectiveness was diminishing while Jimmy Doyle was noticeably less mobile. This was a difficult time for Tipperary. But they were used to being in tight spots before. And then O'Gara, playing heroically, sent a long ball from midfield that rose and rose and drifted away near the end of its flight high over the uprights. The umpire waved the white flag. It brought the sides level.

Boothman Brothers

Dublin were now playing with great freedom and abandon. Within two minutes they were two points up. First Des Foley, hurling powerfully all over the field, placed the fleet-footed Achill Boothman to send over a point. Then Boothman went on another tearing raid. He was fouled. His brother took the free but it was blocked down. The ball however came back to Achill and he clipped it over the bar to put his side two points ahead

A serious blow for Tipperary was an injury to O'Gara at midfield. He was replaced by the experienced John Hough, a solid and reliable player, but O'Gara's departure took one of the inspirational players for Tipperary out of the battle.

But the side in blue and gold reached down deep within themselves for the spirit and grit that was part of Tipperary hurling and they defended with great vigour and attacked again and again.

Two Sent Off

Entering the last quarter of this enthralling battle came the only sour note of a sporting game. In another Tipperary attack Dessie Ferguson was going to pick the ball when Tom Ryan pulled on it, legitimately. Ferguson went down. Lar Foley was incensed by what he saw as a bad foul on his team mate and club mate. He ran across and buffeted Tom Ryan. They got into a scuffle. The referee ran in and sent both of them to the line.

In retrospect it was accepted that Ryan had not deliberately struck Ferguson, that the tangling between Foley and Ryan was not serious and hardly warranted their being sent off. But this incident had a significant effect on the outcome of the game.

'Lar Foley had been playing a storming game. Nobody could get the better of him. He dominated the corner and nobody passed him', said Donie Nealon. 'From then on there was a big space in that corner and it allowed us the room to get vital scores.'

Empty Corner

It was into that corner that Nealon ran to take a good point in the sixteenth minute. But Dublin were quickly back on the attack. O'Brien was called upon to make one of the best saves of the game when Jackson lashed in the ball from a wide angle. It was going for the goal but O'Brien got his hand to it. The ball went off his fingers and over the bar. This was a crucial save. The Tipperary goal was under great pressure at the time — in contrast to the Dublin goal where Gray had to deal with only two balls during the course of the entire game. At this stage Dublin brought on Eamonn Malone in place of Mick Bohan who, like Wall, was tiring.

Vital Switch

Hassett, Maher and Carey had to put all they knew into keeping the ebullient Dublin forwards at bay. On the right wing Mick Burns had played very soundly all through on the dangerous Shannon while John Doyle began to come into the game more and made several rousing clearances out of defence. But the player who undoubtedly turned the game Tipperary's way was Liam Devaney. Tony Wall's knee injury got worse as the game went on and he had no alternative but to come off. Devaney, who often played at centre back for his club, took over from Wall while Sean McLoughlin came into a reshuffled attack.

Devaney gave a display of majestic hurling. He used all his uncanny feeling for the game to be where the ball was, caught it deftly, cleared it away quickly from left or right. He hurled with great fluidity and style as if everything came easily to him. He sent his side into the attack by repeated long clearances.

Dublin defended desperately but it was difficult not to concede frees. Jimmy Doyle put one over. Another attack. Another free. Another point from Doyle to put the sides level. Then the elusive Nealon, with his instinct for an opening, got a ball and ran into the right corner and sent over a narrow-angle point to give Tipperary the lead. And Tipperary still kept pressing. Another attack and another free and another point for Jimmy Doyle. Four points in a row for Tipperary, hurling with all their might against opponents who were fired with a determination that meant every ball was contested with a ferocious urgency.

There was one memorable incident that highlighted the spirit of Tipperary hurling. During these hectic minutes Tipperary attacks were being broken up by the redoubtable Noel Drumgoole, virtually unbeatable that day. His clearances went out ninety yards or more, often sending his side on the rampage. Now he got the ball and was about to make one such clearance. But the courageous Tom Moloughney flung himself into the swing, taking the hurley on his body, blocking the ball down, preventing a rip-roaring, inspiring clearance by the Dublin captain.

Dublin Respond

Dublin were far from finished, however. With five minutes to go they swept back on the attack and once again Achill Boothman sent over the bar for one of the best scores of the game to leave just a point between the sides.

It was in these last few minutes that Devaney made some of his most memorable interceptions, stopping attacks, getting his own forwards on the move.

In the very last minute Dublin were awarded a free over on the left under the Cusack Stand side. The crowd, drained by the continuous excitement of it all, murmured in anticipation.

'It was right on the sideline. A difficult angle even though about fifty yards out', recalls Larry Shannon, who stood over the ball that day while backs and forwards jostled, waiting for what was seen as Dublin's last chance to save the game with a point or even win it with a goal. 'I didn't want to belt it hard in case it went wide. My aim was to loft it just over the bar.'

The ball left his stick, followed by 68,000 pairs of eyes, and sailed into the goalmouth, seeming about to go wide. But Des Foley, throwing everything into the effort, rose into the air and batted the ball towards goal. Instead it went into the side netting and with it went Dublin's final chance.

Only a few seconds later Gerry Fitzgerald blew the whistle to signal full time.

'We really felt depressed when we got back to our dressing-room. All the more so because we had almost pulled it off against all the odds and all the predictions', says Jimmy Gray.

Neither he nor any of his colleagues nor indeed their rivals in the jubilant Tipperary dressing-room next door realised that this was the swansong of Dublin as a serious contender for All-Ireland honours. No one could have foreseen that they would never contest another.

'It was an awful pity. All you have to do is to compare how the Dublin footballers went from strength to strength, especially in the 1970s, once they had won the final. They stayed at or near the top, with new, young players inspired to follow in the footsteps of men who became household names', says Jimmy Gray. 'There is plenty of hurling played in Dublin but it needs the injection of widespread support and enthusiasm that winning the top prize brings.'

In the Tipperary dressing-room there was great relief that they had got by in a close-run thing. They would not have liked to return home having lost two finals in a row.

There was a personal postscript for Donie Nealon. As he sat in the dressing-room amid all the laughs and congratulations he became aware that people were avoiding him. Then a mentor came forward and told him the bad news. His father had collapsed in the Hogan Stand and died near the end of the game. Nealon dressed quickly, collected his hurley and grip and hurried grimly across the pitch. Just as he reached the other side a man came running out to tell him that it was a case of mistaken identity. A person who bore an uncanny resemblance to his father had died.

'I was sure you were dead', a relieved Nealon said to his father afterwards. 'O God I was having my first pint in Ahern's by that time', his father replied.

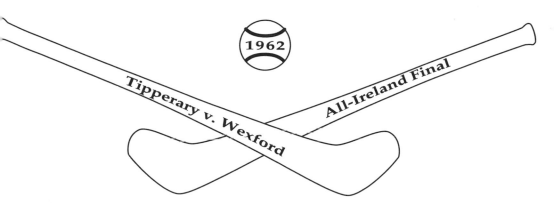

1962

Tipperary v. Wexford

All-Ireland Final

NIGHTMARE START TO GLORIOUS GAME

'A few breaks of the ball could decide this game', said one excited spectator amongst the 75,000 as the referee prepared to start the All-Ireland of 1962.

The Tipperary men, looking confident in their blue and gold jerseys, had one of the most powerful teams ever to emerge from that hurling stronghold. They were reigning All-Ireland champions. They had top players like Jimmy Doyle, Liam Devaney, Donie Nealon, Michael Maher and Theo English. It was a team laden with All-Ireland medals and one player, John Doyle, one of the great backs of the game, had five.

But Wexford, the challengers, had decisively beaten them two years previously in the All-Ireland, against all predictions, with a team which included some of the great hurlers who had brought the county to the hurling forefront at the start of the 1950s. Five of these veterans were now lining out for what seemed likely to be their last All-Ireland: Nick O'Donnell, Billy Rackard, Padge Kehoe, Tim Flood and Ned Wheeler.

Croke Park crackled with the static of excitement. Any time these two teams had met in a big game there had been surging end-to-end play, spectacular striking and sweeping, open hurling that had thrilled and delighted the crowds.

In addition to the massed attendance, another 200,000 people were crouched round black-and-white sets to watch the first All-Ireland televised by RTE. And thousands more were listening to the radio commentary.

It looked like this was going to be a neck-and-neck race from start to finish. Some of the most outstanding players ever to swing a hurley were there waiting for the throw in.

But the Wexford team had hardly had time to get a good grip on their hurleys and the spectators to settle down, when Tipperary had scored two goals. Within ninety seconds of the start. Now, after all the euphoria of expectancy it seemed as if this was about to be one of the most one-sided All-Irelands ever.

Yet the joyful reality was that no All-Ireland final ever began with so disastrous a start for one of the teams yet developed into one of the most pulsating encounters of all time.

First Goal

When the ball was throw in, with midfielders and forwards jostling and elbowing for advantage, Ned Wheeler, the big, fair haired full-forward for Wexford, clipped it into the Tipperary half. It was quickly cleared out by the burly Tipperary full back, Michael Maher, and then went off a Wexford hurley over the sideline.

Matt O'Gara, the spectacled right wing back from Toomevara, cut the sideline ball into the Wexford half. It travelled towards the Tipperary captain, the incomparably skilful Jimmy Doyle, playing at right half forward. He was again being policed by the man who had marked him so successfully two years before, John Nolan of Oylegate. Much was expected from both players by the rival followers and a huge roar went up as they raced shoulder to shoulder for the ball.

When the ball went over the sideline off Nolan, Tipperary's most versatile player, Liam Devaney, playing at midfield, ran over to take the cut. Very skilful with the ground ball, he sliced under it with great precision and power. It took off in a long trajectory. It seemed to be going wide but Donie Nealon, the Tipperary right corner forward, reached over the head of his marker, Ned Colfer, and deflected it towards the goal. The hawk-like, lithe goalkeeper Pat Nolan, blocked it out with his hurley. Ten yards out it ran straight into the hand of the inrushing Tipperary full forward, Tom Moloughney. A strong, muscular player, he shortened the grip on his hurley to avoid being hooked and slammed it to the net.

As the green flag was waved, the stands and terraces suddenly blossomed with blue and gold Tipperary flags. The Wexford followers were stunned. Over a fifteen-year period in top-class hurling few full forwards had scored a more fortuitous goal against the acknowledged prince of full backs, Nick O'Donnell, famed for his alertness and astute positional play.

Tipp's Second Goal

Nolan, a younger brother of the left half back, took the ball from inside the goal and threw it to O'Donnell to take the puck out. The tall full back, with lank, black hair falling across his forehead, flexed his shoulder muscles. He had a powerful stroke and could puck the ball 100 yards. Wexford were playing into the Railway End, with a slight breeze at their backs. Perhaps, in his annoyance at what had happened and determined to land the ball beyond the Tipperary 70 yard line, O'Donnell tried too hard.

Startled players and spectators saw the ball skid off his stick, ricochet off the outstretched hurley of Moloughney and land at the feet of Sean McLoughlin, the tall, sinewy Tipperary corner forward only 20 yards out. He quickly accepted such a rare gift, swung on the ball and sent it rocketing towards the net. Pat Nolan lunged at it but it whizzed past his stick on his right-hand side and shook the net.

The huge roar that rose up in the air over Croke Park was one of astonished delight from Tipperary followers and loud groans of dismay from both Wexford and neutral followers. The game had hardly begun and Wexford were two goals down. The most reliable of full backs, who had captained Wexford to victory two years before, had made a once-in-a-lifetime mishit. The Wexford mentors and substitutes along the sideline looked at one another and shook their heads. But even some of the Tipperary followers were uneasy.

'Two early goals are great — but I didn't put money aside for a ticket and the train fare just to see a bad oul game', said a grizzled hurling lover who had boarded a special train at the Horse and Jockey railway station in Co. Tipperary that morning.

He need not have worried. He and all the other spectators were to see one of the most enthralling games ever seen in Croke Park, with Wexford fighting their way back into the game so that it was indeed neck and neck up until a few minutes before the final whistle.

Great Rivals

All hurling followers had been looking forward to another trial of strength between these two sides. They had virtually the same teams as in 1960. Going into that game Tipperary had been firm favourites. They had a proud record of never having lost an All-Ireland since 1922. It was thought that Wexford were carrying too many ageing stars.

But Wexford, full of fire and vigour and determination, swept the favourites aside. Jimmy Doyle, so dangerous when near a ball, but small and light, had been marked out of the game by the same man now assigned to mark him in 1962. Wexford were cruising to a jubilant victory when the final whistle sounded. The score was Wexford 2–15 to 0-11 for Tipperary.

These two counties had first met in the All-Ireland of 1951. Tipperary, regular champions, had dominated the hurling scene since 1949 and were going for their third title in a row. Wexford, a team of big strapping men from a county which had won only one All-Ireland forty-one years before, had brought a special glamour and novelty to a hurling scene long the preserve of Tipperary, Cork and Kilkenny. It was a thunderous game, with Nick Rackard at full forward for Wexford bursting through for early goals. Lack of experience, on the field of play and among the mentors on the sideline, beat Wexford. But it had been a tremendous contest and Tipperary followers developed a great liking and respect for these sporting rivals.

They had met in the National League finals of 1952, 1955 and 1956. Tipperary had won the first two games with Wexford winning the 1956 final. This latter was one of the most famous games of the decade. With a gale force wind behind them in the first half Tipperary went into what seemed an unassailable lead of 15 points. Wexford had the wind in the second half but few imagined that they would take command in the way they did and emerge winners by four points.

Early in 1962 the teams now about to contest the All-Ireland had met in the Oireachtas final. Another rousing encounter, it had ended in a draw. Tipperary won the replay with six points to spare.

However it was the defeat in the All-Ireland of 1960 that was at the back of the minds of Tipperary followers as they made their way up to the Thurles Sportsfield — now Semple Stadium — to watch the team training in the August evenings.

'They better not think that they are going to get it easy against this Wexford side' was often heard as they watched the veteran, hurling-scarred mentor, Paddy Leahy of Boherlahan, put the team through their paces.

Just the same, there was an air of confidence about the field as the team and substitutes pucked about and raced around the field. The team had matured, were all the time developing a greater sense of teamwork, meshing their many talents to form a hurling machine which, in the mid 1960s, was to grind down most opposition. There was no stopping this team. They had got over the defeat of 1960 and come back to beat Dublin, if only barely, in the final of 1961.

In the semi-final of the Munster championship they had met a very good Limerick side and drawn with them. But Limerick were unable to withstand the power play of the Tipperary men in the replay. They met a depleted Waterford team in the Munster final and won fairly handily.

Sixty miles away, on the other side of the Blackstairs mountains, the Wexford team and selectors gathered in the evenings at Bellefield, the pitch on the heights above Enniscorthy and the river Slaney. Nick Rackard, now a selector, was as dominant a presence as he had been during his playing days.

There was great interest and enthusiasm in the team and the embankment was filled with onlookers from the farmlands, villages and towns about, nodding at one another, commenting, forecasting.

Having overcome Laois rather easily in the Leinster championship, the side had faced Kilkenny in another final. Three goals by Wexford, all within the first eight minutes, settled this game, despite the fact that Kilkenny were a top-rate side of talented players.

'Nothing like early goals to get a team off to a good start', said a commentator in the *Wexford People* newspaper, reporting on that game. This remark was to be ironically apt on the first Sunday in September.

The local newspapers gave the forthcoming match extensive coverage. The sports correspondents of the national newspapers and — for the first time — RTE television visited the two training camps.

The Opposing Sides

It was agreed by all the commentators that the teams were very evenly matched in terms of ability and experience. It was thought that Wexford were likely to be outclassed at midfield, where Theo English and Liam Devaney were two of the surest strikers of a ball, great challengers, able to strike quickly off left or right. Their opponents were to be Phil Wilson and Martin Lyng. Wilson, from Oylegate, had performed well in the Leinster final and Lyng, from the Geraldine O'Hanrahan club in New Ross, had held his own. But they were not considered to be in the same class as their opponents.

There was much speculation about the respective centre backs and their opponents. Billy Rackard had been one of the key players in the rise of Wexford to hurling prominence. He had been playing at centre back for several years and was one of the outstanding players in that position. He had great anticipation under the high dropping ball, was strong enough to stand his ground, and was one of the most consistent catchers of the ball. He was weighty enough to burst past opponents for long clearances that put Wexford on the attack. In the 1960 game he had got the better of the very able Devaney.

Now he was to find himself opposed by a young, bustling player who was solidly built, full of stamina and skilful hurling. John 'Mackey' McKenna from Borrisokane was the man Tipperary hoped would get the better of his more experienced but older opponent.

In Tony Wall, Tipperary had a player who was challenging Rackard for the title of best centre back in the game. A well built player, he studied the game, improved his skills by diligent practice. He was dedicated and controlled in the way he went about his task, backing up his wing men, dominating the half back line. But good and all as he was, he was going to have his work cut out to keep the shackles on Padge Kehoe.

Kehoe, at 37, was a grizzled veteran of big championship games. He was strong and vigorous. He had a great facility, under tight marking, to scoop or hand-pass the ball out to better-placed opponents. But he was accurate when he went for scores himself and he had a very powerful shot.

These two had battled it out in 1960 and Kehoe, by all accounts, had got the better of things. Wall, however, was a learner, a player who studied opponents, worked out ways to combat them.

Wheeler and Maher

For some time the Wexford team mentors had been trying to find a forceful full forward. That year they decided to try their great mid field player, Ned Wheeler, in the position. In the Leinster championship he proved to be a dangerous spearhead. Six foot one inch and 14 stone 8 pounds, he was a muscular, vigorous player. Very agile for his size, he was extremely effective with his overhead striking of high incoming balls.

His opponent was going to be another big man, not quite as big, but fourteen stone, solidly built. Michael Maher had already won two All-Irelands in the position and was a byword for reliability. Nobody was likely to go thundering in on the goalkeeper when he was around. The outcome of the battle of the big men was one of the talking points in the lead-up to the game.

At the other end of the field Tom Moloughney of Kilruane, a strong, hard-working full forward, was thought to have a tough job on his hands in trying to get the better of the king of full backs, Nick O'Donnell.

Corners and Wings

On either side of Maher in the Tipperary full back line were two other big, strong men who used their weight and strength to stop opponents and were able to take the ball away from the danger area near the goalmouth. John Doyle would be playing in his seventh final. He had been in the winning side on five occasions. He was now at right corner back. His assignment was to mark the elusive Tim Flood, who had been his opponent in the 1951 All-Ireland. Flood, from Cloughbawn, was famous for his strong running along the end line with the ball on his hurley and for his accurate striking.

The duel in the opposite corner was to be between Oliver 'Hopper' McGrath and Kieran Carey. One of the fastest men on the Wexford side, McGrath had a jinking style when he got the ball, twisting and dodging, hopping the ball on his stick. Carey, from the Roscrea club, who had marked him well in some previous games, epitomised reliability and physical toughness. He always seemed to be in the right place and McGrath would not find it easy to pass him.

In the battle on the wings on either side of Wall the two Wexford half forwards flanking Kehoe, Jimmy O'Brien and Paul Lynch, were being marked by Mick Burns from Nenagh and Matt O'Gara. O'Brien was fast and industrious, a great passer of the ball; Burns was a tough, tight marker, undemonstrative but very sound. On the opposite side the stickwork and fleet footwork of Lynch would be the challenge before O'Gara. It was Lynch's goal in the first minute of the Leinster final that had helped tumble Kilkenny. The man from Toomevara was a strong, determined player who had overcome the handicap of wearing glasses in a game of hard body contact and flailing hurleys. He was one of the stars of the All-Ireland final of the previous year.

In the contest between the Wexford half backs and Tipperary half forwards Jim English of Rathnure would be marking Tom Ryan of Killenaule. English held the hurley in the right-hand-under grip but he had established himself as the best in the right half back position because of his reliability and effectiveness. He was, however, 31 and had been slowed by a leg injury. There was speculation that he might find it difficult against the speedy Ryan, who had done fairly well against him in previous encounters.

On the other side two other players would also renew rivalry, Jimmy Doyle and John Nolan. The Thurles Sarsfield's man was so good a reader of the play, knowing where the ball would break and so elusive once he got possession that Nolan would have to match him step by step, relentlessly, for every moment of the game.

The Tipperary full forward line had one of the sharpest, energetic right corner forwards in Donie Nealon. Such was his skill and ball control that he could play in several positions, particularly midfield or on the wings. He was going to be watched by a 21-year-old newcomer, Ned Colfer from New Ross, who had shown great capability in the Leinster final, marking Kilkenny's Denis Heaslip. In the left corner the rangy Sean McLoughlin was up against one of the best corner backs in the game, Tom Neville. McLoughlin, a right-hand-under player, looked awkward but was lethal in front of goal and was the leading scorer of hand passed goals on the hurling scene. His opponent from New Ross was a hard-tackling player who made few mistakes and had a good understanding with his full back and goalkeeper.

Both goalkeepers, Donie O'Brien of Tipperary and his opposite number Pat Nolan, were well-established, reliable men. Both were alert and agile. O'Brien had saved his side the previous year in the final against Dublin while Nolan had made memorable saves in the 1960 final.

As the Sunday of the game approached a sense of delightful anticipation took hold of both counties and hurling followers everywhere. CIE laid on special trains, stopping at little stations in Tipperary and Wexford which, in the intervening years, had been closed down one by one.

Two employees of Wexford Corporation set off on the Friday in a horse and a cart which had been converted into a covered wagon — American West style — decked with the Wexford colours. The television rental companies ran advertising campaigns to induce people to watch the game in the comfort of their own homes.

Wexford Battle Back

So, after all the pre-match build-up, there was a great sense of anti-climax when the powerful Tipperary team were two goals ahead with the game hardly started.

But, when the game was restarted, spectators saw the Wexford team rise out of themselves in a tremendous effort to stop the game going

The teams as they lined out were:

TIPPERARY

Donie O'Brien
(Knockavilla)

John Doyle (Holycross)	Michael Maher (Holycross)	Kieran Carey (Roscrea)
Matt O'Gara (Toomevara)	Tony Wall (Thurles Sarsfields)	Mick Burns (Nenagh)

Theo English
(Marlfield)

Liam Devaney
(Borrisoleigh)

Jimmy Doyle, capt (Sarsfields)	John McKenna (Borrisokane)	Tom Ryan (Killenaule)
Donie Nealon (Burgess/UCD)	Tom Moloughney (Kilruane)	John McLoughlin (Sarsfields)

Substitutes: Liam Connolly (Fethard); Tom Ryan (Toomevara); Matt Hassett (Toomevara); Roger Mounsey (Toomevara); Ronnie Slevin (Borrisokane); Michael Murphy (Sarsfields); Christy Hartigan (Newport). *Mentors/selectors*: Paddy Leahy (Boherlahan); Paddy Kenny (Davins); Martin Kennedy (Kiladangan); Philly Dwyer (Boherlahan); Jim Stapleton (Solohead); Sean Ryan (Toomevara). *Assistant trainer*: Gerry Doyle. *Masseur*: Ossie Bennett. *Team doctor*: Dr Paddy Moloney.

WEXFORD

Pat Nolan
(Oylegate)

Tom Neville (New Ross)	Nick O'Donnell (St Aidan's, Enniscorthy)	Ned Colfer (New Ross)
Jim English (Rathnure)	Billy Rackard, capt (Rathnure)	John Nolan (Oylegate)

Martin Lyng
(New Ross)

Phil Wilson
(Ballyhogue)

Jimmy O'Brien (New Ross)	Padge Kehoe (St Aidan's)	Paul Lynch (Shamrocks)
Oliver McGrath (Faythe Harriers)	Ned Wheeler (Faythe Harriers)	Tim Flood (Cloughbawn)

Substitutes: Martin Bergin, Ignatius Gavin, John Kennedy (Faythe Harriers); John Mitchell (St Aidan's); Joe English (Rathnure); Brendan Morris (Ferns); Harry Doyle (New Ireland's, Dublin); Paddy Meyler (Kilmore). *Coach/ trainer*: Nick Rackard. *Team doctor*: Dr Pat Daly.

The referee was John Dowling of Offaly.

away from them so early. They gave everything they had in the race for the ball, in the fierce tussles of what was later described by the *Tipperary Star* as the hardest hour's hurling seen at Croke Park. They often managed to get that few inches ahead of their opponents, to go on full throttle, to be that split second faster on the pull or the catch.

To the surprise of many, Phil Wilson and Martin Lyng established the upper hand at midfield, which they were to hold until the end of the game. Wilson, with a long, fast stride and sure striking won much of ball round the centre of the field and sent raking pucks in to the forwards.

Several promising attacks on the Tipp goalmouth were beaten off by the resolute backs before a move between Wheeler and McGrath ended with the latter being fouled by Kieran Carey. Padge Kehoe came up to take the free and put it over the bar. It raised an encouraging cheer from the Wexford followers. It was exhilarating stuff, sweeping from end to end. Tipperary attacked. Tom Ryan and Jimmy Doyle threatened but the attacks were repulsed by John Nolan and Tom Neville. Jim English frustrated Ryan by one of his well-honed skills — blocking down the ball.

In another Wexford attack Hopper McGrath eluded Carey and came racing in to fire a shot goalwards. It was O'Brien's first real test and a great Tipperary roar went up when he saved it well. The ball was cleared down the field but fell between Rackard and McKenna. The red-haired centre back caught it and sent it on a long flight into the Tipperary square. With Maher and Wheeler grappling, the ball skimmed wide past the post.

Rackard Off Form

The Wexford followers were delighted with this demonstration of the captain's catching and clearing prowess. Rackard, however, was not to dominate the game as expected.

'When I came on the field that day I just wasn't feeling right', he recalls. He liked to practise in his own way and was ill at ease at the training regime in Enniscorthy.

In the first few minutes he and McKenna chased a ball towards the sideline. Rackard tripped and fell forward with outstretched hands near the ball. McKenna pulled on it. His hurley smashed into Rackard's hand and seriously fractured it. Only the flow of adrenalin, the excitement and the unwritten code about enduring pain kept the Rathnure man going.

There was another factor which limited Rackard's effectiveness. The Tipperary mentors and players had studied his stance under the high ball and had a plan to curb him. Most of his opponents stood at his right to pull right-handed on the dropping ball. Rackard was able to hold them off with shoulder and right arm, holding the hurley up for protection while he caught the ball in his reliable left hand.

'We told Mackey to stand on Billy's left and challenge for the ball from there', said Donie Nealon. 'It did not entirely stop Rackard but it certainly gave Mackey some advantage.'

The speed of the game right from the start was exceptional. Wexford had to give their all while Tipperary had to go into full gear to match them. Croke Park was enveloped by the frenzy, the total commitment of the players on the field. The crowd roared and cheered continuously and only drew breath momentarily when the ball went wide or referee Dowling whistled up for a free.

Tipp Keep Ahead

Donie O'Brien made another good save after McGrath, Wheeler and Paul Lynch had raced forward and eluded their markers. But his clearance went to Lynch who hit it over the bar.

Only a moment later Donie Nealon raced on to a ball near his corner, controlled it skilfully and clipped it over the bar. From the puck out Wexford swept back up field. Hopper McGrath, speeding out from the corner with Carey in close pursuit, gathered the ball, spun round and jinked his way goalwards. He sent it over the bar to a delighted yell from the Wexford followers, who loved his daring footwork and style. Wexford were now in arrears by four points: 2–1 to 0–3.

Although he was being closely marked by John Nolan, Jimmy Doyle's skill was hard to curb. He only needed the merest chance to flick the ball accurately and quickly to a colleague, or send it into the full forward line with a neat pull. But it had to be split-second action for Nolan's close attention ensured that he was going to get few free shots at goal. Just the same he sent Tipp attacking twice in succession which ended with a 70 — sent wide by Tony Wall — and a jostled Theo English also missing the uprights. But a free gave Doyle a chance for a point, which he took well.

Watching the Tipperary attacks and how dangerous their forwards were, spectators wondered if Wexford's great effort had begun to peter out. But, in great hip-to-hip challenging, they swept back again. A line ball from John Nolan was well struck and gathered by Padge Kehoe. Wall was at his elbow but he managed to pass it to Paul Lynch who hit it over the bar.

Battle of Big Men

In front of the Tipperay goal was a battle of gladiators. The two big men, Maher and Wheeler, stood hip to hip. They pulled together on every ball. On one occasion a high ball came floating into the goalmouth. They rose together and swung on it. The sharp squeal of ash on ash could be heard above the hubbub and brought out a great roar. The ball fell at their feet. They pulled together again. Another huge roar. The tormented ball skittered behind them. They spun round like heavy tops and pulled again to an even louder roar. When the two of them fell to the ground Donie O'Brien raced out, gathered the ball and cleared it away.

Most of the time Wheeler and Maher were shoulder to shoulder. But a few times they raced for the ball from different directions. Neither of them was going to shirk the thudding impact of bone and muscle. On one occasion, one of the umpires was seen to put his hands to his head in alarm when the two leviathans collided at full speed with a tremendous thump near the goalposts. They both fell to the ground but rose to a gladiatorial roar of encouragement from supporters of both sides.

Tipperary set up another attack but the Wexford full back line was playing well. Nick O'Donnell, always calm, had recovered from the bad start and played very efficiently. Tom Neville delighted the Wexford followers by his vigorous tackling and clearing. Colfer was playing well on Tipp's danger man, Nealon.

Wexford Catching Up

It was from a Colfer clearance that Wexford got their next score. The ball fell in centrefield where Martin Lyng pulled on it and sent it into the square. Wheeler got possession but was fouled going through. Padge Kehoe decided to lob it into the square. Tim Flood, eluding John Doyle for once, came flying in, got his stick to the ball. It skimmed just over the bar with the goalkeeper beaten.

Wexford were now only three points behind and, to the thunderous roar of their followers, visibly redoubled their efforts. John Doyle called on all his experience and endurance to save several dangerous situations; he first scraped the ball off the goal line and then stopped a hard low free taken by the powerful Kehoe. He came running out, tipping the ball before him on the ground, holding off opponents with powerful arms and sent a good clearance down the field. Shortly afterwards Donie Nealon, running like a hare, reached high in the air, caught and cushioned a ball at the end of his stick, brought it down magically into his hand and clipped it over the bar. Tipperary were four points ahead.

From the next puck out Jimmy O'Brien, constantly foraging, gathered the ball and sent a neat puck, straight as a die, to Padge Kehoe, who had got clear of Tony Wall. The Enniscorthy man sent it high between the posts.

It was end-to-end play every minute of the game. Devaney got possession 20 yards out and let fly a great shot. Nolan brought off one of his many great saves as the ball came whizzing in. He turned it out for a 70, which Wall sent wide. But Tipperary came on the attack again. Neville took the ball off the stick of Sean McLoughlin, spun round and sent it out the field. Billy Rackard caught it and got in one of his long pucks. There was a flurry of bodies and sticks and Wexford were awarded a free 30 yards out.

Heartening Wexford Goal

'Put it over the bar, Kehoe', some of the Wexford followers shouted, fearing that the strong Tipperary backs would again clear it if he lobbed it into the square. But lob it he did. Ned Wheeler pulled overhead on it, connected perfectly and the ball shot into the net. A huge cheer of exultation went up from the Wexford crowd. After such a disastrous start they were on level terms.

Wexford attacked again and a similar free resulted. Kehoe again sent the ball into the square but this time it was cleared by Kieran Carey, who blocked down Wheeler's effort and then sent the ball flying away out of danger.

Tipp Respond

Tipperary came thundering back near the end of the first half. They regained some of the initiative. Their talented forwards like Nealon and Doyle were difficult to stop. Two frees resulted from Wexford's frantic efforts to curb the Tipp forwards and Jimmy Doyle, with his impeccable left-handed striking style, put them over the centre of the crossbar. Then, just before the half time whistle, Sean McLoughlin got possession and sent the ball over to put Tipperary three points ahead.

Both teams trailed across the field towards the dressing-rooms to a prolonged handclap. The admiration towards the teams wafted over the pitch like a golden glow. The sense of enjoyment and delight in an epic struggle had the spectators buzzing. Although this was a hard, gruelling physical battle, with heavy shouldering and frenzied jostling, every ball contested with ferocious determination, it was none the less clean and sporting. This was part of the tradition that had been built up between these two teams.

Second Half

Wexford would now be playing towards the Canal end, into a slight breeze. It gave Tipperary followers great confidence that from the throw in Jimmy Doyle, eluding the attentions of John Nolan for once, sent a ball soaring high between the posts. It put the champions four points ahead and augured well for them.

All during the first half the influence of Phil Wilson at midfield was crucial to Wexford's fortunes. Tipperary decided to bring the energetic Nealon out from the corner to midfield and put Devaney on the wing. But despite this the Wexford pair remained much in control.

Wall's Performance

The barrier to the Tipp goal was proving to be their centre half back, Tony Wall. Although he had the difficult task of trying to contain the vigour and wiliness of Padge Kehoe, he was performing very efficiently. He was fast off the mark and raced across to left or right to help out his wing backs. He cleared away many balls with long, controlled pucks that were heartening to the hard pressed Tipp backs. He had learned from his experience with Kehoe in 1960 that the best way was to be ahead of him to the ball on all occasions.

Another Wexford Goal

In every big match between evenly-matched teams there are instances of the unexpected, of good and bad luck. Tipperary were favoured at the start of the game. Now it was Wexford's turn. Jimmy O'Brien just raced a foot in

The Wexford team which defeated Cork in the 1956 All-Ireland final. Front row (*left to right*): Tom Ryan, Mick Morrissey, Jim English (captain), Art Foley, Tim Flood, Tom Dixon, Seamus Hearne. Back row (*left to right*): Billy Rackard, Nick O'Donnell, Ned Wheeler, Jim Morrissey, Martin Codd, Nicky Rackard, Padge Kehoe, Bobby Rackard.

All-Ireland final 1956: Mick Morrissey of Wexford has possession watched by his team-mate Bobby Rackard and challenged by Christy Ring of Cork. The player on the ground is Paddy Barry.

The Waterford team and substitutes which contested the 1959 All-Ireland final replay against Kilkenny. Front row (*left to right*): Paudie Casey, Tom Cheasty, Larry Guinan, Mick Flannelly, Frankie Walsh, John Kiely, Tom Cunningham, Seamus Power, Michael O'Connor, Charlie Ware, Donal Whelan. Back row (*left to right*): Freddie O'Brien, John Barron, Ned Power, Jackie Condon, Martin Og Morrissey, Joe Harney, Austin Flynn, Phil Grimes, Mick Lacey, Joe Coady.

All-Ireland final 1959: Ollie Walsh clears under pressure.

All-Ireland final 1959: Another great save by Ollie Walsh under pressure from Larry Guinan and John Kiely. The Kilkenny right full-back is Tom Walsh.

The Dublin team and substitutes which lost the 1961 All-Ireland to Tipperary. Front row (*left to right*): Christy Hayes, Jimmy Gray, Paddy Croke, Billy Jackson, Noel Drumgoole (captain), Bernard Boothman, Larry Shannon, Eamon Malone, Des Ferguson, Paddy Maycock. Back row (*left to right*): Sean McCabe, assistant secretary of county board, Des Foley, Fran Whelan, Liam Ferguson, Lar Foley, Shay Lynch, Joe Lenihan, Seamus O'Brien, Mick Bohan, Achill Boothman, Mick Kennedy, Mick Ryan, trainer.

All-Ireland final 1961: Paddy Croke, Kieran Carey, Donal O'Brien and Bernard Boothman contest the ball.

The Tipperary team and substitutes which defeated Wexford in the All-Ireland final of 1962. Front row (*left to right*): Mick Burns, Liam Devaney, Donie O'Brien, John McKenna, Theo English, Donie Nealon, Jimmy Doyle (captain), Sean McLoughlin, Roger Mounsey, Christy Hartigan, Tony Wall. Back row (*left to right*): Tom Ryan (Killenaule), Matt O'Gara, Ronnie Slevin, John Doyle, Tom Moloughney, Michael Maher, Kieran Carey, Tom Ryan (Toomevara), Liam Connolly, Matt Hassett, Michael Murphy.

All-Ireland final 1962: Phil Wilson of Wexford and John McKenna of Tipperary tussle for the ball.

All-Ireland final 1962: Pat Nolan, the Wexford goalkeeper, jumps for a high ball while Tom Neville holds off the incoming Sean McLoughlin of Tipperary.

The Wexford team beaten by Tipperary in the All-Ireland final of 1962. Front row (*left to right*): Jim English, Paul Lynch, Martin Lyng, Ned Colfer, Oliver McGrath, Tim Flood, Pat Nolan, Jimmy O'Brien. Back row (*left to right*): Padge Kehoe, Ned Wheeler, Billy Rackard (captain), Phil Wilson, Tom Neville, John Nolan, Nick O'Donnell.

The Cork team of 1966 gave the rebel county one of its sweetest ever All-Ireland victories, bridging a long gap of twelve years. Front row (*left to right*): Gerry O'Sullivan, Colm Sheehan, Paddy Barry, Charlie McCarthy, Gerald McCarthy (captain), Seanie Barry, Finbarr O'Neill, Ger O'Leary. Back row (*left to right*): Jack Barrett (mentor), Denis Murphy, Tom O'Donoghue, John O'Halloran, Tony Connolly, Peter Doolan, Mick Waters, Justin McCarthy, Paddy Fitzgerald, Donal Sheehan, John Bennett, trainer Jim 'Tough' Barry.

All-Ireland final 1966: Paddy Barry about to send the ball upfield.

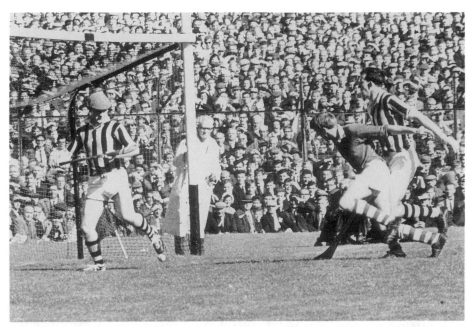

All-Ireland final 1966: Action in the Kilkenny goalmouth.

All-Ireland final 1968: Wexford beat a highly fancied Tipperary side to win what is, to date, their last All-Ireland title. Here, Ned Colfer clears from Michael 'Babs' Keating watched by Eddie Kelly and Dan Quigley.

front of Mick Burns, picked up the ball and sent in a high, stinging shot straight towards the Tipp goal. The heavyweights, Maher and Wheeler, rose together and pulled against one another overhead as the ball came flying in. It was difficult for O'Brien to keep sight of it. The ball went straight into the net without either of them, or the goalkeeper touching it. With only four minutes of the second half gone Wexford were only a point behind.

Tim Flood was finding it very hard to elude the tenacious John Doyle and Padge Kehoe was living off scraps in his battle with Tony Wall. They switched positions. Shortly afterwards Ned Wheeler sent the ball in and only the vigilance of Donie O'Brien stopped it going over the goal-line. He pushed it out for a 70.

Billy Rackard came up to take it. The damaged hand did not prevent him striking a long and accurate shot into the breeze which sailed between the uprights to bring the teams level. All round the ground the purple and gold flags waved.

Wexford Take Lead

They waved again shortly afterwards when a free taken by Martin Lyng was gathered by Wheeler, who slapped it over the bar to give Wexford the lead for the first time. The Wexford supporters felt a great rush of pride that their men could have courageously climbed such a steep incline and managed to reach even ground above.

But Tipperary attacked relentlessly again and again. They were awarded a 21-yard free. Jimmy Doyle, whose mastery of ball control enabled him to direct the ball at will now sent in a low, hard shot. It was cleared by Nick O'Donnell. In Tipperary's next attack Doyle took a heavy shoulder charge which dislocated his own. There were worried looks among the Tipperary supporters as the ambulance men helped him off the field. Tipperary had lost their captain and most skilful player at a crucial juncture of the game.

Doyle's replacement, Tom Ryan of Toomevara, proved to be a handful for John Nolan. He and Liam Connolly, who had replaced Matt O'Gara, were fresh players coming into a game in which energies had been drained by constant neck and neck racing for the ball, by bodily contact that knocked the wind out of men again and again.

Ryan's namesake from Killenaule then managed to beat Jim English for the ball and sent a point over from out on the wing. The teams were level again. But almost immediately Padge Kehoe got possession, shouldered his way past John Doyle with ball balanced on stick. He was fouled, took the free and put it over the bar.

The puck out went to Tim Flood. He raced through and belted the ball over the bar. Wexford had gone into a two point lead with thirteen minutes to go.

Still the play rolled back and forward from end to end. There were near misses and both goalkeepers made great saves. Everybody in Croke Park rose to Nolan on one occasion; a ball from McKenna had passed him on its way to the net when, with lightning reflexes, he spun round and cleared the ball back over his head outfield.

The Wexford corner forwards, McGrath and Kehoe, were staying out from the corners, almost at the half forward positions, to try to escape the attentions of Carey and Doyle. This opened big spaces in front of goal but with Maher blocking Wheeler several balls ran free and Donie O'Brien was able to race out unchallenged and clear them well down the field.

Crucial Tipp Goal

With ten minutes to go disaster struck again for Wexford. Billy Rackard stumbled in going in to challenge Mackey McKenna, who had got possession of the ball. The Borrisokane man, muscular shoulders hunched to protect the ball on his stick went thundering towards the Wexford goal. Fifteen yards out two Wexford backs closed on him. He spotted Tom Ryan of Killenaule racing in and passed the ball to him.

'I chased after Ryan. I could see goal written all over his back. But I couldn't catch him — I had nothing left in the tank', recalls Billy Rackard.

Ryan made space for himself and then swung on the ball. He was renowned for the power of his shot — the ball bulleted into the net for a crucial goal. Tipp were now ahead by a point and the cheering from the spectators was one continuous roar.

But from the puck out Hopper McGrath gained possession and went racing through. He might have scored but two Tipperary defenders threw their hurleys at him for a technical foul. This practice has, thankfully, long been done away with. The referee gave a free which the ever-reliable Padge Kehoe pointed.

Seven minutes to go and the scores were level. The excitement and tension among players and spectators was intense. Tipperary came thundering into attack and only the agility of Nolan in the Wexford goal stopped the ball crossing the line. He scooped it out for a 70. This was taken by Liam Devaney, now making an impression on the game, but it went narrowly wide.

With four minutes to go the ball came flying into the Wexford half. There was a desperate tussle for possession but Nealon got sight of the ball and whipped it over the bar to the thunderous cheers from the Tipperary followers.

Then came two misses that were heart stoppers for the respective supporters. Tom Ryan of Killenaule fired a ball in which ricocheted of the upright and was cleared. Now the ball was swept down into the Tipp half. Tim Flood tipped it over to Paul Lynch who seemed well placed for a score but he gave an agonised grimace as he watched his shot go inches the wrong side of the post.

Younger Team Lasts the Pace

It was in these last minutes of the game, when players had given their all, covered in perspiration, many bearing weals on knuckles and bodies, that it seemed that the great haul back from being two goals down had drained so much energy from the Wexford men. These were the moments when the younger team were those few inches faster to the ball. Some of the veterans on the Wexford team were finding that all their reserves of energy had dwindled.

'Some of us were a bit long in the tooth and it tells in a tight finish like that', says Ned Wheeler.

Tipperary attacked again and Sean McLoughlin of Thurles Sarsfields got possession and rifled the ball over the bar to put his team two points ahead almost on the call of time. Wexford made one last Herculean effort, cheered on by their faithful followers but referee Dowling blew the whistle to bring the great battle to a close.

Tributes

Tony Wall accepted the cup in place of Jimmy Doyle, whose injured shoulder was being treated in hospital. When he praised Wexford for their courage and endurance and their sportsmanship and called for the traditional three cheers, all the spectators and all the Tipperary supporters gave the most sustained and rousing cheer that any losing side ever received after an All-Ireland in Croke Park.

'This was a great game and it took two great teams to make it so', Wall concluded.

There were very few All-Irelands where the supporters of the winners and losers shuffled out of the stadium and along the roadways with an almost equal great sense of delight and joy. Tipperary were jubilant because they had played to the utmost of their skill and stamina and courage — and needed to do it to withstand the great challenge by the men in purple and gold. Wexford followers were full of pride and gratitude that their men came back from such a shattering start to make this one of the greatest games most spectators had seen.

Next morning Paddy Downey in the *Irish Times* referred to the breathtaking power and grandeur of the game that blazed with nerve-wracking drama from start to final whistle. 'Both sides emerged from this memorable final with reputations enhanced in skill, spirit and sportsmanship; and the pity of it was that one of them had to lose.'

In the *Irish Independent*, the veteran GAA correspondent, John D. Hickey said that for drama, tenseness, agonising suspense and valour this spine-tingling hurling inferno capped anything that had been seen on an All-Ireland day.

On Monday evening there were pinpoints of light along the sides of the Devil's Bit mountain as the train carrying the team moved along the flat plain below, heading towards Thurles and a rapturous reception. In the gathering dusk small groups stood about blazing fires near the rounded summits of Keeper Hill and, in the far south of the county, on Slievenamon. These were the bonfires which signalled a tribute to the valour of the men who represented this proud county.

The Wexford team came home to the warmth of a great welcome. They were borne along the roadways of the county on a wave of admiration and gratitude. At Coolgreaney they were met by a man dressed as a pikeman of the rebellion of 1798, riding a white horse. In the rotund oratory of the time there were comparisons between the heroes of that traumatic episode and those of 1962. 'The spirit of Vinegar Hill is still with us', proclaimed one banner.

One of the most remarkable things about this All-Ireland was the deep feelings of goodwill and friendship felt by each county towards the other. This generosity was well expressed by the *Tipperary Star* when it said that if Tipperary played Wexford every day of the week the Wexford men would have an equal share of winning hours. 'It was fire and steel and hell for leather, marked however by splendid sportsmanship. All this week Slievenamon has been smiling across at Vinegar Hill with a warm glow of friendship and rivalry.'

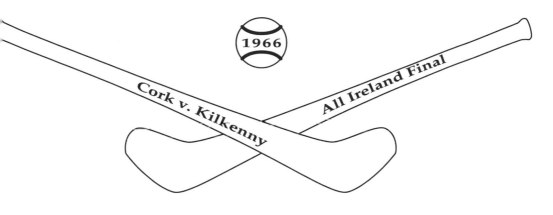

1966

Cork v. Kilkenny

All Ireland Final

CORK'S SWEETEST VICTORY

Nobody would ever pretend that the All-Ireland of 1966 between Cork and Kilkenny could compare with the memorable finals between these two great hurling counties such as those of 1931, 1939, 1947 and 1972.

There was no last-minute winning point scored in an agony of tension for the players and the followers. There were no great passages of top class hurling from two of the counties where skill and style were highly prized.

Yet this final had a significant impact on the hurling world. It ensured that one of the most fruitful fields on the map of the game would continue to grow good-quality players, capable of matching their skills with the best.

Cork had not won an All-Ireland for twelve years. This once-proud bastion had not even contested one for ten. There were thousands of young people who had never seen the men in red win anything.

A Losing Tradition

No county can send out teams year after year and see them beaten again and again, often humiliated, without losing some confidence, without becoming haunted by the spectre of defeat every time they go out to play an important game. Good sides, which should have won All-Irelands, have become immobilised by the ardent hopes of frustrated followers, by the fears and anxieties that shackle those from whom great things are expected, by the pressures and tensions that burgeon in a losing tradition.

Just as much as in counties like Galway, Waterford, Limerick, Offaly and Clare, the three great centres of the game — Cork, Kilkenny and Tipperary — need to win the All-Ireland at regular intervals in order to keep the interest in the game fully alive. Winning at national level promotes the game in the county, from juvenile level to those approaching middle age who play just because they love the feel of a hurley in their hands.

If Cork had not come to the fore after a long absence in 1966 it may not have appreciably diminished the interest in the game in the county. The tradition there is part of the weft and weave of everyday life in the city and the rural hurling areas. However, being in the All-Ireland spotlight — and especially winning — highlights courage and skill and ability and gives these qualities a public accolade. Hurler-heroes emerge from every great game or campaign and their exploits create a climate of emulation among young aspirants. Winning teams create a surge of interest within any county and carry with them armies of followers.

Needed to Win

'There's no question about it — we badly needed to win. For ourselves and for hurling in the county', said Gerald McCarthy, who captained the team that day, one of the youngest players ever to lead a winning side to victory. 'All you had to do was to see the unbelievable scenes in Cork the night we brought the cup back home after a twelve year absence to realise how much it meant to people.'

Eddie Keher, who played for Kilkenny in that final, makes the point that the longer a county goes without winning the more difficult it becomes for them.

'The pressure for a win from supporters builds up as the years go on without an All-Ireland. And supporters include people who are very knowledgeable about the game — winners of All-Ireland medals in the years past, fellows who know everything about hurling and how it should be played, fellows who are training teams, people whose everyday conversation is full of hurling.

'When a team is not winning this pressure gets to GAA officials and team delegates. They can be critical of the selectors and the team manager or coach. They can vote them out of office and sometimes do. This in turn makes the selectors edgy. They try out players, drop them if they don't work out the very first time, chop and change the team, play fellows out of their best positions, sometimes don't give a team time to settle', he says.

Without Ring

There was something unusual about the Cork team of 1966. It was the first time in twenty-five years that a Cork side appeared in the final without the presence of the stocky, messianic figure of the most accomplished hurler of all, Christy Ring. He had played on the winning Cork sides in 1941, '42, '43, '44, '46, '52, '53 and '54. He had been one of the key figures in the last final which Cork had contested, against Wexford in 1956.

Years of Defeat

After all those years of victory Ring, too, became part of the years of defeat that followed Cork's last All-Ireland appearance. It would not be true to say that in the ten years since 1956 the Cork senior team performed badly. They were overshadowed by the rise of two truly great teams in Munster — Waterford and Tipperary. The Waterford side, whose speed and vivacity gave a great boost to the hurling scene, battled for supremacy with a Tipperary team that had some of the greatest exponents of the game in its ranks. Waterford beat Cork in 1957 by five points and by a goal in 1959 in the provincial final.

It was in the Munster final of 1960 against Tipperary that Cork came nearest to regaining the county's place at the top of the hurling scene. This was a hectic, bruising encounter, full of fine hurling and hard tackling. The following year the same teams met again in the final in Limerick before a record, gate-breaking, rib-bruising crowd of over 60,000. The borderline between competitive hurling and tribal violence was crossed a number of times, by some of the players and by people in the crowd. The scenes of rough play evoked anger and vengefulnes even in the mildest souls. There were scuffles between rival groups of spectators. Tipperary won this torrid encounter by eight points and went on to win the All-Ireland.

Humiliation

Cork did not reach a Munster final again until 1964. That year and the following year the team ran up against a Tipperary side that had evolved into one of the most powerful teams ever to play in the championship. So strong were Tipperary that they flattened all opposition in every game they played. In the Munster final of 1964 they trounced Cork on a scoreline of 3–13 to 1–5. This was a big let-down for the thousands of supporters who had travelled so hopefully.

The next year was the nadir of Cork's hurling hopes; they were utterly humiliated not just by a scoreline of 4–11 to 0–5 but by the fact that some of their own supporters were leaving the ground at half-time.

After that inglorious defeat many in the hurling community began to wonder how long, if ever, it would be before they regained their place at the top of the hurling pinnacle. Certainly, nobody expected them to make any impact in 1966.

Kilkenny to Fore

Kilkenny on the other hand had enjoyed great distinction during the same decade. They had beaten the great Waterford side in 1957 against all expectations, coming from behind in the last few minutes as so many Noreside teams had done in finals when all had seemed lost. The following year they had played in one of the legendary semi-finals, by far the best game of hurling that year, when they met Tipperary and lost narrowly to them. The following year they met Waterford once again in a final. This match had everything and is still reckoned to be among the top five finals ever played. It ended in a draw. Waterford won the replay decisively.

The sides met once again in the final of 1963 and this time Kilkenny came out on top in another tremendous game. They were in the final again the following year but were no match for the Tipperary side that had overrun Cork and all other teams that stood in their way. Kilkenny were beaten in one of the most one-sided finals for a long time on a score of 5–13 to 2–8.

But they had put together a side of fine players and in 1966 Kilkenny began to emerge as the top team in the country. Many of the side had a vast amount of championship experience. Most of them were All-Ireland medal winners and had a store of experience of Croke Park on the big days.

Ollie in Goal

They had in goal Ollie Walsh, the man who had given a special glamour to the role of goalkeeper in the modern era. Not alone was he a hawk-eyed wielder of the stick who seemed to make impossible saves but he was able to trap the flying ball and take possession of it. In those days, forwards were allowed to charge the goalkeeper if they got away from the grappling arms of their markers. They sometimes came charging in on Ollie as he came dancing out with the ball. He had the footwork of a Cossack dancer and sidestepped and swerved to the delight of the crowd. Then he would take a mighty swing and hit the ball so hard that it often landed among the Kilkenny full forwards at the far end.

Great Half Back Line

That Kilkenny side had one of the best half back lines seen for many a long day. Seamus Cleere, Ted Carroll and Martin Coogan were players of great ability and had a world of big game experience between them. It was said of Cleere that he was in the mould of one of the most accomplished of all Kilkenny half backs, Paddy Phelan. From the prominent Bennettsbridge club, he was a stylist, a fast striker from right or left, a great reader of the game.

In the centre was Ted Carroll, a tall rangy player not unlike Cleere in stature. He had an instinctive feeling for being in the right place. His greatest attribute was his consistency. He had a calm demeanour and played well and steadily in game after game. On his left was a left-handed player from Castlecomer, Martin Coogan. He had great skill, could hit the ball great distances, seemingly without having to make any great effort. But all his pucks were carefully placed, sent in low to give the forwards the advantage. His sideline pucks were exhibitions of how it should be done. Whenever the ball went over the line along the left touchline anywhere between the half back and half forward line the Kilkenny crowd were wont to shout out, 'Let Coogan take it.'

The kind of balls that Coogan sent in were meat and drink to forwards like Tom Walsh, the small, fairhaired player from Thomastown, who was one of the fastest in the game, able to solo with the ball, leaving markers in his wake and then strike the ball in full flight to a spot in the goal furthest away from the keeper.

Another small but effective forward was Sean Buckley. A product of Patrician College, Ballyfin, it was said of him that he won games for the college on his own. He was a star minor with Kilkenny and brought his nippiness and his skills into the senior team.

Eddie Keher

Even in 1966 Eddie Keher was considered one of the great forwards of all time. He knew where the ball was going to break and once he got hold of it he could hit it over the bar without looking at the uprights, left or right. His skill in lifting, trapping, handling and striking the ball was amazing. He had such smooth skills that he made it look easy. He had a calm, settled temperament which served him well in his role as taker of frees and penalties near the goal.

These and many of the other players on the team were already household names in the hurling areas. Seven of them had played in the All-Irelands of '63 and '64. Four others had been on the losing side in '64. They became even better known early in 1966 when Kilkenny began to make a serious bid for the National League.

League Victories

In the semi-final they met the team they were to meet again in the All-Ireland: Cork. Kilkenny swept the Leesiders away and won easily by twelve points. Not alone did that victory establish Kilkenny as a serious contender for the All-Ireland but, in the minds of many, put the inept Cork side out of the running completely.

The real test of this Kilkenny team was the league final against the side that had beaten them so badly in the All-Ireland of two years before — Tipperary. This was still the great Tipp side and before the game it was impossible to place a bet on them. Kilkenny were the complete outsiders, not given any chance against the burly power and the skill of a team that had been unbeatable since it emerged two years before.

There was an added significance to this game. Kilkenny had not beaten Tipperary in a major game for years and years. It used to be said that the stick artists from Noreside could not match the shoulder-power and hard tackling of the Tipperary men. That league final saw this myth demolished. Kilkenny used their weight and strength like many had never seen them use it before. They were determined to end any talk of allowing themselves to be intimidated by the tough-man attitudes that were a part of the Tipperary hurling tradition. Kilkenny won that muscular encounter by 9 points to 7. They showed an edge of steel as well as traditional skills and were immediately installed as favourites to take the All-Ireland title.

Cork Reorganisation

Down in Cork the selectors set about reorganising the side after the debacle of the league semi-final. They began to look closely at the talent being thrown up by the very promising under-21 side including three McCarthys: Justin, a tall, clever midfielder from Passage; a strong, first-time striker, Gerald; and a small, sharp forward of deadly opportunism and accuracy, Charlie.

The first big break the side got was the surprise elimination of Tipperary by an Eamonn Cregan-led Limerick attack at the Athletic Ground in Cork. Tipperary, perhaps jaded after winning so much or caught by the unexpected power of Limerick, were well beaten. Cork felt far more at ease at the prospect of meeting Limerick than their constant conquerers. However, the side almost went out in the very first game against a very good Clare side, inspired by Pat Cronin. Clare were leading almost on the call of time when Cork were awarded a free nearly 40 yards out. Justin McCarthy was delegated to take it.

'I had no option but to go for a goal', he said afterwards. He rose the ball carefully and hit it with all his might. It flew past hurleys and bodies and smacked into the net to make the game a draw.

One of the emerging stars on the Cork side was a whippet-thin, crew-cut player who held the hurley in the right-hand-under grip, Seanie Barry from Rathcormack. He was clinical in the way he struck every ball that came his way. He had been a star player on the Farranferris team that had won the Harty Cup. He could put balls over the bar from every angle and near the goal could hit bullet-like shots from left or right. In the replay against Clare he scored 2–6 of his side's total to see Cork safely through to the next round.

Game Against Limerick

The next match was against Limerick, the conquerers of Tipperary. It was played on a wet, cool day in Killarney. The Cork mentors detailed Tony Connolly the task of marking Eamonn Cregan. Connolly knew that Cregan liked to roam about, often well out of position, like a wolf waiting for an opportunity to pounce, as he had done to great effect against Tipperary. Connolly, very fit and adept, followed the Limerick star everywhere he went and effectively curbed him. Despite that, with 11 minutes to go Limerick were three points ahead. Then Seanie Barry let fly a left-handed shot that struck the woodwork and bounced out again. But the alert Charlie McCarthy whipped the rebound into the net to make it a draw. It was typical of the many scores this player was to get in the years ahead.

Barry seemed to have won the game for his side with a palmed goal shortly afterwards. But Limerick had no intention of going out tamely. It took one of the great performers that day for Cork, the experienced Paddy Fitzgerald of Midleton, to save his side from at least a replay. It was his alacrity that turned a last-gasp goal-bound ball by Limerick over the bar.

Wondering About Ring

Notwithstanding being on the winning trail again there was talk about the need for more forceful forward play. Although he had been in effect passed over by the Cork selectors in 1964 the thoughts of many now turned to the 46-year-old Ring. He was playing well in the club championship, slower in the sprint but as clever and skilled as ever and still a figure of extraordinary lustre.

There were some tentative moves to sound him out but he was very sensitive about allowing his name to go forward for selection and then ending up as a substitute. His pride in his reputation would not allow this. Whether he might make himself available required the kind of delicate handling was never the forte of GAA officialdom. Ring effectively dropped out of the reckoning, although his name was still being mentioned as a remote possibility right up to the final.

There were many in Cork who said that this new, young team should not be burdened with rumours about a possible return of Ring. However, his name and personality had been central to Cork hurling for so long that he was not easily put out of mind.

If Cork were looking for a forward of experience they found one in John Bennett from Blackrock. At 33 years of age, he was a player who had been in hundreds of close encounters at county and club level and would use his skills and energies well in the corner and scrambles round the square.

He was not the only seasoned performer in the side, despite its being constantly referred to as a 'young side'. Players like Denis O'Riordan, Peter Doolan, Jerry O'Sullivan and Paddy Fitzgerald had soldiered through Cork's most dismal days, known nothing but defeat over the years. For some of them 1966 was the end of the road, their last chance to reach an All-Ireland, let alone win one. There were other fine Cork hurlers, like the great Jimmy Brohan, who had already retired without ever being able to win an All-Ireland medal which so many ex-players in Cork from other eras had in abundance.

In the Munster final against Waterford, Bennett justified his recall by scoring two fine goals and helping Cork to a six point victory. It was by no means a memorable game and did little to lift the perception of Cork as outsiders for the final. They seemed to be scraping through each time they played and to have more than a fair share of luck on their side.

Within the team itself a spirit of determination was growing with each game, with each training session.

'We developed a tremendous fighting spirit. We began to mould together as a team, to become fiercely loyal to one another, to understand one another's play', says Gerald McCarthy. 'We knew that the Cork followers wanted so much for us to win and we wanted to win for them and for ourselves. We were inspired by this feeling. We were a very hungry side, determine to do or die.'

Jim Barry

Trainer of the side was the impeccably dressed and elegant figure of Jim 'Tough' Barry, a tailor from Washington Street. He had been associated with Cork teams for years and years, had known days of celebration and glory and, in the previous twelve years, disappointment and dismay. He was a cheerful, fatherly figure, who had a great human concern for all the players.

'His nickname was not really deserved. In fact he was a bit of an old softie', recalls Gerald McCarthy. 'His presence made for a happy family of players. He had a very warm and caring personality and we all felt at ease with him. He was of immense value to the well-being and morale of the team.'

Kilkenny in Leinster

While Cork were gradually forcing their way out of Munster the Kilkenny side first took on Offaly at Portlaoise. It was a rugged game but the fleet-footed Tom Walsh scored two goals to settle the matter. It was the familiar Wexford-Kilkenny pairing in the Leinster final. Wexford were leading 2–5 to 0–7 at half time but the introduction of the 22-year old Claus Dunne of Mooncoin helped turn the tide for Kilkenny in the second half. He went to centre forward and although marked by the redoubtable Dan Quigley he opened up the Wexford defence by his skilful touches and clever play.

Midfield Pairing

At midfield Kilkenny had a real powerhouse that day in John Teehan from the St Lactain's club in Freshford. Tall and strong under the dropping ball, he was a tireless forager, and struck some great balls into the forward line. Teehan's companion at midfield for the final was the left-handed Paddy Moran who was one of the stars of a great Bennettsbridge side. He was one of those who had won an All-Ireland medal in 1963 and played in the 1964 final as well as being consistently picked for Leinster. Moran was a player who had grown in skill and ability from year to year and now, at 28, was at the height of his hurling career. He and Teehan had dominated midfield during the testing league final against Tipperary.

Defenders

In the defence was one of the most determined, lion-hearted players ever to don the black and amber jersey, Pat Henderson from Johnstown. He had learned much of his hurling at Thurles CBS and had gone on to be a stalwart in Kilkenny minor and junior sides. Another defender who distinguished himself that day was the stocky Jim Treacy of Bennettsbridge. He was to establish himself as a corner back of great tenacity who won the ball consistently and cleared it away with powerful strokes.

Among Kilkenny's skilful forwards who had played well in the Leinster final was another young player from Mooncoin, Joe Dunphy, who had been a minor star and had played with Leinster in the Railway

Cup two years previously. He was the typically nippy Kilkenny corner forward.

The Full Positions

Named at full forward for the All-Ireland was a tall, sinewy farmer from Freshford, Pa Dillon. Here was a teak-tough man who battled for the ball, would break up the play, stop his opposite number clearing the ball and keep the ball in the danger area. He was to turn from poacher to game-keeper in the following years when he became one of the staunchest full backs the county ever produced.

At full back that year was a young but experienced player of 6 ft 1 ins who weighed 14 stone, Jim Lynch. Like so many of his colleagues he had been good enough to be picked on the Leinster side for the Railway Cup at a time all players in the province strove to be selected.

Kilkenny Look Unbeatable

As Kilkenny and Cork began their preparations for the final there began a buzz of excitement that always attends the prospect of a game between these two sides. The only thing that served to dampen the expectation somewhat was that most people in Kilkenny and many hurling lovers outside the county could not see them being beaten. Indeed many wondered if it might not be a one-sided affair, in which the Croke Park experience and traditional skills of the Noresiders might overwhelm the newcomers to the scene.

As the Cork side underwent preparation under Jim Barry and the sharp eyes of one of the legends of Cork hurling, Jim O'Regan, they had to cope with a shoulder injury to one of their best, Denis O'Riordan. In the end, to his great disappointment, he could not assume his customary place at centre half back. The selectors were fortunate that a player of equal ability, Jerry O'Sullivan, had recovered from injury. He had starred as a midfielder in the championship but a player of his quality was equal to the task at centre back and that is where he went for the final.

The goalkeeper, Paddy Barry, a low-sized but very alert goalkeeper, had been put to the test in the Munster championship and had pulled off some great saves. One of the veterans of the side was Peter Doolan of St Finbarr's. He made a point of getting first to the incoming ball. His clear-ances were prodigious. Both the full back, Tom O'Donoghue and the man in the other corner, Denis Murphy were tight-marking players. Murphy was exceptionally agile for a corner back of that era, able to flick balls away from opponents. No Kilkenny forward could expect to get free shots from either of these, although it was considered that Murphy would have his work cut out minding the mercurial Tom Walsh.

The Cork half back line, although not as illustrious in reputation as their Kilkenny counterparts, had all played very soundly in the cham-pionship. Connolly was a close-tackling half back, very quick off the mark, as he had shown against Cregan of Limerick. On the other side of O'Sullivan in the centre was the experienced Fitzgerald, who had also come into his own in the four Munster games.

Newcomers

At centrefield were two comparative newcomers, Justin McCarthy of Passage and a player who had been called into action during the course of the Munster championship, Mick Waters of UCC. How they would fare against the force of Teehan and Moran was seen as crucial to keeping Cork in the game.

At centre forward was another player from the UCC side that had come to the fore in the fiercely competitive Cork county championship, John O'Halloran. Like most of the Cork outfield players he could keep the ball moving by first-time pulling. So could Gerald McCarthy, now the captain of the side. Some doubts had been expressed about his lack of big time experience early in the campaign but he had proved his worth by his skill and his utter commitment on the field. Seanie Barry on the other wing and McCarthy were certainly going to be tested by players of the calibre of Coogan and Cleere.

McCarthy's St Finbarr's namesake Charlie had now become a fixture in the right corner. A razor sharp opportunist with a rapier-quick hurley, the small cornerman was fast off his line to meet and strike the low incoming balls that Gerald often sent in when they played for their club.

The bustling Colm Sheehan was a forager for the ball in the square, blocking and harrassing the backs, breaking the ball for the two corner opportunists, McCarthy and Bennett.

'Our side were not as well known nationally as the Kilkenny fellows but we didn't let that bother us. Nor did we mind being underdogs. That only fired us up further', says Gerald McCarthy.

Kilkenny Training

In Kilkenny, as the team trained under Nick McGrath and Fr Tommy Maher, there was some emphasis on ground hurling. The mentors there correctly assumed that the Cork side would keep the ball flying low along the ground in order to stifle the Kilkenny penchant for getting the ball in the hand before twisting and turning elegantly to strike it over the bar or send a pin-point pass to a better placed colleague.

'We looked forward to the game against Cork. We always liked to play Cork because they had a lovely style of play, they relied a lot on skill and good team work. We liked to beat them but they were always a great team to play against', said Eddie Keher.

Tradition of Rivalry

The two counties had begun a fine and exciting tradition of rivalry when they met in the final of 1893. Cork won that game and the next one in

1903. They met again the following two years and in 1907 when Kilkenny were the victors on each occasion. The Leinster representatives won again in 1912.

It may all have seemed a long time ago but these games and the men who played in them became part of the folklore of places like Mooncoin and Blackrock. Some of the leading players, their skill and physical endurance, became legendary at a time of nationalist fervour when the country badly needed home-grown heroes.

Survivors

In 1966 there was an actual survivor of the Kilkenny team which had dominated the All-Ireland series from 1904 to 1913. Sim Walton had played in all the finals contested by Kilkenny in that period and was the only living Kilkenny man who held seven All-Ireland medals. There were five players still living who had played in one or more of those finals, their names revered, greatly respected in their old age.

Cork Pride

The Cork team's appearance in the final also engendered the great pride and deep feelings about hurling and those who had played it down the years. The streets and roadways about Blackrock, the Lough and Blackpool, or flat fields in places like Dungourney were redolent with the memory and the feats of past teams and exponents of the game. Besides being skilful, players had to be courageous and physically tough. In the bars and clubs about the city there were oft-told tales of thrilling games, of fierce encounters, of wounds and weals, of memorable scores.

There were cul-de-sacs and quiet roadways and gable ends in the city and suburbs where young players had developed their ball control. Every paving stone in places like Blackpool could tell a story of tenacious play, of anger and of delight, of skills diligently acquired, of rows and of handshakes as young boys came of hurling age.

1931

It was in 1931 that the modern rivalry of Cork and Kilkenny raised the profile of hurling in the country. They met in the final that year and played a thrilling draw that was widely reported in the national media. Each side had players of exceptional hurling ability. Lory Meagher who led the Kilkenny side and Eudie Coughlan who captained Cork were still alive in 1966, their exploits with hurley and ball told and retold down the years. The replay also ended in a pulsating draw. An injury-depleted Kilkenny finally succumbed to their southern rivals. Those three games attracted a combined total of almost 100,000 spectators and aroused an unprecedented interest in the game which grew steadily in the following years, as evidenced by the rising numbers attending games.

The 1947 final between the sides has been acknowledged to have been one of the best games in terms of skill, of thrills and spills and a nail-

The teams as they lined out were:

CORK

Paddy Barry
(St Vincent's)

Peter Doolan	Tom O'Donoghue	Denis Murphy
(St Finbarr's)	(Sarsfields)	(St Finbarr's)

Tony Connolly	Gerry O'Sullivan	Paddy Fitzgerald
(St Finbarr's)	(Glen Rovers)	(Midleton)

Justin McCarthy   Mick Waters
(Passage)   (Blackrock)

Seanie Barry	John O'Halloran	Gerald McCarthy, capt
(Rathcormac)	(UCC)	(St Finbarr's)

Charlie McCarthy	Colm Sheehan	John Bennett
(St Finbarr's)	(Eire Og)	(Blackrock)

Substitutes: Ger O'Leary (Blackrock); Con Roche (St Finbarr's); Donal Sheehan (Na Piarsaigh); Finbarr O'Neill (Glen Rovers); Teddy O'Mahony (Cloughduv). *Trainer*: Jim Barry. *Selectors*: Jim O'Regan (UCC); Billy 'Long Puck' Murphy (Ballincollig); Dan Coughlan (Glen Rovers); Tony O'Shaughnessy (St Finbarr's); Denis Hurley (Sarsfields).

KILKENNY

Ollie Walsh
(Thomastown)

Pat Henderson	Jim Lynch, capt	Jim Treacy
(Fenians)	(Mooncoin)	(Bennettsbridge)

Seamus Cleere	Ted Carroll	Martin Coogan
(Bennettsbridge)	(Lisdowney)	(Castlecomer)

John Teehan   Paddy Moran
(Freshford)   (Bennettsbridge)

Eddie Keher	Claus Dunne	Sean Buckley
(Rower-Inistioge)	(Mooncoin)	(Freshford)

Tom Walsh	Pa Dillon	Joe Dunphy
(Thomastown)	(Freshford)	(Mooncoin)

Substitutes: Dick Dunphy (Mooncoin); Pat Delahunty (Mooncoin); Tommy Murphy (Rower-Inistioge); Pat Carroll (Knocktopher); Ned Connolly (Mooncoin); Tommy O'Connell (Eire Og); Jim Bennett (Bennettsbridge); Wattie McDonald (Mooncoin). *Coach*: Rev Tommy Maher. *Trainer*: Nicky McGrath. *Team assistant*: Mick 'Chew' Leahy. *Selectors/mentors*: Dan Kennedy; Tom Nolan; Mick Fripps; Nicky Purcell. *Team doctor*: Dr Kieran Cuddihy.

The referee was Jimmy Hatton of Wicklow.

biting finish which Kilkenny won with a last-second point by Terry Leahy.

Now, nineteen years later, they were due to meet again. A huge crowd converged on the capital by car and bus and train. Judging by the banners flying before the game began that Sunday it seemed as if the Cork supporters outnumbered their rivals by two to one.

'Welcome back, Cork', Michael O'Hehir shouted in the RTE commentary box as the men in red and white ran onto the field to a frenzied roar from their starved supporters. The cheer for the Kilkenny side was more muted — they and their followers were quite used to being there and they saw nothing to get over-excited about.

On the fiftieth anniversary of the Easter Rising, a contingent of survivors of that historic event were in places of honour in the Hogan Stand, as were two key figures from that period, President de Valera and the Taoiseach, Sean Lemass.

Windy Day

It was not an ideal day for hurling, with a strong wind blowing into the Railway end and a risk of showers between the bright spells. The turf was damp from a spell of rain on the Saturday.

Jim Lynch won the toss and elected to play with the wind and sun, to put Cork at a disadvantage during what was seen as an initial settling-in period. Certainly it seemed as if the Cork players could well do without any such additional pressures. None of them had ever played before a crowd of 68,000 before. Most of them had never played in Croke Park before. There were even some who had never *been* to Croke Park even as spectators. And there were many young people among the Leeside supporters for whom this was the first outing to Headquarters, who had never seen their side play in an All-Ireland. This was a first-time experience for many.

All round the stadium the red and white flags waved with verve and with hope while the Kilkenny colours remained sedately confident.

Cork's Whirlwind Start

As soon as the ball was thrown the Cork side came like a whirlwind. They raced to every ball and, if they could not pick it and hit it from the hand, they pulled on it first time. This was a startlingly fierce onslaught on their opponents.

'Part of our plan was to keep the ball moving, not to let the Kilkenny players settle on it, get it into their hands and begin to dictate the pace of the game', recalls Gerald McCarthy.

This resulted in a good deal of scrappy, broken play all over the field but it meant that Kilkenny were unable to take full advantage of the wind. In fact it was Cork who made the first real attack and the ball went over the end line off a Kilkenny hurley for a 70. Justin McCarthy hit it as hard as he could but the wind caught it and slowed it down and it fell into the safe grasp of Ollie Walsh. His puck out went high in the air, reached its apex somewhere over centrefield and was carried along by the southwesterly wind until it dropped only 20 yards from the Cork end line. It was an indication of how important the wind was going to be in the match.

Cork, closing down, blocking the Kilkenny players and hitting the ball quickly went into another attack. Charlie McCarthy suddenly broke loose from Jim Treacy and took a lightning-fast whip on the ball. To the relief of the Kilkenny team and supporters Ollie Walsh blocked it and dealt with it capably. There was a reassuring cheer from the Noreside followers who felt that their great goalkeeper's reliability at this early stage was a good omen despite the inability of their stylists to get clean strokes of the ball.

Seamus Cleere, though being given little chance to display his skills by the first-time pulling of Gerald McCarthy, repelled another Cork attack. The ball went down to the far end and a rasper shot towards the Cork net. But Paddy Barry made the first of several great saves and the danger passed.

Seanie Barry and Martin Coogan had the first of many tussles which ended even — Barry was going to be denied the kind of scoring freedom he was allowed up to now while Coogan was not going to be able to send his side attacking with carefully flighted balls in front of the forwards. This was a pattern of play that was going to be repeated round the field — the skill and experience of Kilkenny held well in check by the energy and drive of the underdogs.

Pat Henderson

Barry did get away early on but was fouled going through. The resultant free could not be got over the bar against the wind and was cleared. Even at this early stage the hard determination of Pat Henderson was coming to the fore. He had a great pair of hands to catch a ball but he found it difficult to come bursting out to clear in his customary fashion because of the tenacious marking and challenging of John Bennett.

Even after four minutes the pattern of first half play had emerged — the utterly relentless marking of the Cork backs frustrating all the efforts of the wind-aided Kilkenny forwards. It was left to the midfielder, John Teehan, who got his side's first score, a point, from a pass from Eddie Keher.

First Score by Keher

The light, fast Tom Walsh tried to run through but was fouled. Eddie Keher came up to take the first of his frees. He was a meticulous performer. Everything had to be right as he stood over the ball, laces tight, jersey tucked in. He looked at the posts, held his left hand well down the hurley for better control in lifting the ball, rose it and sent it over carefully, to the delight of the Kilkenny supporters, who were relying so much on him.

Kilkenny attacked again but got little room to steady up. Gerry O'Sullivan baulked Claus Dunne just enough to make the centre forward send the ball wide from far out. Dunne went racing through shortly afterwards but, with the Cork supporters holding their breath, Peter Doolan came thundering out and dispossessed him at the very last second.

Then it was Cork's turn to attack which brought a fine save by Ollie Walsh before the ball was eventually sent wide. In the 13th minute Kilkenny forced a free 40 yards out and Keher sent it over for his side's third point.

Cork were doing well yet they had not scored as the game moved into the second quarter. Justin McCarthy was just wide with an effort from out the field. It was a disappointment for Cork to see his effort being pushed outside the post by the wind. But they were holding the vaunted Kilkenny forwards so tightly, stopping them developing any pattern of play, hampering any efforts at the kind of team work that were their hallmark. And McCarthy and Waters at midfield were getting the upper hand on two players, Teehan and Moran, who had distinguished themselves in the league final against Tipperary.

A minute later Seanie Barry opened the account for Cork when he pointed a free. Those who had not seen him play before saw him bend over the ball awkwardly with the hurley in the left hand grip. But he was calm and accurate and the ball went over the bar. He took another one shortly afterwards but the wind carried it to the left.

Wind Spoiling Play

This was a day on which there were going to be many misses and wides by both sides. Some of them, from play, could be ascribed to the tight marking, spoiling and scrambling. But a good many could be legitimately blamed on the wind. It was strong enough to move the ball an inch or more between the time a player rose it or threw it up to hit it. It was hard for players to time their swing on a wind-blown ball so that they hit it with the sweet spot of the boss — an area no larger than a 10p piece.

'I've always said that a strong wind can spoil a game. You can cope much better with rain or wet on account of a new ball coming in so often but the wind can be endlessly frustrating on players trying to hit the ball with any kind of accuracy or force', comments Eddie Keher.

One advantage of the wind was the extra length it added to Ollie Walsh's puck outs. One landed almost in the square. Pa Dillon got hold of it and running out with Tom O'Donoghue on his heels managed to get a pass to the ever-alert Eddie Keher to score a point in the 18th minute. The Rower marksman again scored two minutes later from a free to put his side five points to one ahead.

Great Shot, Great Save

Keher was the best of the forwards but even he was being closed down again and again by Paddy Fitzgerald, with no free man to give a pass to or take a pass from. Just the same he came running into the square in the second quarter and unleashed a bullet which brought an astounding save from Paddy Barry. On another occasion, near the end of the first half he sent in a pile-driver that went inches wide.

In goal, Barry was having an inspirational game. He had far more to do than his opposite number in the first half. Several times he averted dangerous situations by having the courage and confidence to come running out to catch the incoming ball, dodging charging forwards as he ran with it to send it down the field.

He was greatly helped by the solid play of his full back and of Denis Murphy in the left corner, who all the time ran step for step with the dangerous Tom Walsh. In the other corner Joe Dunphy had little chance to display his forward skills because Peter Doolan was always there, strong and forceful and winning ball after ball. He was one of the few players of either side who seemed to be able to master the conditions and consistently hit the ball long distances. Tony Connolly did an equally good job of close marking on another fine ball player, Sean Buckley.

Kilkenny Half Line Subdued

Even in the first half, with the sun and wind behind them, the strong Kilkenny half back line had a great deal of pressure on them, with the Noreside forwards tied up and their midfield struggling. And these three fine players, Cleere, Carroll and Coogan, were never allowed time to take the ball in hand, step gracefully to one side and send in good forward balls. Gerald McCarthy, John O'Halloran and Seanie Barry kept tussling for every ball, sometimes pulling hard on it, sometimes kicking it when they got the chance. As a result the key Kilkenny line never made the contribution it might have been expected to make.

Rousing Goal

Then in the 21st minute came a score that raised the rafters in Croke Park and in the houses of all those listening to radios all over Cork city and county. The Leesiders were awarded a free from midfield. Gerry O'Sullivan, playing a capital game, took it. This resulted in another free from the 21-yard line. Seanie Barry stepped up to take it. Everyone assumed he would send it over the bar in his clinical fashion. It may have been the wind but he hit the ball near the edge of the boss. It went in low, bounded off the crossbar, came out, was grabbed by Colm Sheehan who sent in a hard shot that went whizzing past backs and forwards and into the net.

The Cork players were even more galvanised. With only ten minutes to go to half-time they were only a point behind. They were getting the better of the favourites all over the field.

Great Goal Disallowed

Just after that came a controversial incident. Tom Walsh, using all his adroit stickwork, got the ball on the 21 and went sprinting goalwards. On the run with the ball on his hurley, he eluded one foul tackle, and hit the ball with all his might. It went like a missile goalwards. Even Barry couldn't stop this one, though he got his hurley to it. Afterwards Walsh was to say this was the best goal he got in his career.

Unfortunately for him and for Kilkenny this score did not count. The referee had not allowed him the advantage and had whistled play back for a free. There is no telling what a goal at this stage might have done for Kilkenny's spirit, as the team struggled to get some kind of rhythm going. Eddie Keher took the free. It seemed he intended to go for a goal for he hit the ball low and hard and it skimmed just over the crossbar with no hurley in the way to stop it.

After these escapes Cork came right back and Charlie McCarthy, racing out to meet a ball hit first time at waist height by his namesake Gerald, neatly clipped a delightful point off the ground.

Kilkenny Substitution

By this time the Kilkenny mentors had decided to replace Pa Dillon with Tommy Murphy. In retrospect this was seen as a mistake for while Dillon did not get scores he was a tower of strength in his tussles with an equally tough opponent Tom O'Donoghue and kept the ball in the square. Though Kilkenny switched the forwards about during the rest of the game and actually replaced Murphy with Pat Carroll late in the second half they effectively missed the power that Dillon had provided.

On the call of half time Sean Buckley at last got clear of his marker to send over a fine point and leave the score Kilkenny 0–7 to Cork's 1–2.

Half-Time

'We left the field glowing', recalled Gerald McCarthy. 'We had grown in confidence and resolve as the first half went on. We knew we had adopted the right tactics to contain a very talented Kilkenny side. And we knew we had the wind in our favour in the second half.'

The Kilkenny supporters wondered why their side had fallen far below the standard displayed in the league but the fact of the matter is that they were being hounded and hustled out of the game by a side imbued with a ferocious hunger for success.

Cork Keep Up Pace

When the Kilkenny team took their places for the second half Tom Walsh was at full forward and Tommy Murphy in the left corner. The second half began as the first had ended — Cork full of unquenchable fire and vigour, running hard all the time. Many Kilkenny followers nurtured the hope that the underdogs could not keep up the pace, keep up the frenzied concentration and the mental effort for the entire game.

In the third minute the captain, Gerald McCarthy, who was not in awe of his renowned opponent, Seamus Cleere, sent a ball over the bar from 35 yards out. As the umpire waved the white flag McCarthy gestured with clenched fist to his team-mates. A minute later the goal scorer, Colm Sheehan, who was being well policed by Jim Lynch, was fouled as he tried to get through.

Seanie Barry bent over the ball and sent it over. An exultant roar of encouragement and delight went up from the huge Cork contingent as the white flag was waved and the scoreboard operator changed the figures to show that the teams were now level with only three minutes gone in the second half.

Kilkenny struck back, trying hard to put their forward game together. They attacked, with Joe Dunphy and Sean Buckley combining to send the ball towards the goal but Gerry O'Sullivan cleared off the line. Kilkenny went on the attack again, with Claus Dunne, Murphy and Walsh trying desperately to shake off their markers, make and take passes, get into gear. Perhaps they sensed that the game would really go away from them if they could not change the pattern soon. All their efforts resulted in a free. Eddie Keher, by far the most dangerous of the forwards despite having to cope with Paddy Fitzgerald, put it neatly over the bar to put his side ahead again on a score of 0–8 to 1–4.

The Testing Moments

This was one of the testing periods of the game. The initiative might have been wrested from the Cork side. However, the Leesiders struck back with great determination. Charlie McCarthy baulked Jim Treacy, preventing him getting a good clearance, and the ball flew about, back and forward in front of goal. Colm Sheehan gathered and, with his back to the goal, flicked the ball one-handed to the net with Ollie Walsh unsighted by the backs and forwards tussling in front of him.

Cork had taken the lead for the first time in the game and the team's hungry followers began to sense that the time might be at hand. This feeling was reinforced when Seanie Barry managed to elude Martin Coogan, who was marking him well, and sent one of the best points of the game over the bar. The score now stood at 2–5 to 0–8.

Kilkenny Claw Way Back

But by now the Kilkenny attack were beginning to cope better with their tenacious Cork markers. They kept trying, switching players about, moving away from their opponents. John Teehan came into the attack and sent a powerful shot just wide. This drew a roar of relief and applause from the Cork supporters. Not long after Keher got free and sent a point over and then Joe Dunphy slipped away from Peter Doolan to score a neat point.

Cork were now only one score ahead despite their dominance and a goal for Kilkenny might have altered the balance of power and mental attitude. This was when the Cork backs held their nerve and hurled with great vigour. No one was more inspirational then the dark-haired Peter Doolan who time and again came racing out, grabbed the ball and sent huge clearances that, aided by the wind, landed near the Kilkenny end line. The Cork crowd loved this kind of jaunty, demonstrative hurling and gave a great cheer every time Doolan went for a ball.

In the 19th minute came the most decisive score of the game. By that time Kilkenny were beginning to hurl with more authority and to move well as a unit. It was a worrying time for Jim O'Regan and Jim Barry on the sideline. Nobody knew better than they how dangerous Kilkenny could be to a team who had controlled the play but who had not gone far enough ahead. Cleere, Carroll and Coogan were coming into their own, calling upon their repository of experience. Paddy Moran was now helping to break the midfield hold of their opponents. The game-wise players in black and amber knew how to get out of difficulty, to turn the trend of play in their favour.

Cork's Third Goal

Then John O'Halloran, who had had a tough time on Ted Carroll, raced out to the right wing and got possession. He sent in a high ball, trying for a point. Ollie Walsh in goal thought it was going over. In an instant it had hit the upright and bounced down behind the goal line for an astonishing goal. Ollie Walsh whipped round and scooped it off the line but by that time the umpire was reaching for the green flag. It all happened so quickly and unexpectedly that even the players crowding about the square were taken unawares. Later it was said that the ball had actually hit the shoulder of Colm Sheehan before it crossed the line.

The immense roar of the Cork supporters at this unusual goal was a signal for a continuous bout of cheering that went on and on until the end of the game. Cascades of sound rolled down from the stands and the terraces on to the field, firing up the men in red to give it their all with the winning post in sight.

'This was a fantastic sound to hear, tens of thousands of voices shouting and roaring, flags waving, hands clapping', said Gerald McCarthy. 'Our supporters had a big role in the game that day and nowhere more than after that goal. They lifted us and inspired us and we owed a lot to them.'

There were those who said that this goal, which clinched the match for Cork, was a lucky break. Eddie Keher would not agree. 'I always contend that a team makes its own luck. If a team is exuberant, if its players are hungry, they will be racing for that vital ball rather than waiting to see where it is going to break.'

Shortly after that goal Gerald McCarthy hit a ball from 40 yards out and it went over the bar for a wonderful point. It was a captain's inspirational score.

Last Kilkenny Effort

In these last minutes Kilkenny, with defeat now staring them in the face, began to play really well. In one attack Claus Dunne shot barely wide though under great pressure from the close-tackling defence. It was a reprieve for Cork and they came thundering back. Seanie Barry got a point for them in the 25th minute and two minutes later Justin McCarthy, now playing in the half forward line, scored another one.

Now Kilkenny were playing some of their best hurling and went on the attack. They were awarded a close-in free. All their forwards moved into position. Nobody had any doubt but that Keher would try for a goal. He swung hard on the ball but it was blocked by the Cork defence and carried out by them to a thunderous roar from their supporters, who were now looking at their watches, asking one another how long there was to go.

Kilkenny went on another attack. Eddie Keher got a pass to Tom Walsh who whipped the ball past Paddy Barry for his side's first goal.

'We were beginning to put our game together a bit better at that stage but it was too late', says Eddie Keher. 'My view is that Cork had the game won before Kilkenny really woke up.'

Danger of Being Favourites

This was a game where the label 'favourites' did no good to the team on which it was stamped.

'We were not able to handle it. It was the first time in any big match that that the team had been made favourites and it was difficult not to believe what so many of our supporters and the media were saying about the game. You have to have fire in your belly to win an All-Ireland, be utterly urgent about winning. Being favourites can sap that essential element from a team's make-up. That is what happened in 1966. But we learned a lot from it', said Eddie Keher.

The last score of the game came, appropriately, from the man who had been brought back in to add experience to the side, John Bennett. He had had no easy game against the most forceful of the full backs, Pat Henderson, but almost on the call of time a free taken by Seanie Barry was pushed across the square and he got clear to send over the final point. The score stood at 3–9 for Cork to 1–10 for Kilkenny.

Explosion of Joy

By that time the exultant Cork supporters were crowding onto the sidelines, whistling at referee Jimmy Hatton to end the game. When he blew the final long blast it was the signal for a great charge of flag-bearing followers onto the field from every corner of the ground. The players had hardly time to shake hands with their opponents before they were engulfed by ecstatic supporters, young, old, middle-aged, male and female. They were kissed and hugged and backslapped, pushed this way and that about the grass.

Enough of the Cork players broke free of their excited admirers to surround Jim Barry and carry him on their shoulders towards the presentation podium on the Hogan Stand. When they got him there they pushed him up the steps so that he was near Gerald McCarthy as he received the Liam McCarthy.

'Tough' Barry Weeps

This grey-haired, elderly man, who lived for Cork hurling and who had been associated with senior teams since 1926, wept unashamedly for joy. He had seen the September sun sinking behind the spires and tall brick houses to the west of Croke Park on many such occasions in the past. This was to be his farewell. This man, who epitomised Cork's almost mystic love of hurling, died two years later.

There was an uninterrupted ten minutes of cheering from the Cork supporters massed beneath the stand before the presentation ceremony got under way and McCarthy made his victory speech of thanks, congratulations and, to Kilkenny, generous praise.

Huge Crowds Meet Victors

Next evening in Cork a huge deluge of people covered every foot of ground in and around Glanmire railway station and the streets leading out of it. A great roar echoed under the glass roof as the hollow rumble of the train was heard at the round black mouth of the tunnel and it emerged and slid into the curve of the platform and came to a stop.

The scenes of delight and of joy were unprecedented as the team was carried along the streets to the Victoria hotel in the victory parade. The county's pride in the team's expression of skill, endurance, courage and will-to-win was almost frenzied. There were 30,000 people thronging the streets that night. The intensity of that welcome was awesome and unlikely to be experienced again.

Cork Humour Over All

When the team and mentors eventually came out on the balcony of the hotel and waved at the crowd below the typical Cork mischievous humour came to the fore. The Lord Mayor, Alderman Sean Casey, wearing his chain of office, stepped up to the microphone to begin his formal address of welcome. Someone shouted out 'Never mind all that speechifying — sing us a song.' And so he did and led the singing of 'The Banks of My Own Lovely Lee'.

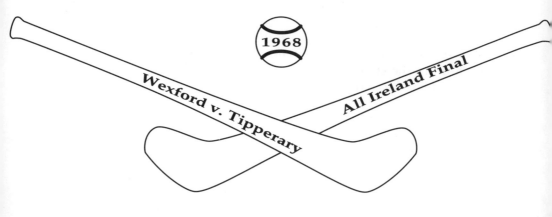

'THIS CAN'T BE REAL'

As the Tipperary team entered the dressing-room at half-time, glowing with the power and brilliance of a first-half performance that had overwhelmed their stunned opponents, Donie Nealon turned to Michael 'Babs' Keating.

'I'm looking at All-Irelands a long time — and this can't be real. There's no way an All-Ireland can be won as easily as this', said the Burgess school-teacher who had won the first of his five winner's medals ten years before.

Tipperary were leading by eight points on a scoreline of 1–11 to 1–3 but this in no way reflected the superiority of the Munster champions. They had hurled the Wexfordmen off the field with an awesome display of teamwork, strength and individual skill.

'We played incredibly good hurling in that first half', recalls Nealon. 'We did everything right, combined marvellously well, played our markers out of it, used all our experience and skill to the utmost. We had Wexford at sixes and sevens.'

The Tipperary captain, Mick Roche, had given one of the most memorable displays of centre back play ever seen in Croke Park or anywhere else. So uncanny was his sense of positional play that the ball seemed to seek him out wherever he went. He rose almost languidly to trap it overhead with outstretched hurley, to catch it in his hand and to clear it away, from his hand or on the ground. Sometimes he pulled first time — against the oncoming ball or with the outgoing ball — and hit it every time with the sweet spot of the hurley, sending his side into the attack. He did everything with such style and grace that it even seemed as if he were unhurried, even casual in his approach.

One Point Only

So outplayed were Wexford that coming up to half time all they had managed to score was a single point from play. The other two points came from frees. Then Jack Berry got a Wexford goal to take the humiliating look off the scoreboard.

The Wexford players trudged off the field at half-time with heavy steps, aware of their vast army of disappointed supporters in the crowd of 63,461 who had had no reason to wave their purple and gold flags or to raise their voices.

It was not as if the players had not tried. They had run and challenged and struck the ball and tried all they knew. But it was like being in a nightmare where nothing seemed to work, where they seemed to be beaten not alone by their markers but by the ball itself. Despite their weeks of strenuous physical preparation by Ned Power, the best trainer in the county, they seemed leaden footed, floundering after their fleet and ebullient opponents.

Exhibition by Tipp

Most of the hurling neutrals would have preferred a stirring, evenly-matched first half. But no hurling lover would have wanted a neck-and-neck race at the expense of the quality of the hurling.

Nobody, commentator or spectator, could have envisaged how different the second half was to be. No member of the Tipperary side had an inkling of how forcefully the rug was about to be pulled from under their boots by the most astonishing and unbelievable come back in the history of All-Ireland finals. Probably nobody on the Wexford side expected the kind of dramatic transformation that had this team thundering forward for a victory that seemed no more than fantasy at half-time.

Tipp Tipped

Tipperary were favourites to win this match because of the high level of ability, of vigour, skill and grit which had made the county the leading exponent of the game in the 1960s. They had been champions in '61 and '62 then again in '64 and '65. The team of those last two years had been so powerful that they had simply flattened all opposition. Nobody could match them, including Wexford who were badly beaten in the final of 1965. It was said of that side that they had become so jaded with winning that they were taken by surprise by a young Limerick side in the championship of 1966.

But Tipperary were back in the final of 1967, minus a few of their great veterans of the glory years. For the first time since 1922 Kilkenny defeated Tipperary in an All-Ireland and after that some of the team's great figures went into retirement — John Doyle, Kieran Carey, Tony Wall, Theo English.

Many thought that the break-up of the all-conquering side of the early '60s might signal a period of relative obscurity for the county. But the resounding victories of the near past, the feats of skill and spirit, had evoked a great surge of hurling enthusiasm in the county. The county championships were fiercely contested. The interest in the game among ambitious young hurlers had never been higher.

Ambitious Players

There were top-rate players who had been on the periphery of the senior side for a number of years and were now getting their chance. There were outstanding young players coming on the scene who could not be ignored by the selectors. And there were honour-laden players from the great side of the past who were still hurling well — Roche, Keating, Nealon, Devaney and the incomparable Jimmy Doyle.

It was almost as expected that the team would do well in the National League of 1967/68 and it was no surprise that they reached the final. There they met Kilkenny, their conquerors in the All-Ireland of the previous year. It was a tense encounter.

After a superb first quarter there came an unsavoury flare-up, with harsh words exchanged, hurleys swung, punches exchanged, jostling and buffeting. Tipperary won by two points in a very close finish and collected another league title.

There was one significant and negative outcome of the match. One of Tipperary's most vibrant young players, John Flanagan of Moycarkey, was suspended for six months and would be out of contention for the championship.

Tipp Path to Final

In the first round the Clare forward line scored three goals in the first nineteen minutes and were in front at the interval. However, the Tipperary forwards struck in four goals in the second half to put paid to the Bannermen. There were some in Tipperary who were saying 'God be with the days of Carey, Maher and Doyle — there would be no three goals going in when they were there.'

Tipperary met Cork in the Munster final before a crowd of 43,238 spectators on a boiling hot day in Limerick. Tipperary had what all winning teams must have — a good half back line — and Burns, Roche and Gaynor made up the launching pad for a nine-point victory. Keating gave a magnificent display, scoring 1–3, showing his strength, ability to take the high ball, hit left or right with great power and accuracy.

It was little wonder therefore that the side were favourites to win another All-Ireland. Some in Tipperary were hoping that it might be a re-match against Kilkenny, to avenge the defeat of the previous year.

Wexford Hurling on Wave

In Wexford itself there was much more confidence in the team than among the commentators and media pundits and the traditionalists of the hurling world. This was in good part because hurling was on a wave in the county since the start of the 1960s. The minor title had been won for the first time in 1963 and again in 1966. Now the minors were in the 1968 final against Cork and there was even talk of a Wexford double.

In 1965 the county had won the under-21 title and the following year it had taken three games in the final before Cork overcame them. Over the same period St Peter's College in Wexford town began to challenge for the Leinster and All-Ireland senior colleges title. They contested several national finals, winning in '61, '67 and '68 while Wexford CBS won a provincial final in the B section.

All of this successful hurling activity at under-age level seemed to herald a new dawn for the county. It threw up several first-rate players who were challenging for places on the senior team.

Ned Power

Ned Power, who had trained the St Peters, minor and under-21 teams, was now bringing his talents to the senior side while Padge Kehoe, the strong-willed veteran of many great Wexford victories, was manager.

These Wexford and Tipperary teams were by no means strangers to one another. They had met twice already that year in the National League. Wexford were the holders of the title and they beat Tipperary rather easily by eleven points in one of the preliminary games. However Tipperary won their remaining games and qualified to meet Wexford at Croke Park in a play off on 24 March. This was a thrilling match, memorable for two things — the long range scoring by Jimmy Doyle for a personal tally of eleven points and the five goals scored by Wexford. Tipperary won on a scoreline of 1–19 to 5–5 and went on to beat Kilkenny in the tempestuous final.

Wexford were not anything as impressive in the Leinster championship. They were well held by Dublin for three-quarters of the game and only snap goals by their big red-haired forward Tony Doran and the lightest man on the field, Christy Jacob, turned the game their way. It also confirmed the form of a player who had been in and out of the team for several seasons — 30-year-old Paul Lynch who played exceptionally well at midfield.

Wexford only just got there in the Leinster final against the reigning All-Ireland champions. A crucial factor was the hurling of Phil Wilson at midfield as Kilkenny came with a great last gasp effort. Wexford were a point ahead when the referee's whistle sounded.

The Players

When the hurling-wise and the commentators in the media and in the pubs and homes began to assess the relative strengths and weaknesses of both sides there was great emphasis on the strength of both half back lines and on how the outcome of the game might depend on them.

Tipperary had Roche back in the centre after a spell at midfield. He was flanked by two tenacious tacklers who often got free to send long low balls down to the forwards, Len Gaynor and Mick Burns. In the centre for Wexford was the biggest man on the team, Dan Quigley of Rathnure, who had starred on the under-age teams of the recent past. His flankers were Willie Murphy and Vincie Staples, two players not unlike their Tipperary counterparts for their aggressive attacking approach to their game.

Nine of the young Wexford side so well beaten by Tipperary in 1965 were still there, anxious to atone for that decisive defeat. Nine of the Tipperary side of that year were on the current team. Two of the full back line, John Costigan and John Gleeson, and centre forward Jimmy Ryan were contesting their first final.

The combination and cohesion of the Tipperary forward line, with top-rate players of vast experience like Keating, Devaney and McLoughlin in the ranks, was regarded as superior to the Wexford sextet. The only fly in the ointment was the heel injury incurred by Jimmy Doyle in training; he rested it during the last few days of preparation. The most versatile member of the attack, Donie Nealon had now been asked to go to midfield to try to strengthen what was seen as a vulnerable area.

Wilson Fit

In Wexford there was some concern in the county about a a shoulder injury that midfielder Phil Wilson had sustained.

'Thankfully that injury had healed well before the final — you have no business going out to play in an All-Ireland if you are not 100% fit. No game you'll ever play is as fast or as tough', says Wilson. 'You can't be holding back going for 50/50 balls for fear of aggravating an injury. As well as that you have to be mentally fit going into a game — be full of determination. You have to be mentally prepared to give it all you have because you have only one hour and then it's all over.

'Even a good player who is physically and mentally fit can have a bad game. No matter how good you are you may be due a bad game — and you can only hope that it won't be in the All-Ireland', he reflects.

Wexford Forwards

The Wexford forward line was not considered anything as effective as their rivals but they had eager players like Tony Doran and Jack Berry as well as the most accomplished ball-player on the side, Paul Lynch.

Some 63,000 spectators made their way to Croke Park on a breezy day of sunshine and the odd threatening shower. There seemed more Wexford followers than Tipperary judging from the flags and colours waving in the breeze.

It was a great encouragement to the men in purple and gold that their minor side beat Cork in a great final. It seemed to augur well for them.

The teams as they lined out were:

WEXFORD

John Nolan
(Oylegate)

Tom Neville	Eddie Kelly	Ned Colfer
(New Ross)	(St Aidan's)	(New Ross)

Vincie Staples	Dan Quigley, capt	Willie Murphy
(Rosslare)	(Rathnure)	(Faythe Harriers)

Phil Wilson	Dave Bernie
(Ballyhogue)	(Ferns)

Paul Lynch	Tony Doran	Christy Jacob
(Shamrocks)	(Buffer's Alley)	(Oulart)

Jimmy O'Brien	Seamus Whelan	Jack Berry
(New Ross)	(St Martin's)	(Kilmore)

Substitutes: John Quigley (Rathnure); Mick Jacob (Oulart); Teddie O'Connor (Rathnure); Mick Kinsella (Buffer's Alley); Pat Nolan (New Ross); Ned Buggy (Faythe Harriers); Seamus Barron (Rathnure); Mick Browne (Faythe Harriers); Jim Furlong (Adamstown). *Coach*: Padge Kehoe. *Trainer*: Ned Power. *Selectors*: Nick Rackard (Rathnure); Syl Barron (Rathnure); Mick Hanlon (Horeswood); Tom Donohoe (Buffer's Alley); Nick Cardiff (St Martin's). *Team doctor*: Dr Bob Bowe.

TIPPERARY

John O'Donoghue
(Arravale Rovers)

John Costigan	Noel O'Gorman	John Gleeson
(Clonakenny)	(Newport)	(Moneygall)

Mick Burns	Mick Roche, capt	Len Gaynor
(Nenagh)	(Carrick Davins)	(Kilruane)

Donie Nealon	P.J. Ryan
(Burgess)	(Carrick Davins)

Michael Keating	Jimmy Ryan	Jimmy Doyle
(Ballybacon)	(Carrick Davins)	(Sarsfields)

Liam Devaney	John McKenna	Sean McLoughlin
(Borrisoleigh)	(Borrisokane)	(Sarsfields)

Substitutes: Matt Stapleton (Borrisoleigh); Seamus Shinnors (Newport); Francis Loughnane (Roscrea); Patsy Roland (Roscrea); Brian Kenny (Carrick Davins); Phil Lowry (Upperchurch); Jimmy Ryan (Carrick Davins). *Trainer*: Ossie Bennett. *Assistant trainer*: Gerry Doyle. *Selectors/mentors*: Paddy 'Sweeper' Ryan (Moycarkey); P.J. Kenny and Eddie Lyons (Carrick Davins); Jimmy Hennessy (Dundrum); Martin Kennedy (Kiladangan).

The referee was John Dowling of Offaly.

The referee was John Dowling of Offaly, later to be president of the GAA. He called the captains, Roche and Quigley, together for the ritual handshake and the toss up. Roche won the toss and elected to play into the Railway end goal, with the fitful breeze at his back.

Game Gets Under Way

From the throw in three of the most influential players in this game were immediately involved. Keating broke away but his puck was stopped by Quigley who cleared the ball downfield where it was collected and sent over the bar by Lynch for the first score of the game.

This raised a great cheer of anticipation from the Wexford followers, still flushed after cheering on their minors. But from now on there were to be few happy shouts from the great army of faithful followers who had moved up along the east coast in their thousands by coach, bus and many excursion trains.

Tipperary went on a series of confident quick-silver attacks, marvellous fare to watch. Within a few minutes the midfield pattern had emerged — the veteran Nealon and the burly P.J. Ryan were getting the better of Wilson and the young, inexperienced Dave Bernie.

Tipperary on Top

There was a great whoosh of ten thousand intakes of breath as Jimmy Doyle collected the ball with effortless style and, sidestepping and weaving like a wisp, headed for goal. He was brought down. He took the free himself. This was the first time in the game that the attendance could watch his free-taking artistry, the easy way he lifted the ball, the wide left handed stroke that sent the ball over the centre of the crossbar. Freetaking looked simple and matter-of-fact when this small, dark-haired man of gentle temperament performed.

Pat Nolan began to be very busy in the Wexford goal. With Tipperary seeming to be in control all over the field the attacks came one after another. Eleven years minding the county net, Nolan had to call on all his experience, all his alacrity, to keep the ball out. First Sean McLoughlin, the lanky, predatory player who was deadly with the handpass, sent in a difficult shot which Nolan managed to save. Not long afterwards John 'Mackey' McKenna, whose bustling style hid great skill in using the ball in tight corners, clipped in another. Nolan got his hurley to it and cleared it out.

'Mark Up'

The Wexford goalkeeper shouted at his backs to mark up. McLoughlin's marker was the determined Tom Neville who had a sudden burst of speed and always tried to bring the ball with him. Marking McKenna was Eddie Kelly whose anticipation and ability to keep the forwards out had served him well in the Leinster championship. Now, however, he found McKenna racing away out to collect balls, and trying to follow him created a lot of space in front of goal. In the other corner Ned Colfer, small of stature but strong, was considered to have the most trying prospect before him — watching the versatile, sharp-shooting Devaney, who was a key player in a line that passed the ball to one another automatically, instinctively knowing where the better-placed colleague would be.

All the Wexford backs were under continuous pressure and when Vincie Staples failed to connect on a ground ball, Jimmy Doyle took it, weaved away from the challenge and ran forward to send the ball over the bar.

Keating to the Fore

It was becoming apparent that Keating, on the right wing of the Tipperary attack, was on song. Willie Murphy, normally so fluid and fast in his striking and determined in his tackling, seemed tense and hesitant. Keating was quick onto a pass from P.J. Ryan to send the ball over the bar, hitting it fast, close to his body.

Wexford's disarray was momentarily halted when Whelan collected in the corner and sent a pass to Berry who passed to the inrushing Tony Doran who swept the ball to the net. The referee, however, had already called back play for a free. Paul Lynch, the neatest striker on the team, sent it over the bar.

Tipperary got the next score, a pointed free by Jimmy Doyle. It was given away by Dan Quigley, who with Murphy and Staples was fighting a desperate battle to stem the flow of attacks into the Tipperary full forward line. One of Quigley's rare long clearances in this half went in to Whelan who was fouled going through. Lynch again took the free and sent it over.

Tipperary on Full Power

It seemed that, despite the disparity in power and ability, Wexford were managing to keep in touch. Now however, Tipperary began to make their dominance felt on the scoreboard. Keating, running fast, swept in from the right wing and, drawing the backs, placed his old colleague, Devaney, for a point. At that stage they switched positions, something that came second nature to both.

Now the Tipperary half back line was totally in control. Roche was intercepting every ball that came down the middle, rising to catch or pull on the ball in the air, sidestepping nimbly to send his side on the attack. Tony Doran tried all he knew but he looked awkward and was ineffective. On the wings Burns and Gaynor had the better of it with Jacob and Lynch in the individual tussles. Seamus 'Shanks' Whelan threw himself about the square, fighting for every scrap that came his way. He had no thought for his safety and took two blows to his legs that slowed him up a good deal. And little was achieved for his pain.

'Their half back line was so in control that they kept sending the ball well into our half. As a result our half backs were being forced back, backing into the full backs. There was a lot of confusion back there', recalls

Phil Wilson, who just could not get into the game at centrefield, hard and all as he tried.

Jimmy Doyle increased the lead with a free. Keating and Devaney ran and passed and ran again and in the space of two minutes the burly Ballybacon man, equally adept as a footballer, had sent over two further points. Wexford switched the experienced Neville over to the left corner to try to curb the Tipperary duo but it did not make much difference. Tipperary attacks were coming on both wings and from one of these Sean McLoughlin sent over a point when McKenna got the ball and though bottled up, passed it out to the tall Sarsfields man.

Time and time again the hawk-eyed Nolan had to leave his line and take possession of the ball, weave his way out of trouble and clear it away. On several occasions he got in front of dangerous hopping balls skidding towards the line. At this stage it could be said that he was keeping his hapless side from being totally overwhelmed.

Goal from Doyle

But even Nolan could not stop the next shot. The ball went over the sideline from a Wexford hurley. Donie Nealon, running all over the midfield area to keep the Tipp momentum going, came up to take it. He had a fine cut on a sideline ball and sent it in at shoulder height, hard and fast. The Wexford backs seemed like statues as Jimmy Doyle leapt nimbly in the air and with a neat flick of his fluid wrists deflected the flying ball into the net for a fine goal.

This brought a great cheer of appreciation not alone from the Tipperary fans but from those who loved to see a stick-artist perform a difficult feat and do it with such grace. However, Doyle's moment of achievement had a serious price. As he met the ground after his balletic leap he landed on his vulnerable left heel and felt it go. From then on he was hobbling.

Trying to Curb Roche

The score now stood at 1–9 to a mere three points for Wexford. No Wexford supporter could but agree that this no more than reflected the reality of the play.

The Wexford mentors tried to curb the exuberant play of Roche by switching Doran to his customary place on the edge of the square and sending out Berry to the 40. It was hoped that Berry's strong unorthodox style and uncompromising challenging might curb Roche somewhat. It made some difference but not that much and in any case P.J. Ryan and Nealon were continuing to hurl Wilson and Bernie out of it at centrefield and keeping the winning rhythm going.

At this stage also it was taking Dan Quigley all his time to try to keep Jimmy Ryan from doing more damage — the Davins man scooped out passes to the wings, kept the ball moving, stopping his marker from making the long clearances for which he was famous.

Tipperary attacked again. Keating, the scourge of Wexford, sent out a neat pass to Devaney. His shot was deflected at point blank range by the tough, determined Neville. The ball went across the end line for a 70. This was taken by Mick Burns. It was a well-struck and beautifully flighted ball that sailed high between the uprights. It got a great cheer from the Tipperary supporters and from the many onlookers who were now coming to regard this game as something of a hurling exhibition by the masters, but one without too much competitive excitement.

Unexpected Wexford Goal

Yet, from the puck out the Wexford centrefield men got the ball forward. Christy Jacob, who never stopped trying despite the dominance of Burns, now got hold of the ball, slipped his man and, running in, got out a pass to Jack Berry. The muscular Kilmore player lashed it to the net, regardless of the best effort of John O'Donoghue who up to that had ably dealt with all that had come his way.

A Wexford accented roar went up from the stands and terraces of Croke Park. It was full of relief. At least it would take the bad look off the scoreboard. It was the first Wexford score for what seemed like an age. Perhaps it might lift whatever paralysis had taken hold of the Slaneysiders from the start.

As if to tell them that this was no more than a ripple against the tide of the play, Tipperary again attacked and Wexford, to prevent another goal, had recoursed to fouling. By this stage a limping Jimmy Doyle, his speed slowed by his injury, had moved to full forward. His injury did not curb his free-taking style and he sent it over the bar to leave the half-time score: Tipperary 1–11 to Wexford 1–3.

Half-Time

'We really owned the game in that half', said Michael Keating, who had caught every ball that came in his vicinity. But, like Jimmy Doyle, Keating had aggravated an injury picked up playing football some time before and he was limping a little as he left the field.

'It was hard for us not to feel a sense of security as we walked off the pitch to a great round of applause', recalls Donie Nealon. 'We had played unbelievably good hurling. All the forwards were playing like a dream. It looked a foregone conclusion', he says.

Watching and waiting for the Wexford players trudging in from the field were two of the legendary figures of Wexford hurling, Nick Rackard and Padge Kehoe.

Padge Kehoe's Tirade

The stories, apocryphal or exaggerated, of Kehoe's tirade at his charges in the dressing-room are part of Wexford hurling lore. His anger at their helplessness, his anguish at their flatfootedness, his calls not to go under so tamely, to uphold the fighting tradition of the county, are supposed to have been emphasised by the flat of a hurley whacking down on the table again and again, with crockery being smashed and one GAA official peeping in the door in alarm.

In the Tipperary dressing-room there was a justifiable air of confidence. The only worrying factor was the loss of their free-taker and inspirational score-getter, Jimmy Doyle. He told the mentors he did not feel able to play in the second half. They asked the young, eager Francis Loughnane to get ready to go in. However, after Doyle had had a rubdown and rested his foot he felt a lot better and changed his mind about resuming. The mentors were relieved.

John Quigley gets his Chance

Wexford, however, had no option but to replace the injury-hampered Shanks Whelan. On to the side for the second half came a 19-year-old player of great promise, John Quigley of Rathnure, brother of Dan. He went into the right corner forward position. Jimmy O'Brien went to right half forward.

The Wexford mentors had made another change that was to be significant. Paul Lynch was now at centre forward. He had the unenviable task of playing the pivotal forward role while opposed by Roche. Lynch was a skilful ball-player rather than a marker and when he took his place as the teams lined out to restart the match there were many in the Wexford camp who wondered how this might work out. Jack Berry was now top of the left.

Second Half Starts

As soon as the game was restarted it seemed that the pattern established in the first half would resume. Tipperary, the team that always had the capacity to deliver hard, disabling blows to a floundering opponent at the most opportune time, now went on the assault.

They set up attacks one after the other. But Eddie Kelly, Ned Colfer and Tom Neville showed a renewed vigour and Kelly whipped the ball away from Jimmy Doyle, who had fumbled a ball he would normally have sent over the bar. The next attack had Liam Devaney fire in a hard shot from an angle. This looked like a goal but Nolan made a great save. This was a crucial incident. It stopped Tipperary nailing Wexford's coffin shut and gave great heart to the beleaguered Wexford team.

In another attack, Doyle again showed the fumbling effect of his injury and the ball was cleared out of the way by the backs.

Tipperary were awarded a 70 — a small enough reward for their efforts. The fair-haired Burns, always good with the long ball, came up to take it. To the dismay of Tipperary followers his shot went wide. In the first few minutes of the game Tipperary had lost the chance to put their opponents away and lost the initiative as well.

From the puck out Wilson collected at midfield, made a devil-may-care foray into the Tipperary half, sent the ball in to Berry who sent it over the bar to a great cheer from the beleagured Wexford followers.

Wilson's colleague, Bernie, began to come into the game and he helped set up another attack. This was when John Quigley gave an indication of the impact he was to have on the game. He raced out, collected the ball, controlled it well on the hurley and turned towards goal. He sent it in to Doran. The big red-haired Buffer's Alley player was bottled up but he was strong enough to get out a pass to the inrushing Christy Jacob, who sent it to the net. To Wexford's annoyance the whistle had gone for a foul on Doran. This was further compounded when the free was missed.

Lynch and Roche

But it was now clear that Wexford were taking control with a vengeance. There was a key battle on the 40-yard mark between Lynch and Roche. They were both skilled sticksmen, both played an open game, always played the ball and not the man. Lynch was as good an overhead striker as Roche and he was equally adept at pulling on or with the moving ball.

'Well he practised and he practised, every kind of stroke. He lived in the ball alley in Enniscorthy, perfecting his skills', said Phil Wilson.

Lynch managed to keep the ball out of the hands of Roche and he kept it moving with deft flicks and pulls on the ground, left or right. No player could be expected to get completely the better of someone of Roche's quality and he had his moments and his clearances. He remained the best of the Tipperary backs but he was no longer the dominant attacking centre back of the first half.

Doran Goal

It was from a ball tipped on by Lynch that Berry got possession. He was foiled by O'Gorman and Costigan, now under severe pressure in the full back line. At that moment Phil Wilson, running all over the field, came thundering in, took the ball on his stick and passed to Doran. It was a high ball but this was Doran's forte. With his unorthodox grip he kept the marker away with his left shoulder and arm, catching with his right hand. On this occasion he collected well, turned like a top and went for goal. John Costigan had moved to full back to try to curb Doran but it was a difficult task on a player that had found his feet after a frustrating first half. Doran, strong and hard-muscled, burst past several tackles and slammed the ball to the net.

This goal was a great boost for Wexford morale. They had looked leaden-footed and awkward in the first half. Now they were playing with great verve and dash. The transformation of the team was epitomised by Willie Murphy. Strained by tension in the first half he now opened his shoulders and played with abandon. He beat Keating to the ball again and again and cleared it with the fast, close strokes that were part of his game. Keating was labouring under his injured foot but nobody expected he would be eclipsed in this way.

'Wexford had played so badly in the first half that they just threw caution to the winds in the second half and hurled with great power and freedom', says Donie Nealon.

Dan Quigley

A player who did this most markedly was Dan Quigley. The big man, tall and heavy and strong, got under every ball that came his way, caught it, shouldered and burst his way to free space and sent huge clearances that went right down into the Tipperary goalmouth where Doran, Berry and Quigley were waiting. This was a heroic display that raised great cheers from the stands and terraces from followers and hurling lovers who loved to see the underdog get up off the floor.

Quigley's immediate rival, Jimmy Ryan, was playing with a broken thumb and was hampered by it. But there was a certain code of endurance in hurling which said that you didn't ask for concessions, didn't ask to come off because of a broken finger or broken teeth. Only if a player were visibly unable to hurl or to run would he be taken off by the mentors.

'Wilson came into his own at midfield. He was all over the place, winning the ball and racing away. He kept going past me like a train and there was nothing I could do about it', said Donie Nealon, who was moved to the full forward position midway in the half.

From a Lynch delivery Jack Berry got the ball and sent it over the bar. Wexford were now only one goal behind.

Tipp try to Regain Control

It was now that the indomitable veteran of the Tipperary side, Devaney, tried to stop the Wexford flow of play and bring his own team back in. He came racing in, with McLoughlin and McKenna waiting for the break but the Borrisoleigh man was judged to have overcarried the ball even as he palmed it wide. A free out was given.

Wexford attacked again and to the cheers of the Wexford supporters Doran got the ball once again and went charging in. But a timely challenge by John Gleeson resulted in Doran sending it wide.

Then it was Tipperary's turn to go on the rampage, doing all they could to get going again. In a hectic goalmouth scramble Devaney took the ball from Eddie Kelly and was about to strike to the net when Ned Colfer came charging across and intercepted and struck the ball away. Tipperary were back a minute later. There was a gasp of dismay when Neville slipped and McLoughlin got clear. Nolan faced him and made a fine save. These two escapes came at a pivotal time in the game. A goal at that stage might have wrested the initiative from the Slaneysiders.

John Quigley and O'Brien had just exchanged places when Quigley, revelling in the freedom of the wing, came racing in and sent in a rasper.

The tall O'Donoghue made a brilliant save and cleared the ball out with great aplomb.

At this stage the ball was going from one end of the field to the other and when it came to the wily Nealon in front of the Wexford goal only another well-timed shoulder from Colfer averted the danger.

Tipp Still Ahead

In the 14th minute Sean McLoughlin gathered the ball in the corner and sent a neat pass out to Devaney who put it over the bar to keep Tipperary ahead. Devaney was now placed at the forty yard mark to try to curb Quigley, an impossible task as the big Rathnure man became unstoppable. He had a great understanding with his wing men and whenever he was bottled up got the ball to Vincie Staples or Willie Murphy, who invariably cleared away down their respective wings.

At this stage the mentors called in the limping Jimmy Doyle and sent on the Roscrea player, Loughnane.

Devaney's point and the introduction of the hard-running Loughnane, who made his presence felt, raised Tipperary hopes of holding on until they could get their breath back again. But Wexford were on top down the middle, with few balls passing Quigley, Wilson lording it all over the midfield area, Lynch tipping on many balls into the full forward, where Doran was like a red-maned lion preying on the goal.

Wexford Keep Pressing

From the corner Jimmy O'Brien nipped in to send in a flashing drive. It just skimmed the crossbar as O'Donoghue lunged at it. Once again a high ball came into the Tipperary goalmouth and once again Doran grabbed it. As he was shouldered to the ground he managed to get a shot in but the reliable Tipp goalkeeper saved again.

Yet the balls kept coming in — high deliveries from Quigley or faster, lower balls from Lynch or passes from the rampaging Wilson. It was a case of fouling Doran or letting him through for a goal. He caught a ball and was wrestled to the ground. John Dowling blew for a 21-yard free. All Lynch's hours of ball alley sharpshooting came to the fore now. He placed a pile-driver clear of the goalkeeper — the one most likely to stop it — and it rocketed into the net. After being eight points down at the end of the first half Wexford were now level going into the last quarter.

Eight Scoreless Minutes

The gauntlet had been thrown down to Tipperary. The Munster champions took it up. Wexford may have taken the initiative but there was no way that Tipperary, with their proud hurling tradition, were going to go under. For the next eight minutes both sides battled for supremacy without conceding a score. The ball flew up and down the pitch, bobbled and spun in the goalmouths, dribbled along the grass as players shouldered and pulled.

It was to the great credit of both sides that not once did the referee have to issue a caution for dangerous play to any player. This was a tough, tempestuous bout of play but exceedingly sporting, despite the pressure the players were under, with families and friends and loyal supporters willing them on to win each individual battle.

At midfield P.J. Ryan began to come back into the picture but Bernie and Wilson still held the upper hand for most of the time.

And Dan Quigley stayed in control at centre back, sending the ball down to the Tipperary goalmouth.

As the scoreless minutes passed by, with the sides level, both sides knew that the next score would be vital and that the next goal might well decide the issue.

Decisive Goal

Finally it was Wexford who broke the deadlock. A Dan Quigley clearance went to Lynch. With his deft wristwork he was able to send in a pin-point pass to Doran. The big man burst through two hard tackles to send the ball into the net. This goal raised the biggest cheer that day in Croke Park, for it signalled the never-say-die attitude of the Wexford men.

Now that the impasse had been broken Wexford raided again and Jimmy O'Brien sent over from the corner to put his side four points ahead.

When Willie Murphy conceded a free Michael Keating went for a goal but it was saved and cleared. Tipperary, with Loughnane winning several balls, came again and Wexford gave a 70 away. Mick Burns took it, sending it right under the crossbar. John Nolan saved it well, despite the tussling that went on beside him. These two goal attempts by Tipperary showed how dangerous they could still be despite the game going against them.

Coup De Grace

Then Wexford delivered the *coup de grace* to their harrassed opponents. Once again Lynch's wristwork came to the fore when he flicked a pass to Jack Berry, who scored his second goal. Nothing but a miracle could save Tipperary at this stage. And Wexford held on to the initiative. John Quigley kept pulling Len Gaynor out of position with his running, collecting and attacking and from one of these forays the ball went to Doran who this time was content with a point.

With four minutes to go Wexford were eight points ahead. It seemed an incredible transformation of a game that had seemed well and truly lost at half-time.

Late Tipp Scores

Yet Tipperary showed that they too had the never-say-die spirit. With the game almost beyond reach they went on the attack. In a goalmouth scramble Pat Nolan almost had the ball in his hand when McLoughlin snapped it away and sent in a goal.

Almost from the puck out Tipperary came again. Loughnane, hungry for action grabbed the ball and raced into the goal. He was pulled down and a 21-yard free awarded. The Tipperary players looked at the muscular Keating, master of this kind of placed ball.

Like Lynch, Keating had perfected his free taking in a ball alley and could place the ball where he liked. He never believed in running forward to scoop the ball and gain a few yards before striking the dropping ball.

'If you run forward you risk losing the balance that is vital if you are to strike the ball with the sweet spot and get power into it', he explained. On this occasion he rose the ball perfectly and rocketed it to the roof of the net well away from the most likely obstacle — the razor sharp hurley of John Nolan. Now there was only two points between the sides. But in the stands and terraces, along the sideline there were whistles to the referee to remind him that time was up.

Shortly afterwards John Dowling blew the long whistle to bring an end to this remarkable contest.

When Dan Quigley went up to take the trophy from Seamus O Riain, president of the GAA, the delight of players and supporters at this stunning victory knew no bounds. For the Tipperary captain, Mick Roche, this was a great disappointment. For the first time ever, Tipperary had lost two finals in a row and he had been captain on both occasions. Yet, three years later, he gave another memorable display of centre back play when marking the most difficult centre forward of the time, Paddy Delaney, as Tipperary beat Kilkenny.

That day in 1968 the state of hurling in Wexford never seemed higher. As well as their inspirational victory, the county had, for the first time, won both minor and senior titles together. The Wexford newspapers spoke of the dawn of a new epoch in Wexford hurling.

Few could have predicted that this great hurling county would not win another final to the present time. They contested the finals of '70, '76 and '77, being beaten by Cork on each occasion. Then the county went into a decline from which it has not recovered. There were to be no more minor titles either and many days of frustration and disappointment for the faithful followers. Yet the memory of their great comeback in 1968 is warmly remembered in the county. It may help to inspire this great stronghold of the game to stride to the All-Ireland some day in the near future.

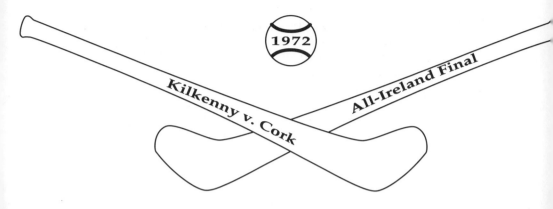

KILKENNY'S GREAT RESURGENCE

Twenty minutes into the second half Cork's left half back, the redoubtable Con Roche, face red with determination and exertion, got hold of the ball near the left sideline. He eluded his marker and ran forward a few steps to take one of his characteristic swings at the ball.

He was a marvel of accuracy from long range but this was over 80 yards away from the Kilkenny goal. The ball shot away from his hurley, rising and soaring over the midfield, followed by 66,137 pairs of eyes squinting in the blazing sunlight. The tiny white dot kept travelling like a satellite over the green of the pitch, seen against the roofs of the stands until it began to lose height.

Then at the end of its long flight it passed between the two tall white uprights that marked the Kilkenny goal and hopped on the ground behind, scattering some officials and photographers.

As a huge cheer went up from the delighted Cork supporters in the crowd. Several others, waving red and white flags like dervishes, raced out to congratulate the St Finbarr's player. His great score put his side no less than eight points ahead and seemed to spell the end of the road for a fine Kilkenny side. The Noresiders had tried everything they knew to contain a talent-laden Cork team which boasted some of the most lethal forwards ever to play the game of hurling.

Great Game, Great Teams

Even at that stage this had been a pulsating game between two of the best teams to contest a final, with beautiful hurling, great displays of skill, marvellous scores, full-blooded physical challenges which demanded courage and endurance from the players. If, as seemed likely, Cork had pulled away to win by a handsome score no follower of the game, apart from ardent Kilkenny zealots, could have complained. The entertainment had been lavish from the start, with tremendous duels between talented men on the field and the tacticians on the sideline.

Another reason this turned out to be such an entertaining contest was that Cork and Kilkenny had a great respect for each other and allowed each other to hurl.

After Roche's point few could have foreseen that the best of this exciting game was still to come; that they would see an astonishing example of what can happen when all the members of an apparently beaten side begin to motor as one unit and develop a surge of hurling that overwhelms the opposition. The comeback by Kilkenny from imminent defeat was carried out in a way that went into hurling legend and made the game without any doubt one of the greatest of all time.

Two of the Best

When these two teams qualified to meet in the final there was a growing hum of expectation in the hurling world. The sides were among the very best put forward by their respective counties and it was only fitting that they should meet to test their mettle and their skills on centre stage.

Both sides had been developing for some time, adding players, dropping some, selecting others to make up the panels. There were players on both sides who had played against one another in the All-Irelands of 1966 and 1969. There were newcomers on the two teams who were striving to match the quality of their colleagues and were waiting for an opportunity to do so.

Both sides had reached a pinnacle of maturity by 1972. Cork had won the All-Ireland of 1970, against Wexford. The following year Kilkenny had taken on Tipperary in the final and had lost after a fine game. Now Kilkenny were back, fully determined not to lose two All-Irelands in a row.

This was a Kilkenny side which was to provide immense delight and entertainment for the first half of the 1970s, contesting five All-Irelands in a row and winning three of them. It had one of the all-time great centre backs in Pat Henderson and forwards whose feats are now part of hurling lore — Keher, Delaney and Purcell.

The Cork team was spearheaded by forwards that were a most exciting spectacle to watch. Charlie McCarthy, Ray Cummins and Sean O'Leary made up the most lethal full forward line in modern times and all three were to be the foundation on which the Cork three-in-a-row triumph later in the '70s was to be built.

All-Ireland Experience

The only players on the Kilkenny side making their first appearance in a final were Morrissey, O'Brien, Crotty and Kinsella. Eddie Byrne and

Kieran Purcell had played in the final of the previous year. All of the others held All-Ireland medals won in either in '63, '67 or '69.

On the Cork side Paddy Barry and the three McCarthys — Gerald, Justin and Charlie — won medals in 1966. Maher, McDonnell, Looney, Roche, Hegarty and Cummins had been on the winning side in 1970.

Cork Regarded as Best

It was the style and consistency of the Cork team which made them favourites in the eyes of the hurling public for the final of 1972. Along with their two All-Irelands of recent times they had also won the National League in '69, '70 and '72. That game in May had been one of the best finals seen for a long time. Against a Limerick side which put on a great spurt of power in the second half Cork showed style and verve and made some delightful scores to hold out for a good win.

Then in the Munster championship they were put to the test when they met the reigning champions, Tipperary in the semi-final. With 20 minutes of the second half gone Cork found themselves 11 points down. Yet they were resilient and their forwards incisive enough to fight their way back for a draw. They improved for the replay and dethroned the champions in another hard-fought game. In the Munster final they utterly demolished Clare by their superiority all over the field, with Ray Cummins unbeatable as full forward.

Powers of Recovery

Kilkenny proved that they too could come from behind. Against Wexford in the Leinster final they were seven points adrift in the third quarter of the 80-minute game but managed to claw their way back into contention through a last minute point by Mick Crotty. Both sides scored 6–13.

After that draw some of the exacting supporters were critical of Noel Skehan, who had succeeded the incomparable Ollie Walsh in goal. But, in the replay, the Bennettsbridge man rescued his side by a series of astonishing saves and Kilkenny pulled ahead in the last part of the game to win by eight points. They easily overcame Galway in the semi-final.

'You will have Hurling'

Now the scene was set for the battle between these traditional rivals. 'Whenever you have Cork and Kilkenny in a final you will see hurling — I am certain you will have hurling', said the white-haired trainer of the Cork side, Jim O'Regan. He was one of the stars of the three pulsating games it took to decide the issue between the sides in 1931. Those matches, more than any others, created a nationwide interest in the game and ensured that from then on the attendances at finals would grow steadily to the point that the quest for tickets became a ritual connected with the event.

O'Regan was pointing to the fact that each county had great respect for the other and usually allowed hurling rather than hustling to decide the issue. Since the championship began near the end of the last century they had met thirteen times with Kilkenny victorious on seven occasions.

Eighty-Minute Final

This was the first 80-minute final between them. The Cork team were marginally younger on average than their opponents and some Cork supporters were hopefully predicting that the Kilkenny men would run out of steam in the last ten minutes, especially if it was a warm sunny day. Fr Donal Coakley from St Colman's College, Fermoy, was charged with ensuring that the physical fitness of the players would reach a peak for the game.

At Nowlan Park in Kilkenny the physical training was planned and carried out by a former athlete, Mick Lanigan. He said he had no doubts his men would last the pace come rain or shine. It was likely to be shine, for there was a long spell of settled summer weather, with clear skies and warm temperatures, and it looked likely to last at least until the first Sunday in September.

The man in charge of the team was one of the most forward-looking mentors, Fr Tommy Maher, who had made a study of the game, its tactics and was introducing elements of teamwork that were to be adopted by all other counties and eventually become part of the way the game is played today.

New Rules

There was another important factor which added to the expectations of hurling purists. This was to be the first final between the sides under the new rules which protected the goalkeeper and did away with the contentious third man tackle. Full backs were no longer picked for their weight and ability to grapple or even intimidate forwards who might try to charge the goalkeeper and dump him — with or without the ball — in the back of the net.

'These new rules made a tremendous difference to the game. They put the emphasis on hurling, opened it up completely. From then on full backs had to be able to hurl as well as to mark their men', said Eddie Keher.

Injuries

No All-Ireland final is quite complete without rumour and speculation about injuries, serious and slight. The newspapers repeated the doubts about the fitness of the Cork captain, Frank Norberg, who was trying to recover from a knee injury to take his place in the half back line. Fan Larkin, the Kilkenny corner back, was also battling against the after-effects of a leg injury. Pat Hegarty, the Cork half forward, and Frank Cummins the Kilkenny midfielder were also carrying recent injuries.

The unease and the interest about injuries was by no means spurious. No one who knew about the utter physical effort required in an

All-Ireland had any doubt but that it was no place for an injured man or indeed one not at the top of his physical form.

The Cork captain, Norberg, of Swedish ancestry, would be the first representative from the Leeside village of Blackrock to lead the side since 1931. Eudie Coughlan had done so then; he was still hale and hearty and offered words of caution about underestimating the opposition. The Kilkenny captain of that era, Lory Meagher, was still alive, a bachelor farmer living at Tullaroan, and he too was careful about making any jaunty predictions.

When the hurling-wise and the commentators began to sum up the chances of both sides they honed in on a number of key personal duels on which they felt the match might turn.

The teams as they lined out were:

CORK

Paddy Barry
(Sarsfields)

Tony Maher	Pat McDonnell	Brian Murphy
(St Finbarr's)	(UCC)	(Nemo Rangers)
Frank Norberg, capt	Seamus Looney	Con Roche
(Blackrock)	(St Finbarr's)	(St Finbarr's)

Justin McCarthy   Denis Coughlan
(Passage)   (Glen Rovers)

Gerald McCarthy	Mick Malone	Pat Hegarty
(St Finbarr's)	(Eire Og)	(Youghal)
Charlie McCarthy	Ray Cummins	Sean O'Leary
(St Finbarr's)	(Blackrock)	(Youghal)

Substitutes: Teddie O'Brien (Glen Rovers); Donal Collins (Blackrock); Martin Coleman (Ballinhassig); Paddy Crowley (UCC); John Rothwell (Blackrock). *Coach/selector*: Jim O'Regan (Kinsale/UCC). *Trainer*: Fr Donal Coakley (St Colman's College). *Selectors*: Fr Bertie Troy (Newtownshandrum; Pat O'Leary (Sarsfields); Dan O'Mahony (Passage); Frank Murphy, county secretary.

KILKENNY

Noel Skehan, capt
(Bennettsbridge)

Fan Larkin	Pa Dillon	Jim Treacy
(James Stephens)	(Freshford)	(Bennettsbridge)
Paddy Lalor	Pat Henderson	Eamon Morrissey
(Bennettsbridge)	(Johnstown)	(James Stephens)

Frank Cummins   Liam O'Brien
(Blackrock)   (James Stephens)

John Kinsella	Pat Delaney	Mick Crotty
(Bennettsbridge)	(Johnstown)	(James Stephens)
Ned Byrne	Kieran Purcell	Eddie Keher
(James Stephens)	(Windgap) ·	(Rower-Inistioge)

Substitutes: Mossy Murphy (Mullinavat); Martin Coogan (Erin's Own, Castlecomer); Paddy Moran (Bennettsbridge); Ollie Walsh (Thomastown); Wattie Murphy (Rower-Inistioge); Senan Cooke (Kilmacow); Nicky Orr (Fenians). *Coach*: Rev Tommy Maher. *Trainer*: Mick Lanigan. *Team doctor*: Dr Kieran Cuddihy.

The referee was Mick Spain of Offaly.

Curbing Cummins

Would Pa Dillon be able to curb the prolific Ray Cummins? Dillon had been persuaded to come out of retirement that year and without him Kilkenny would not be in the final. This big man, almost 14 stone in weight, had the height to command the air and the physique to hold his stance under the dropping ball. He had held Wexford at bay in the drawn game and the replay.

Cummins was 6 ft 4 ins, a lanky player who was exceptionally agile. He had a marvellous facility to catch the ball, a long, bony figure rising into the air to grab a dropping ball or bending to snap up one hopping round the square. He had developed a finely tuned sense of teamwork with the two corner men, O'Leary and McCarthy, flicking fast and accurate balls to them after he had drawn the backs.

Handpassed goals were allowed at that time and the fair haired full back from Freshford would have to ensure that Cummins did not take two or three of his long strides to palm the ball to the net.

In the Corners

Four relatively small men were going to battle it out in the corners. Sean O'Leary always looked deceptively weighty. Those who played against him knew of his rocket-like bursts of speed which could leave opponents trailing in his wake as he raced for goal. He was a supreme stick-artist and goal-opportunist who never strayed far from the square. Marking him was the tigerish Fan Larkin, son of an equally well-known Kilkenny hurler. The presence of this small, light player emphasised how the rule changes had begun to affect the structure of teams. Here was no traditional beefy stopper but a lightning-fast player who made it his business to race out to get the ball first. Larkin had the confidence to do something most corner backs avoided — he pulled first time on the incoming ball no matter how fast it was coming. Rarely if ever did he miss this spectacular gambit which delighted the crowd for its skill and devilry.

In the other corner the duel would be between Treacy and McCarthy. The St Finbarr's player created scores by his sharply honed skills and his ability to read the game, know where a ball was going to break. He had scored goals pulling at waist-height on fast balls but some of his best scores came off the ground, the ball hit on the half-volley just an inch off the turf. He could perform this feat from his left or his right and he had a cheekiness about the daring way he played that made him a favourite with the Cork followers.

His marker that day was a stocky, weighty man whose hair had prematurely whitened. Treacy was no creaking veteran however. He was an astute assessor of the play, of how to mark opponents out of the game. He always kept between the goal and the man he was marking. He had the weight to knock forwards off the ball. He had a good pair of hands and once he got the ball he was hard to dispossess.

Henderson

One of the problems for the Kilkenny full back line was to mark their opponents without giving frees away. Part of Kilkenny's plan would be to limit the amount of dangerous ball coming in to the front line trio. The key man in this task was the big, sandy-haired man from Johnstown, Pat Henderson. He had emerged as one of the great centre backs of the modern era. He had a commanding, inspirational presence in the centre of the line, a figure of great courage and drive. With a great pair of hands he caught the ball amid swinging hurleys and then used his weight and physique to come bursting through harrassing forwards to clear the ball defiantly down the field. Henderson was always at his best when his side were under pressure, rallying his colleagues by his refusal to even contemplate defeat.

The man he would have to control was a fast-running, bustling player, Mick Malone, who had come to prominence by his power play on under-age teams. There was a great urgency about the way he went into the clash for a ball. He pulled hard on the ground or overhead but he could catch it too and when he did he was fast and agile, able to round his man and race goalwards. He was a workhorse centre forward from whom players like Gerald McCarthy and Pat Hegarty could feed.

Half Backs and Forwards

Some of the Kilkenny followers wondered how a newcomer to the All-Ireland scene, Eamon Morrissey would measure up against a player of vast experience and ability, Gerald McCarthy. Both had the same kind of sturdy stature. McCarthy, fiery captain of the side that brought Cork back into the hurling limelight in 1966, was tough and vigorous, a man who had tirelessly practised hitting the moving ball, striking against it or pulling with it, until he did it automatically, sending it exactly where he wanted it to go, an art which has largely died out today. Morrissey had accumulated a great deal of experience on the Kilkenny minor team, on which he played for three years, and on the under-21 side. He had been severely tested in the two tempestuous games against Wexford and had emerged as a reliable half back who covered well and made few mistakes.

Paddy Lalor of Bennettsbridge played at right half back and would be marking Pat Hegarty. Lalor had developed an uncanny instinct for knowing where the ball was going to break and where to be. For that reason he always seemed to have all the time in the world to clear the ball down the field. He had a finely-tuned playing relationship with Fan Larkin and always ran into position to take the pass from the corner man and strike the ball way past midfield. 'Who's supposed to be marking Lalor, for God's sake?' irate supporters of the other team were wont to cry out when they saw him striking the ball unimpeded.

Lalor's first job in the All-Ireland would be to mark the very accomplished Pat Hegarty from Youghal. He had played very well in the

All-Ireland of 1970 and had scored some great points and a few memorable goals during Cork's victorious league campaigns in '69, '70 and '72. He had played consistently well during the games in the Munster campaign but he was now carrying an injury which had only just cleared up.

Midfield

At midfield Cork had the tall, muscular Denis Coughlan from the Glen Rovers side and Justin McCarthy from Passage, one of the stars of the 1966 win. Coughlan was an elegant hurler who made it all look easy, rising and reaching back behind his head for overhead balls, sending long pucks down the field, always being in the right place at the right time.

His opponent on the Sunday was a man he knew well, Frank Cummins, then a Garda stationed in Cork and playing outstanding hurling with the Blackrock side. Cummins was a strong, barrel-chested man only a few pounds off 14 stones, who dominated the centre by his power and energy. He used his weight legitimately to knock opponents about in the exchanges. He could run with the ball and sometimes did. Despite his stature he was fast enough to get clear of opponents. Then this left-hander would bring his hurley almost full circle to hit one of the hardest shots ever seen in modern times.

Cummin's partner at centrefield was the ball-juggling Liam 'Chunky' O'Brien from the James Stephens club. He was light and fast, very skilful. He got out of tight situations by racing away with the ball seemingly glued to his weaving hurley. He always seemed to have time to slow down, steady himself and score a long-range point. His marker would be an equally skilful hurler, Justin McCarthy, who was one of the real stylists of the game, full of pace and balance in the way he hurled, a great striker of the ball. McCarthy had vast experience and he was the kind of thoughtful player who learns from year to year and gets appreciably better. The Cork fans knew his qualities and were expecting a lot from him.

Looney v. Delaney

Another key duel that the knowledgeable ones were debating in pubs and indeed on the terraces of the old Cork Athletic Grounds and Nowlan Park as they watched the teams in training, was Seamus Looney versus Pat Delaney. The tall slim Looney had played in several positions since he first came to prominence and there was some criticism of the mentors for playing him at centre back, a position for which his free-flowing style was not fully suited. His fast footwork and quick striking during the 1970 All-Ireland when he played at midfield, had helped his side overcome Wexford.

Whoever marked Pat Delaney, the strong, tough farmer from Johnstown had better keep the ball away from him. He had a pair of strong large hands which could catch the ball anywhere and when he got possession he always took his man on, shouldering his way through. Many backs found that the only way to stop him was to foul him. He had a habit of sending goalwards the high incoming ball by flicking it overhead to his right, often with one hand on the hurley. Delaney was the powerhouse of the Kilkenny attack. One of the great strengths of that team was the way he and Purcell — at full forward — could interchange positions if they were having a difficult time in their respective positions.

Purcell, from Windgap, had starred in the All-Ireland of the previous year, racing through the Tipperary defence, cleverly dodging the charges of backs, controlling the ball like a juggler, twisting and turning until he hit a bullet-like ball into the Tipperary net. Purcell had a great pair of hands and a great facility to take hold on the dropping ball. He had broad shoulders and a powerful shot along with delicate skills. He was as powerful at centre forward as he was at full forward.

Marking Purcell was Pat McDonnell, one of the most accomplished full backs playing. In match after match he played exceptionally well, very fast around the square, able to twist and turn with great agility. He had been a bulwark of the Cork defence in the 1970 final and had later been picked as the Texaco Hurler of the Year for his exploits.

Personal Duels

From game experience many knew that these personal duels often do not count. Players cancel one another out. Sometimes both play well. Sometimes one gets on top for a while and then loses out. Sometimes a player changes position and loses the run of the game. Other times a new position can liberate a man who is having problems getting away from his opponent or getting into his stride.

Many Kilkenny followers wondered if it was wise to confine a player of Keher's versatility and opportunism to the corner. His scoring ability could easily be wasted there because it was not uncommon for the corners to see a minimum amount of action in a game. And Keher would be marked by a man who would stick to him like a barnacle, Tony Maher. Maher had marked corner forwards completely out of the game since he began to play for Cork. He was a resourceful player and he had weight to hold his feet in the bodily clashes.

The other corner of the Cork defence had a young player in Brian Murphy of Nemo Rangers who was a natural athlete, equally adept at football as well as hurling. At 20 he was one of the youngest players on the field but during the Munster campaign he had made the left corner his own and he would win great renown there in the years ahead.

Murphy was going to be giving away a lot in terms of weigth. The man he would be marking was the heaviest on the field, the 6 ft 2 ins, 16 stone Ned Byrne from the James Stephens club. He and Purcell made up a lot of physical power in the full forward line. Byrne, as he had done in the Leinster campaign, would break the ball down for the other forwards, do a lot of the hard physical work round the square and keep the ball there, blocking clearances.

Roche and Norberg

In front of Brian Murphy was the great enthusiast of the Cork side, Con Roche from St Finbarr's, in his left half back position. He played with great vigour and commitment and his clearances sailed off down the field into the opposing goal area. No matter how much pressure he was under he hit the ball dead on — right on the sweet spot of the hurley. His opponent was John Kinsella from Bennettsbridge who had been on the fringe of the team since coming on as a sub in the All-Ireland of 1967. He had played on the minor and under-21 sides and was the typical Kilkenny sticksman, nippy and full of skilful touches.

The Cork right half back Frank Norberg would need to be fast on his feet to handle the tall, lanky Mick Crotty, who kept moving all the time, often well away from his own position. Against Wexford he had roamed freely on his long-striding legs, getting possession anywhere from midfield to the right corner and in every game he invariably scored. He was the kind of forward who foraged tirelessly for the ball all over his half of the field. A fully fit Norberg had played some excellent games in Munster but there was now a question mark over his injury.

The Goalkeepers

And there were the goalkeepers. Kilkenny's Noel Skehan, was a small, stocky player from Bennettsbridge. He was the captain of the side. He had been understudy to Ollie Walsh for a long time and only got his chance between the posts when that great net-minder retired in 1971. For some time Skehan was under critical scrutiny from followers who were used to the style and flamboyance of Walsh and felt he could never be replaced. The players on the Kilkenny team already knew how good he was and in the years to come he was to be very favourably compared to his illustrious predecessor.

His opposite number was Paddy Barry, one of the stars of the 1966 triumph when his great saves in the first half ensured that his side were poised for victory in the wind-aided second half. Since then his goal-keeping had been one of the linchpins of the side in All-Ireland and National League victories. He had a dash about the way he saved that endeared him to the fans.

Warm and Sunny

The day of the All-Ireland was one of the warmest September days on which a final was played. There was a clear blue sky and little or no wind. The Croke Park sod was dry. It was a day for all the fans to enjoy but the heat and the blazing sun were certainly going to test the stamina of the players.

After the minor game, won impressively by Kilkenny when they beat Cork, there was a parade to protest at the occupation of the GAA grounds at Casement Park in Belfast by the British army. There was turmoil, terrorism and terrible loss of life in the North that year. The complexities of the situation were not yet fully understood or accepted by many in the Republic and there was some florid oratory heard in Croke Park that afternoon.

President de Valera, his near blindness making the occasion one of ceremonial attendance only, took his place in the stand. Beside him was the Taoiseach, Jack Lynch, one of Cork's hurling heroes of the past. He would have to leave the game at half time to fly to Munich, where a meeting had been arranged with the British premier, Edward Heath, to discuss the violence in Northern Ireland.

The referee was Mick Spain of Offaly. He called Norberg and Skehan together for the toss and Kilkenny decided to play into the sun in the first half, a decision which had a bearing on the outcome as Paddy Barry would have the hard sunlight in his eyes in the second half as the September sun began to decline.

The ball was thrown in at 3.15 p.m. to a great roar from the crowd, most of them in shirtsleeves or summer frocks, many in the sun-facing terraces and Cusack stand wearing sun-glasses.

Kilkenny Score First

Cork went on the attack right away but the ball went wide. Then John Kinsella, on the right wing of the Kilkenny attack, cut a good side line ball into the Cork goal area. The tall Crotty, lank black hair falling across his forehead, grabbed it and with his characteristic sharp stroke, sent it over the bar for the game's first score.

Devasting Response

Cork's response was instant. The awesome power of their forwards was displayed. Ray Cummins showed how lethal he was when Justin McCarthy sent in a long centre from midfield. Despite Pa Dillon's best efforts the tall Blackrock player got the ball and then weaved his way goalwards. Noel Skehan had no chance with the shot that went to the net.

This raised a huge cheer from the crowd, especially the massed Cork contingent on Hill 16 where it looked as if a hurricane was tossing the red and white flags about. This was a great start for Cork, a morale-booster for the team.

Kilkenny came back. They were awarded a long range free. This was the domain of Pat Henderson. He stood over the ball, legs close together, bent his knees, put his hurley beneath the ball, lifted it carefully from the tinder-dry grass and sent it over the bar. This was a confident start for the big centre back.

Henderson was in the action again shortly when he got possession, came shouldering his way past red-shirted opponents and, though now surrounded, managed to get a pass out to Liam O'Brien. The James Stephens man controlled the ball beautifully and then made space to steady himself for a long ball that soared over the bar and brought the sides level.

Cork went on the attack. Larkin and Treacy clung close to the dangerous O'Leary and McCarthy but the Kilkenny defence gave away a 70. The Cork captain, Norberg, centred this ball but in a great clash before the goal the ball was beaten out and was swept down to the other end with some delightful striking. Eddie Keher got it but Tony Maher, strong and resolute, hardly gave him room to breathe and Keher sent the ball narrowly wide of the upright.

Kilkenny Level

At this stage the two tall men at centrefield, Coughlan and Cummins, were largely cancelling one another out but the Cork player got in a few good strokes on the ball. O'Brien and Justin McCarthy, two skilled ball-players, were both playing well, proving that at centrefield it is possible for immediate opponents to both have a good game. In the eighth minute O'Brien, who shared the long-range frees with Henderson, took one from 60 yards. His measured swing on the ball sent it over the bar to put Kilkenny ahead.

Cork surged into an attack but the teak-tough Henderson came bustling out with the ball once again. He was fouled and sent the free well into the Cork goal area where another free was awarded to the Noresiders. This was Eddie Keher's first free. As usual he settled the ball carefully, flexed his shoulders, shifted his feet so that the balance was exactly right, put his left hand well down the hurley for full control, lifted the ball carefully and struck it over. It was something he had practised thousands of times.

Fast Hurling

Under the hot sun, on the dry sod, the ball flew from end to end. All the touches of skill and ball control were being shown by both sides. Skill was necessary because the game was being played at such a fast pace, the marking was often so tight that a player only got a split second to tip on a ball, pull on it, block it down. There were bone-shaking challenges but this game was being played in an admirably sporting spirit and it was to remain so right to the end.

The spectators were lifted by this hurling spectacle, shouting and laughing, turning to one another when a beautiful stroke was played or a courageous gambit paid off. Strangers nudged one another, exchanged comments, bonded by the splendour of the hurling spectacle before them.

Cork Playing Well

Cork were beginning to edge ahead in advantage. Coughlan was making characteristic catches, stretching up into the air for the ball and then sending it goalward towards the tall figure of the full forward, Ray

Cummins. He was seen as the danger man because it was nip and tuck between Gerald McCarthy and Eamon Morrissey and Pat Hegarty and Pat Lalor. They each in turn showed their skills in the few seconds the ball came their way but there was no time for any of them to settle on the ball.

Cork attacked twice in succession and the Kilkenny backs gave away two 21-yard frees. Charlie McCarthy, with his characteristic short-stepped trot, came out to take them. He was a figure of compact, controlled energy in his play and he took frees with the same sense of neatness and control, as well as a certain self-confident swagger. He put both of them over the bar.

At the other end Brian Murphy was keeping the strong man of the Kilkenny attack, Ned Byrne, in check but Pat McDonnell had his work cut out minding the wily and dexterous Purcell. The Windgap man it was who got the next score when he made a fine catch and then spun about to send the ball flying over the bar.

Up to this Seamus Looney had managed to keep the ball out of the hands of Pat Delaney, to flick it away from him. But his preoccupation with Delaney meant he could not make the kind of inspirational clearances that his opposite number, Henderson, was making as Kilkenny were being subjected to an increase in Cork pressure. Fan Larkin, grim-faced and beetle-browed in his hard tussling with his heavier opponent, O'Leary, got a free out. He had a great stroke on a ball and sent it way down the field to set up an attack. It ended in a free for the Noresiders which Keher put over.

Great Skehan Save

The Kilkenny supporters held their breath when the ball came flying down to their goal. Charlie McCarthy whipped quickly on it. The ball was flying netwards when Skehan made the first of his miraculous saves at close quarters. He was a goalkeeper of great courage whose front teeth had long since been knocked out in goalmouth tussles. He had lightning reflexes, helped by his razor-sharp alacrity as a champion squash player. However the ball bounded out to the prowling Cummins. Dillon ensured that his way to goal was blocked but the tall full forward sent it over the bar.

Cork forced a free from 40 yards out and Charlie McCarthy cantered out to take it and sent it over the bar to level the scores. In the next attack Noel Skehan brought off a spectacular save that stopped a certain goal. Saves like this effectively put an end to all doubts in Kilkenny about his ability to fill the boots of Ollie Walsh.

In the next attack Charlie McCarthy got free of the attentions of Jim Treacy. He flicked a pass out to Cummins, who kept moving in and out in front of goal to create space, and Cummins put it over the bar.

At this stage the Cork backs were looking well in control, limiting the opportunities for the opposing forwards, but just the same Paddy Barry had to handle a few difficult balls. He did so with his usual style and panache.

At midfield the bushy-haired 'Chunkie' O'Brien began weaving his way into the Cork half, hurley glued to ball, acting as an extra forward. However this gambit left Justin McCarthy loose and he in turn sent in low balls to the corner forwards. O'Brien took the next middle distance free and sent it over the bar.

In the next Cork raid Mick Malone got into his stride, running strongly, crouched to shoulder opponents out of the way. The ball went away from him for a few seconds but he finished this raid with a fine point.

There was more Cork pressure and the dust rose in the sunlight as Dillon and Cummins grappled, boots scrabbling against the hard ground, while Treacy and Larkin tried all they knew to keep their men under control. In one of these goalmouth scuffles Skehan went on his knees to block a ball, something he did often in order to limit the chances of the ball going between his shins or past his wide-bossed hurley. He got knocked over as bodies came crashing down on top of him and had to receive medical attention before he resumed.

'That fellow is a hardy whore', said a Wexford-accented voice in the crowd as Skehan dusted himself off and took the ball for the puck out.

Roche Long-Distance Free

Con Roche was playing with great fire and vigour, shouldering hard in races for possession and getting long clearances down the field. He now took a free from 65 yards out and sent it over the bar.

Kilkenny's forward difficulties, with so many good forwards tied up, was forcing them to depend on frees. This was emphasised once again when their next score came from a placed ball, a free from 50 yards out which the unerring O'Brien once again sent over.

Opportunist Goal

By now Mick Malone, who had got few chances against Pat Henderson, had swopped with Charlie McCarthy. This move paid off in the 32nd minute when a long, speculative shot from the left wing deceived Skehan. Malone was in like a shot to finish it to the net. The Leesiders now had a four-point lead on a score line of 2–7 to 0–9.

John Kinsella got away from Frank Norberg a half minute later and sent over a good point to cut Cork's lead to three points. There was great cheering when Looney and Delaney clashed on the 40 yard line. The Cork man was proving a good marker for the burly Delaney. But there were times that he stopped Delaney going on one of his characteristic runs by fouling him and it led to a number of frees.

Keher Tied Up

In the corner Keher was having a frustrating time against Maher. Keher was famous not just for his skills but for being able to spot a gap at the back and to be gone through it with the ball before anyone knew what was happening. At this stage Maher was at his side, limpet-like. Keher was also used to feeding off the bustling endeavours of Delaney and Purcell but he was only getting a few scraps in the corner and Maher saw to it that he could make little use of them. The battle of wits, of brawn, of skill between these two raised a great cheer whenever the ball came their way.

Keher's next score was again off a free, taken 35 yards out. Accurate as ever, he sent it over. Charlie McCarthy did likewise at the other end.

At this stage Frank Norberg, who was showing signs of his injury under the fierce pace and passion of the game, had no option but to go off. It was a sad departure for the Cork captain, who had done so much to bring his side to the final and now had to sit it out in frustration. He was replaced by the experienced Teddie O'Brien.

The next score came when Crotty, ever foraging for the ball, got hold of it and sent it over for the last point of the first half. The half time score stood at Cork 2–8 to Kilkenny 0–12.

Half-Time

Many spectators felt that Cork should probably be further ahead than a mere two points, considering that they were doing well at midfield and had the edge in many of the other positions about the field. Seven of Kilkenny's points had come from placed balls. But as the two sides, jerseys dark with perspiration, trooped off the field there was a prolonged round of applause for thirty men who had already given an exhibition of how the game should be played.

Game Resumes

The teams returned to the pitch to a welcoming cheer not alone from supporters of either side but from the highly-entertained spectators who had no particular affiliation. Ned Byrne, who had found it hard to find his form, had been replaced by Mossie Murphy on the Kilkenny side.

At the start of the second half it looked as if Kilkenny were going to assert themselves more. They went on the attack and Cork gave away a free which Keher sent over from 35 yards. He made it look easy. A point always seemed inevitable each time a free was given within his range. He had the temperament for the big occasion, the cool nerve, the methodical approach to his free-taking.

About a minute later Liam O'Brien got the ball around midfield and shot a spectacular point, high into the air between the uprights. It brought the sides level. It was his fifth and a measure of his endless energy as he roamed about the midfield. Their was something defiant about his scores in the confident, stylish way he took them.

Malone Goals Again

Then Cork began to really turn on the power. They sent the ball again and again into the Kilkenny half. If it had not been for Henderson, a giant force in the centre, the Noresiders would have been in serious trouble. Then Gerald McCarthy, not having an easy time with the close marking of Eamon Morrissey, sent in a hard ball into the goalmouth. Skehan made a great save but the ball skittered about while Fan Larkin toppled over, injured, and in the scramble Kilkenny failed to clear the ball. Malone drove it to the net for his second goal. It was a great boost for Cork, a reward for a lot of their outfield effort.

Coogan Comes On

Doughty warrior though he was, Larkin had no alternative but to limp to the sideline. He was replaced by the veteran Martin Coogan from Freshford, who would bring his years of experience to the fore in this game. But it did not look exactly promising for him when the first ball that came into the area was grabbed by Seanie O'Leary and sent over the bar from a narrow angle. Cork were now four points ahead and hurling well all over the field.

The Kilkenny followers gasped when the next ball came into the Kilkenny goal. The High King of full forwards, Ray Cummins, went up for it and caught it. All Pa Dillon could do was ensure his way to goal was blocked. Cummins clipped over a neat point to put his side five to the good. The Cork supporters, sensing that their side were now getting the upper hand and might be poised to kill off the Kilkenny challenge, set up a continuous cascade of sound from Hill 16.

Decisive Move

It was at that moment that one of the most decisive moves of the game took place. Fr Tommy Maher, the Kilkenny strategist, was following the patterns of play and the man-to-man duels from high in one of the stands. He was in contact with the mentors in the dugout below by walkie-talkie. They concluded that if Kilkenny did not do something to get their talented forwards going then the match would go away from them.

The word went out to Eddie Keher to leave the constrictions of the corner and come out to the greater freedom of his customary position on the left wing. As the master scorer was moving out to his new position, Tony Maher was seen looking towards the sideline for a signal to follow him out. None came. What did come was Keher's first point, from play stylishly struck, from out near the sideline. As it went over the bar many Kilkenny followers wondered why he had been confined to the corner in the first place.

Sun-Aided Goal

Then Keher struck again. It was a dramatic score. He saw Chunky O'Brien starting a run, holding his hurley like a magic wand which the ball could not leave. Keher ran parallel to him. When O'Brien was challenged he tipped the ball over to Keher.

Maher came racing out to take him but Keher was now going fast and he did a neat sidestep. He saw Purcell and Delaney also moving in towards the goal. He let fly a fast, curving shot from about 40 yards. It came dipping in to Paddy Barry, straight out of the sun and the glare from the roof of the Hogan stand. The ball seemed to hit his chest and go spinning into the back of the goal.

It was an unfortunate goal for Barry but it aroused a great cheer of relief from the beleagured Kilkenny fans. It also aroused the spirit of the black and amber men as they saw that, despite the great and skilful scores Cork had got, their side were now only one point in arrears.

Two Hammer Blows from Cork

Cork's response to this setback was swift and decisive. Line by line the ball was whipped along until it flew into the Kilkenny goal. Once again the high-catch expert Cummins rose to grab it some nine feet off the ground. He rounded Pa Dillon. A few lanky steps and he was at the goal line and Skehan had no chance with the palmed ball to the back of the net.

This seemed like a killer of a goal from the unstoppable full forward, whom nobody could mark on a day like today.

There was more to come. Thirty seconds later the ball came in again and Sean O'Leary used all his agility and skill with the stick to reach it, twist, turn and whip it into the net. The roar of delight that went up from the Cork crowd seemed to signal the end of this exceptionally entertaining encounter. And when the tearaway Con Roche landed his point from 80 yards the Cork victory celebrations began on the sidelines, on the terraces and in the stands.

The two goals seemed to demonstrate who was master of this game. They made scoring look easy, as if the Leesiders could put on extra power when it was really needed. To many the game as a contest was just about over.

Amazing Comeback by Kilkenny

How and why did Kilkenny come thundering back into this game in a way that was awesome in its intensity? First of all it was not in the Kilkenny tradition go down tamely, no matter how marvellously talented the opposition might be, no matter how hopelessly far behind they might seem to be.

'I believe that Cork had got so much on top at this stage, had knifed through for tremendous scores — goals and points — that they relaxed their grip', recalls Eddie Keher, who says this was the best All-Ireland in which he ever played. 'I said to myself that now is the time to hit them when they are relaxed.'

Kilkenny Transformed

Keher also noticed something else. All of the Kilkenny team were fired by Cork's thunderous goals, stung by the celebratory antics of some of the Leeside followers on the sidelines. They began to radiate power. They all began to motor together. They encouraged and inspired one another. The team blazed with a great release of energy from some source deep down within it.

Henderson, who had been playing well all along, became even more dominant now. None of his several markers could make any impression on him. He blocked and caught balls and came charging out, shouldering aside all challengers and sending defiant balls away down the field. He raced back and forward to the wings where Pat Lalor and Eamon Morrissey began to get the better of their men.

Pat Delaney was like a man transformed. Now he risked his hand amid flailing hurleys and caught ball after ball. Whenever he did he whipped round, solid on the ground with his heavy thighs and muscled legs, and shouldered Looney and the other Cork backs out of his way as he began a goalward run.

He led a charge that resulted in a 21-yard free. A goal opportunity had been created. All eyes were on Keher as he came over to take it. When he moved well back from the ball everyone in Croke Park knew that he was going for goal. He stood there ramrod straight, his dark helmet making him look like a Roman centurion. Nearby spectators could see his chest heave as he took deep breaths, composing himself.

Keher had practised so diligently over the years that he could direct the ball wherever he liked and hit it at speeds in the region of 100 mph. The huge crowd were momentarily hushed as he ran up to the ball, scooped it up, pulled hard on it and sent it like an almost unseen missile into the net.

'Come on Kilkenny, you're not done yet', roared an elderly man from the stands, standing up to shake his fist, while those behind him called on him to sit down and let everyone see the match.

Frank Cummins Opens Up

At midfield Denis Coughlan had had the edge on his opponent Frank Cummins in a great battle of skill and weight. Now the Kilkenny man began to open his shoulders and hurl with great abandon. He started to win every ball at midfield on his side of the pitch while O'Brien did the same. Cummins used his weight to make space for himself and send in low left-handed balls to the forwards. The Cork backs conceded another 21-yard free from one of these pulsating raids.

Keher came up to take it. Many of the spectators thought he would go for another goal. But the experienced Keher knew that what was needed at this time to keep the momentum going was another certain score. He put it straight over the bar without ado to leave Kilkenny only four points in arrears.

Cork responded with a series of counter attacks. Two of them were broken up at the half back line by the towering Henderson and his two colleagues. Con Roche, battling valiantly in a rearguard that was showing signs of wear and tear under the Kilkenny onslaught, sought to loft a few balls over Henderson's head, to drop them to Ray Cummins and the corner forwards. But the resourceful Martin Coogan, drawing on his keen ability to read the play, kept running round the back of Henderson to pick up the overhead balls before Cummins could reach them.

Coogan Clearing

Coogan made himself master of his corner. On one occasion after a bone-shaking clash of bodies with the weighty O'Leary he kept his feet to come racing out to lift the ball off the turf with the hurley in his left hand, then pulled hard on it for an almighty clearance that had the Kilkenny followers in ecstasy. In the other corner Treacy began to completely curb McCarthy, decisively winning two great balls and striking them far away to safety.

Ball-Hopping Delaney

From these rip-roaring clearances by the Kilkenny backs the forwards went on the rampage. One of the most memorable sights was that of Pat Delaney, his brown helmet and dark curly hair making him look like a gladiator, tearing along hopping the ball off the ground as if it were made of rubber. His strong arm and ball control enabled him to perform this gambit while thundering along — the rules allowed him to handle the ball twice while bumping past opponents but he then hopped the ball off the ground to put another two catches in his armoury for the next encounters. After one such mesmeric run, with the specators marvelling at his skill and daring, he finished the gambit with a fine point to leave only a goal between the sides.

Thundering Goal

Ninety seconds later Frank Cummins won the ball at midfield and began a run through the centre of the Cork defence. The strongest man on the field, he seemed to grow in size as he came thundering along. Cork backs who came to challenge him were brushed aside.

'When we saw him going through we knew what he was doing so we scattered and made room for him', recalls Eddie Keher.

Cummins was about 30 yards out when the spectators saw the familiar back-swing from his left hand side and then the hurley swinging forward to rocket the ball for an unstoppable shot that went at an angle across the goal and billowed the side netting. Paddy Barry, good and all as he was, had no chance with this one. Incredibly, the sides were now level, with 11 minutes to go.

Cork tried to compose themselves and get attacks going but the Kilkenny backs had cut off the supply to the formerly lethal Cork full forward line.

Kilkenny in Lead

As if to show that the lead could be taken with style, Keher flighted a beautiful ball over the bar from near the sideline. In the next Kilkenny attack, Mossie Murphy, who was now getting free of the sound Brian Murphy, collected a ball and sent it over the bar to put his side two points ahead. Now Kieran Purcell also began to come into his own after battling away with the very effective Pat McDonnell for much of the match. He ran far out and got possession of a ball, twisted about and struck it all in one balletic movement. The ball went high between the uprights like a rifle shot.

By now the Kilkenny supporters were delirious with the spectacle of powerful hurling by a side that had seemed about to sink to defeat. Not alone Kilkenny followers but all the spectators marvelled at the last quarter transformation of the men in black and amber. It was a rare and wonderful sight to watch a full team take flight and to do everything with such style and vigour.

Delaney made another pulsating run through the middle, cheered on by spectators of every hue and sent over another point. Another Kilkenny attack. Another free given away by Cork. Another point by Keher.

'They came at us with such force that we were taken aback and we had not time to pull ourselves together before the whistle went', says Gerald McCarthy. 'I believe we were capable of coming back into the game, despite being steamrolled, but we just had not the time to do it.'

In the frayed Cork defence only Roche was now playing up to his form. At this stage it made little difference. The Kilkenny attacks could now only be staved off by giving frees away and from two of these on the 21-yard line Keher sent over two more points. It brought his personal talley to 2–9.

It fell to the muscular centre forward, Delaney, to send over the last point of the game as the stewards began to prepare for the presentation of the cup to the goalkeeper, Noel Skehan, playing in his first All-Ireland. The final score was Kilkenny 3–24 to Cork's 5–11.

When Mick Spain blew the final whistle on that glorious day in September those who had been there knew they had witnessed one of the great finals between two of the greatest teams of modern times. Many came out on the turf just to walk the grass where such drama had been played out. They were there, wandering about, wiping their faces with damp handkerchiefs, long after the presentation was over and the crowd was drifting away in the warm evening sunlight.

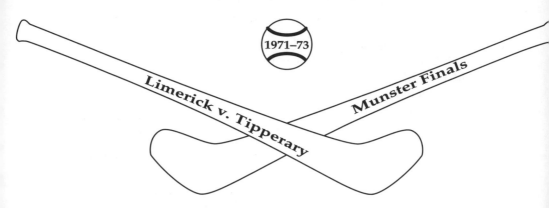

THE LIMERICK-TIPPERARY SAGA 1971–73 'WHAT ARE WE DOING IN THIS PLACE?'

This was the question posed between two bulky middle-aged men, faces grey with anguish and disappointment, clothes soaking wet, sodden shoes squelching as they made their way across the field at Fitzgerald Stadium, Killarney after the Munster final of 1971.

Mick Mackey in his playing days had been the jaunty leader and powerhouse of the Limerick side that hurled its way onto the national scene at the start of the '30s. Their flair and flamboyance, their strength and courage and their stickwork had endeared themselves to hurling lovers everwhere. Mackey loved playing, relished the rough and tumble of thumping bodies and flailing hurleys. More than anyone he was saddened by the state into which his county's hurling had declined after he and the members of that great team had finally hung up their boots.

He, like thousands of other Limerick supporters in the crowd of 31,000, was bitterly disappointed that these new, talented representatives of the county had lost a game they could have won. Crossing the field when it was all over, and when the torrential rain had eased off, his remark was directed to his old hurling team-mate and now coach of the Limerick side, Jackie Power.

Frustrated and annoyed that the prize had slipped from their grasp on the wet grass, in the endless downpour, they and others wondered if it would have been better to have tossed with Tipperary for a home venue rather than opt for this place so remote from the hurling areas of the province and one where the surrounding mountains tended to drag cloud down and turn it into rain.

The deep ache at losing was acute not just because a last-minute point had decided the issue but because a once-great hurling power had failed in a brave attempt to fight its way back to hurling renown.

No Hopers

Limerick had been the no hopers of the province. There was still a glow about their name because of the exploits of the legendary team whose swan-song had been the All-Ireland win of 1940. Now they were ritually beaten each year, not only by the two dominant counties, Cork and Tipperary, but on occasion by Clare and Waterford as well.

Their own followers yearned for some kind of resurrection of the county as a hurling power once more. Those in charge of the game did their best but they were not able to make the breakthrough and the longer it went on the more difficult a task it seemed.

Brief Dawn of 1955/56

There was a brief resurgence under the guidance of Mick Mackey and the drive and artistry of Dermot Kelly and others in 1955. For the first time in fifteen years they won the Munster final but were overwhelmed in the semi-final by the powerful and hungry Wexford side of that era. The following year that team, which carried much hope for a renewal of hurling in the county, went out to Cork in a Munster final where Christy Ring exploded into life in the last ten minutes to score three goals. After that Limerick reverted to their customary role as championship cannon fodder, knocked out each year, sometimes painfully humiliated. Their loyal band of followers grew less with each outing. Many of them had never seen their side win a major game.

The memory of the great days and the great players of yesteryear became like a weight round the necks of the current players. 'Every time Limerick put out a team there were references to our great predecessors among followers and in the media and it was hard not to feel that we were being unfavourably compared with them', says Pat Hartigan, one of the men who would shoulder the burden with great resolve and help to write a new chapter for the county.

Harty Cup Hope

Some of the first sentences were written in Sexton Street Christian Brothers School. There determined hurling enthusiasts encouraged the game among the pupils and developed a series of first-rate teams that won the senior colleges title, the Harty Cup, in four successive years from 1964 to 1967. Twice in that period the team went on to win the All-Ireland colleges championship.

Hartigan himself was one of those who came to the fore in those teams, along with players like Eamonn Grimes, Eamonn Cregan, Sean Foley and Christy Campbell. These players began to build up a winning mentality and a determination which would serve their county well in the years ahead.

There had been other hopeful signs that Limerick might begin to come back onto the national hurling scene. Good minor sides won out in Munster in 1963 and in 1965 and reached the All-Ireland. They were however beaten on both occasions, with Cregan the captain of the '63 side.

Slow Road Back

Then came 1966. A young, unfancied Limerick side took on the giants of the game, Tipperary, in the first round of the Munster championship. Tipp were the unbeatable reigning champions for the previous two years, a powerful side that habitually flattened all opposition, so much so that all their games were one-sided affairs.

That day in Cork they were taken asunder by a fast moving Limerick side, with Cregan spearheading the attack. A tall, sinewy, blond-headed player, he was exceptionally sharp to go through an opening and very determined about doing so. He had a keen eye for the weak spots in an opposing side. Whipping balls off the ground around the goal to send in bullets became a characteristic of Cregan's play.

However, that Limerick side made an unfortunate exit to Cork in the next round, played at Killarney. They were beaten by two points in a titanic finish by a Cork side that went on to win the All-Ireland.

Fast Game Style

But now Limerick were definitely on the way back. Even though their growth was slow they were developing an attractive, fast striking style, moving the ball quickly. More notice began to be taken of them. Yet they found that it was extremely difficult to translate will and skill into winning major games. They went out to Clare, Cork and Tipperary respectively in the Munster championship of the following years. In 1970 they had a galling experience, playing very well against a very good Cork side but giving away easy scores after all their great effort.

Defeats Spurred Determination

These defeats no longer deterred the breed of players that was now emerging. It only fired their determination to make the breakthrough. Pat Hartigan, a big strong man who loved to come out and gather the ball and send it flying down the field, was now at full back. His brother Bernie was another strong player who operated in the midfield area. Another player from the South Liberties club, Eamonn Grimes, had established himself among the forwards; he was a light, fast winger with great ball control who was very good on the ground ball.

Then there were players from the Patrickswell club like Sean Foley, a very forceful player who loved to tip up the moving ball with his hurley

All-Ireland final 1968: Ned Colfer stretches for the ball, challenged by Sean McLoughlin of Tipperary.

All-Ireland final 1968: Backs and forwards watch anxiously as the ball drops into the Tipperary goalmouth.

The Kilkenny team which beat Cork in one of the greatest of all All-Ireland finals, in 1972. Front row (*left to right*): Pat Lalor, Jim Treacy, Liam O'Brien, Noel Skehan, Pat Delaney, John Kinsella, Eamon Morrissey. Back row (*left to right*) Ned Byrne, Mick Crotty, Pa Dillon, Pat Henderson, Eddie Keher, Frank Cummins, Kieran Purcell. The right corner back, Fan Larkin, was having his ankle bandaged in the dressing room by Dr Kieran Cuddihy. When an official shouted to him that he would miss the team photograph, Larkin responded, 'I came up here to win a medal, not to get my photograph taken.'

All-Ireland final 1972: Seanie O'Leary and Jim Treacy.

All-Ireland final 1972: Ned Byrne and Brian Murphy chase the sliothar.

All-Ireland final 1972: Martin Coogan, who replaced the injured Fan Larkin in the second half, is about to clear Kilkenny's lines.

All-Ireland final 1972: Charlie McCarthy of Cork in full flight.

The Leinster senior final of 1974 between Kilkenny and Wexford was one of the finest contests between these two great rivals. Here Tony Doran watches as Fan Larkin and Nicky Orr clear the ball for Kilkenny.

Leinster final 1974: Fan Larkin, Jim Treacy, Christy Kehoe and Tony Doran chase a loose ball.

When Galway beat Cork in the All-Ireland semi-final of 1975, they marked their return to the big time. It would be five years before they won the All-Ireland, but this victory started them on that long journey. The team was, front row (*left to right*): P.J. Molloy, Gerry Coone, John Connolly, Marty Barrett, Padraig Fahy, Niall McInerney, Joe McDonagh. Back row (*left to right*): Iggy Clarke, Sean Silke, Sean Murphy, P.J. Qualter, Michael Conneely, Frank Burke, Paddy Lally, Joe Clarke.

The Kilkenny captain, Nicky Orr, holds the Leinster trophy aloft after the 1974 victory against Wexford.

All-Ireland semi-final 1975: Michael Conneely, Joe Clarke, Jimmy Barry Murphy and Gerald McCarthy contest the loose ball.

All-Ireland semi-final 1975: Gerald McCarthy of Cork has the ball, pursued by Joe McDonagh.

Niall McInerney of Galway about to clear the ball in the All-Ireland semi-final of 1975.

and pull hard and accurately on it without catching it. Richie Bennis held the hurley in the unorthodox grip, yet he became the established free-taker for the side, rising the ball with the point of the hurley, seeming to shorten his grip as he swung and often as not sending the ball straight over for points from way out. His brother Phil was a tenacious wing back, with a great will to win which made him into an attacking half back.

Gathering Strength

At the end of 1970 the team decided to make a real bid for the league, to grow and develop the team in the process, to build up game experience and to make a renewed effort for the championship the following year.

There were two significant personalities now involved with the team. Jackie Power, one of the greatest of all the players during Limerick's era of glory, had taken over as coach. In his playing days he had been so exceptionally good that he had been played in almost every position. He had known the good and the bad days, especially when the side went into decline as players got old or retired. He knew the kind of fire and grit that was needed to win Munster finals. Power was greatly respected by the players.

At the same time a forthright northerner, Joe McGrath, took over as team trainer. He had come from the disciplined Down tradition where the belief was that training must be well organised and done on a planned basis over the playing year, that players from whom much was expected must be well cared for. His own enthusiasm rubbed off on the players and as the league progressed they trained to attain the keen edge needed to prevail in close-run games.

Three Limerick-Tipp Games

The real saga of that 1970/71 league campaign was the three battles between Limerick and Tipperary. Tipperary were still regarded as kingpins, even though many of the great players of the previous decade had now retired. They had the winning ways about them, the big game experience, that indefinable edge that comes with tradition and that is so hard to acquire or indeed to re-acquire if it is ever lost.

Tipperary had some of the top-class players that had been part of the 1964/65 hurling machine. Mick Roche, a marvellously skilled hurler, in air and ground, left or right, renowned for his ability to read the game, to win duels purely on his pin-point stickwork, was playing. So was the barrel-chested Michael Keating, a player of immense courage who had honed his hurling skills almost obsessively until he became a supreme ball juggler.

'Babs could chop down on a ball and make it hop straight into his hand, right in the middle of a ruck, with everybody pulling hard. He could roll the ball up and down the edge of his stick like something you'd see done in a circus. And he was as strong as a horse and could run all day', one contemporary said of him.

Also on the Tipp team, although now slowed by injuries suffered over the years, was Jimmy Doyle of Thurles Sarsfields. This left hander had the most astonishing ball control.

'It was as if he had the ball on a string the way it came to him from all angles. The reality was that he could reach out his hurley and trap it and pull it in to him', said Donie Nealon, one of the stars of the team of the '60s now in the role of coach to the Tipp side.

Doyle's ball skill was uncanny. He lifted the ball effortlessly, scored points without stopping to measure the distance or see where the posts were, and was totally reliable from the placed ball.

First League Encounter

In mid-April Tipperary and Limerick met at the Ennis Road grounds in a game to decide a place in the semi-final of the National League. Tipp were expected to win. However for much of the second quarter the Limerick side got on top. The problem was that, like many outsiders, they were unable to translate their superiority into scores. Then Tipperary brought on one of their best players, Noel O'Dwyer from Borrisoleigh. A big forceful red-headed player, he was not long on the field before he burst through for a goal.

The new Limerick side refused to be upset by this score. Mick Graham more than held his own against Roche at midfield. Graham was a very vigorous player, who challenged tenaciously for every ball and roused the team by his spirit. In the backs the tall, lanky Jim O'Brien from Bruree came into his own. He and Christy Campbell drew roar after roar of applause from the home crowd as they repulsed repeated Tipperary attacks. The man who was to captain Limerick in the championship, Tony O'Brien, played an inspirational game. In the end Limerick won by two points.

Second League Game

This result meant that the teams now had to meet the following Sunday, in Croke Park, in a play off. This was a thunderous game. Both sides piled into the fray with abandon. The pulling and physical encounters were uncompromising. No harder hurling had been seen in a long time, though it did not spill over the narrow border of violence. Scores were level ten times. Only one score out of thirty-three decided the issue. Each side had to recover from repeated setbacks. There were some great scores, including a spectacular point by John Flanagan for Tipperary. The Moycarkey man was bottled up in a corner but controlled the ball under heavy shouldering to get free and send the ball over from the narrowest of angles. Willie Moore's opportunist goal for Limerick helped to seal the issue for his side on a score of 2–15 to 1–15.

With each game the Limerick following was getting bigger and bigger. They were now seen as a side to match the best in the country. The defeated Tipperary side still had a chance because of the complexities of the league system. Incensed at this second defeat they put everything into winning their last-chance games against Kildare and Cork. They won out and once again Tipperary lined out against Limerick. This was the final, played in Cork.

By now the opposing players were getting to know one another very well and the marking was tight. This was yet another thrilling game, neck and neck all the way. It was decided by a free taken in the dying seconds by the unflappable Richie Bennis. When he sent it over and the whistle went, hundreds of Limerick followers, starved of any kind of trophy over the years, raced out onto the field to cheer their men.

'Will they meet again in the championship?' the newspapers asked and followers of both sides hoped that they would. Their rivalry was now intense and some players had skinned knuckles and barked shins to show for it.

First Win Over Cork in 33 Years

The first real test of Limerick mettle was when they found themselves up against Cork in the Munster semi-final. All right to win the league on dull, drizzly days in winter and early spring but the championship was very different. This was when the Big Three of hurling, Cork, Kilkenny and Tipperary, gave it their all, used all their experience and canniness, had well-developed strategies to overcome opposition. 'Any of the outsiders has to be twice as good as them to be able to beat them in a championship game', was a dictum of some truth.

In a classic game at Thurles Limerick beat Cork for the first time in 33 years in a championship game. After that game Limerick were accepted by all as now being in real contention for All-Ireland honours. When Tipperary beat Clare the stage was set for yet another encounter between the sides.

The Venue

The Tipperary officials suggested tossing for home venue. The Limerick mentors, anxious not to risk a disadvantage at such a crucial time for the team, insisted on a neutral venue. This is how rain-prone Killarney came to be the chosen.

A huge Limerick following travelled by car, bus and train to Killarney to see their men once again, after so long an absence, centre stage again. Few of them had any doubt that their side was well capable of winning out. Most neutral followers were hoping for a Limerick win in order to break the monotony of the Big Three — and occasionally Wexford — vying for the championship title year after year.

The Tipp Side

Tipperary were well trained by Donie Nealon. They were a self-confident side. They had All-Ireland medal holders in their midst. They had players who knew what it was like to face out into a great crowd, thousands of eyes glued on every move, and to play their best.

'We felt we had an advantage. Limerick were tipped to beat us but a team that has beaten you three times may feel it does not have to hurl so well to beat you the fourth time', said Donie Nealon. 'As well as that it is difficult for any team to keep up that kind of pattern. So we knew we were in there with a good chance no matter what anyone might say. It's a big advantage to be underdogs; there is euphoria if you win and if you lose nobody gives out to you.'

However, Michael Keating did feel a certain burden of responsibility. 'There were some players, Mick Roche and I in particular, who had come in as the newcomers on the great team of '64/'65 that had won all round them. We were still playing and there was an expectation that we would lead the way in bringing an All-Ireland back to Tipperary. We had been beaten in the finals of '67 and '68. At that time people in Tipperary expected us to win often — and five years had gone by since the last win', he reflected.

Pouring Rain

From early morning, as the special trains came in to the station one after another and the roads were clogged with long lines of cars stretching back into the countryside, it was raining. The clouds had come down low and were unloading sheets of water down on the town and on the grass at Fitzgerald stadium. There was a very light breeze which would make little difference to the play but hurling lovers hated the idea of a game being spoiled by slipping and falling players, by the ball skittering dangerously about in the goal area, ready to hop or slither over the line for freak, unearned goals.

There was nothing for it but for the teams to take the field. That was sport — one had to take the good days with the bad. Many Limerick supporters felt these conditions were far from suitable for the kind of game their side played — whipping the ball from wing to wing, sending in low, fast balls to the forwards, playing a fluid sort of game that demanded stamina and was seen to its best on a dry sod.

Limerick Dominate

When the ball was thrown in the players from both sides went at it hammer and tongs as if it was a bright dry day. So great was their intensity in the bodily clashes that they ignored the deluge which soon had their hair and their jerseys soaking wet.

Cheered on by their great following in the crowd Limerick began to play hard methodical hurling, sending the ball along the ground despite

The tams as they lined out were:

Tipperary

Peter O'Sullivan
(Cashel)

Noel Lane	John Kelly	John Gleeson
(Lorrha)	(Cappawhite)	(Moneygall)

Tadhg O'Connor, capt	Mick Roche	Len Gaynor
(Roscrea)	(Carrick Davins)	(Kilruane)

Seamus Hogan   P.J. Ryan
(Kiladangan)   (Carrick Davins)

Francis Loughnane	Noel O'Dwyer	John Flanagan
(Roscrea)	(Borrisoleigh)	(Moycarkey)

Jimmy Doyle	Michael Keating	Dinny Ryan
(Sarsfields)	(Ballybacon-Grange)	(Sean Treacy's)

Substitutes: Liam King (Lorrha); Roger Ryan (Roscrea); Paul Byrne (Sarsfields); John O'Donoghue (Arravale Rovers); Jack Ryan (Moneygall); Michael Jones (Newport); Jim Fogarty (Moyne). *Trainer*: Donie Nealon. *Assistant trainer*: Gerry Doyle. *Mentors/selectors*: Sean Ryan (Toomevara); Jim Lanigan (Sarsfields); Kieran Carey (Roscrea); Jimmy Hennessy (Dundrum); Theo English (Marlfield). *Masseur*: Ossie Bennett. *Team doctor*: Dr Paddy Moloney.

Limerick

Jim Hogan
(Claughaun)

Tony O'Brien, capt	Pat Hartigan	Jim O'Brien
(Patrickswell)	(South Liberties)	(Bruree)

Christy Campbell	Jim O'Donnell	Phil Bennis
(Old Christians)	(Doon)	(Patrickswell)

Bernie Hartigan   Sean Foley
(Old Christians)   (Patrickswell)

Richie Bennis	Mick Graham	Eamonn Grimes
(Patrickswell)	(Claughaun)	(South Liberties)

Donal Flynn	Mick Cregan	Eamonn Cregan
(Cappamore)	(Claughaun)	(Claughaun)

Substitutes: Willie Moore (Doon); Eddie Prenderville (Old Christians); Con Shanahan (Croom); Jim Allis (Doon); Davy Bourke (Garryspillane); Leonard Enright (Patrickswell); Frankie Nolan (Patrickswell). *Coach/selector*: Jackie Power. *Trainer*: Joe McGrath. *Mentors/selectors*: J.P. Ryan (Garryspillane); Dan Hickey (Young Irelands).

The referee was Frank Murphy of Cork.

the sodden turf, getting first to the ball for a quick pull or to take the ball in the hand.

Tipperary were finding it hard to come to terms with their opponents or the elements. They were being out-hurled and out-run by the men in green. Several players were trying to lift the greasy ball and fumbling it. Passes went astray, were sometimes blocked by their opponents and whipped away. Contrary to some expectations, the Limerick style of open, first-time pulling was not suffering under the conditions.

Mick Graham was proving a handful for Mick Roche. The Carrick Davins man was unable to impose his customary command and Graham sent in several of the low, fast balls that the Cregan brothers liked. Eamonn Cregan's roving tactics, moving about wolfishly, restlessly, ready to strike, made it very difficult for a conventional corner back like Noel Lane.

Two Goals

Before nine minutes had gone by the ball had come flying low along the ground into the Tipperary goalmouth again and again. Donal Flynn and Eamonn Cregan scored a goal each. Limerick's tactics of racing up the sideline to whip in low forward balls was paying off and Tipperary were giving away frees as they attempted to stop this gambit.

'I remember the goal I got. It came in fast from the wing and I managed get in behind Lane to send it to the net', recalls Cregan.

At midfield for Tipperary Seamus Hogan was finding it hard to get into his stride and P.J. Ryan was hurling in spasms. Hartigan and Foley were having the better of these great clashes where players collided like battlewagons on the slippery grass, where hurleys flew out of the grip, where men were sent flying by shoulder-charges.

The Limerick crowd, ecstatic at seeing their men gaining the upper hand, watching the scoreboard operator building up their sides total, were delightfully soaked along the open terraces. Their team were playing with the same style and vigour as they had done against Cork in the semi-final.

Keating and Hartigan

In front of the Limerick goal two of the great hurlers of the era were locked in combat. They had laid down the gauntlet to one another several times before. Hartigan was taller and he caught a number of incoming balls but he did not dare come running out to make his great clearances in case Keating, with his ball skills, might whip the ball off his hurley. These two were cancelling one another out. But Hartigan's colleagues, Tony and Jim O'Brien, had the advantage in height and weight over Jimmy Doyle and Dinny Ryan, especially in the heavy going over the drenched ground.

Noel O'Dwyer fought tigerishly for every ball and grabbed several but it was another matter to make full use of possession when the forwards were at sixes and sevens. The once-great Jimmy Doyle was perceptibly slowed by all his old injuries. His only score was a free, which he pointed with ease. John Flanagan did shoot a beautiful long-range point but he was well policed for most of the first half by the hard-tackling Christy Campbell.

Tipp Goal

The game might have gone beyond the reach of Tipperary altogether but they kept playing by instinct. Peter O'Sullivan was in top form and he saved two certain goals when the ball came flying goalwards though the rain, with backs and forwards grappling in front of him. And P.J. Ryan scored a goal when he sent a ball in and it ran over the line with Hartigan and Keating struggling for it, unsighting the goalkeeper Jim Hogan.

When the referee blew the whistle for half-time Limerick were a well-deserved six points ahead on a scoreline of 2–10 to 1–7. The rain was still coming down though it was not quite the monsoon that had prevailed in the first half.

The Dressing-Rooms

There was talk afterwards that the Limerick dressing-room was full of euphoric supporters, telling the team that they had it won. Eamonn Cregan discounts this. 'Not really. I do remember Mick Mackey coming into the dressing-room to lend us his support. He told us we were only 40 minutes away from victory and to go out and give it all we had. There were some other well-intentioned people saying the same thing and perhaps we were not quite used to all this.'

There was a different atmosphere in the Tipperary dressing-room. There was an air of deflation. The players knew they had played badly.

'I think there was a feeling in the first half that the team would have to contain the Limerick side — watch this fellow and watch that fellow instead of going out to play our own game', said Donie Nealon. 'We said to the team — look, you can't play any worse. Throw caution to the winds and go out there and hurl, have a go at them. And you have a full 40 minutes to do it — a long time.'

He made the point that in the 80-minute game, now wisely discarded, no player could keep up the kind of pace being set by Limerick. He took the subs aside and told them to be ready, that any of them might have an important role to play.

Key Tipp Changes

The Tipperary selectors made two key decisions at half-time. They took off the injury-slowed Jimmy Doyle and in his place brought on Roger Ryan, a strapping big player whose strength would be needed in the wet conditions. Ryan went to full forward, leaving Keating free to go to the left corner. Liam King, a more mobile type of player, came on for Noel Lane. King's task was to follow Cregan everywhere he went, not an easy task by any means against a man famous for losing his marker.

Michael Keating recalls, 'Before we went out to restart the match Roche said to me 'The first ball I get I'll send it into you. Be ready for it.'

For whatever reason, Limerick seemed to have lost some of the urgency that had characterised their first half play. Within a minute Francis Loughnane, the low-slung, left-handed forward had put the ball over the bar. Still, Limerick were five points ahead and this score was not seen as significant.

Roche to Keating

Then came the score that really turned the game and gave the initiative to Tipperary. Roche did indeed get the ball. As he did, Keating raced forward, heading towards the front of the goal. Roche flighted a beautiful ball over the Limerick half back line that dropped right in front of the running Keating, who had eluded Tony O'Brien. 'Roche dropped it right into my pocket', said Keating who kept running, made an angle for himself and sent in a good shot. Hogan seemed to have it covered but to his own consternation the ball slipped through and into the net.

The soaked Tipperary supporters, gloomy for much of the first half, now broke out in a roar of applause. Roche began to take full control at centre back, with Tadgh O'Connor and Len Gaynor getting the better of their opponents on the wings. Another carefully weighted Roche delivery set the hard-running Loughnane into action. With hurley on ball he made for goal. Stocky, he was hard to dispossess legally. He was pulled down and Tipperary were awarded a 21-yard free.

New Ball Incident

This was to lead to one of the incidents which is part of hurling folklore in Limerick and Tipperary. As Keating got ready to take the 21, the ball had disappeared into the crowd. But Keating was cut over the eye and Nealon ran out with a towel to wipe the blood that was impeding his vision.

'Have you a ball?' he asked Nealon. The coach had several in the pocket of his raincoat and he gave one to Keating, who put it down on the ground. Just then the original ball was fired back in from the crowd. It hopped in front of Nealon, into his hand and he put it in his pocket and ran off to the sideline as Keating prepared to take the 21-yard free.

'There was no intended deviousness about this. This was a time when balls were often pocketed as souvenirs when hit into the crowd behind the goals or over the sideline. All goalkeepers had several balls in readiness to hit out quickly and get their side into an attack rather than having to wait for a ball to be returned from the crowd. And mentors and coaches had them too', explains Nealon.

There was a difference, however. The ball that had been in play was sodden and heavy. In those years the new, light, water-proof ball had not yet come into being. A wet ball went out of shape when hit, often sliced away to one side. A new dry ball could be hit at much greater speed.

'I don't believe it would have made much difference', says Eamonn Cregan. 'Babs Keating was all fired up that day and, wet or dry, he had a powerful stroke on the ball.'

Keating's 21

Not alone had Keating a powerful stroke but he could place the ball wherever he wanted. He had spent hundreds of hours in a ball alley directing a ball at specified spots on the wall.

The Limerick players stood in readiness on the line in the pouring rain. Keating lifted the dry ball well, swung hard on it with his powerful wrists and shoulders and sent it whizzing into the back of the net. Suddenly Limerick's lead had been wiped out and Tipperary were in control.

Dinny Ryan, now in the half forward line, won several frees by his determined running along the sideline. Francis Loughnane was equally dangerous while John Flanagan performed the feat for which he is best remembered — sending over points from far out, often on the turn under pressure and sometimes right on the sideline.

Limerick had lost the initiative. They had lost control at midfield too where P.J. Ryan began to win ball after ball, a key factor in turning the tide against Limerick.

'That was a fine Limerick side but when a team loses its rhythm it can be very hard to play its way back in again', says Michael Keating.

Another Tipp Goal

It was Keating who put Tipperary four points ahead. He and Dinny Ryan combined in another attacking foray. Keating rounded Tony O'Brien, who had played so well in the league games, and sent a rasper into the net for his third goal. Then John Flanagan sent over a point and Tipp were five points ahead, with their supporters uncaring of the rain that was still falling.

Players like Noel O'Dwyer were coming into their own now and keeping control for Tipperary. Big and eager, he fought for every ball, won some, prevented others from being cleared by Jim O'Donnell and was a thorn in the side of the Limerick defence until he got injured. His replacement was Paul Byrne of Thurles Sarsfields, son of a famous father, Mickey 'Rattler' Byrne.

'There is no doubt about it but we lost concentration', says Eamonn Cregan. 'But we had no intention of just caving in.'

Limerick's Fighting Spirit

Despite the obvious disorganisation of the Limerick side they showed their fighting spirit. They tried might and main to play their way back into a game they seemed to have sowed up for much of the time. As had happened all during the game, most of the frees won by the forwards were sent over the bar by Richie Bennis.

Pat Hartigan caught a high ball in the square and thundered his way out, knocking Tipperary forwards out of his way. Thirty yards from his own goal he belted a huge clearance. The ball soared up into the grey sky and travelled the length of the pitch before falling to earth at the feet Eamonn Grimes. He timed his pull exactly right and sent the ball into the net to reduce Tipperary's lead to a single point. The score now stood at 4–14 to 3–16.

Disallowed Goal

Then came an incident that was a turning point of the match. Grimes's goal injected great heart into the Limerick team and all over the field they ran and challenged with a renewed sense of urgency. They swept back into the attack and Willie Moore, who had come on as a substitute for Donal Flynn, came bursting past several backs and struck the ball into the net. A huge cheer went up from the Limerick supporters and the players raised their hands and their hurleys in delight that they had struck back to take the lead. There was utter dismay on the Limerick side when they realised that the referee had whistled for a free, for a foul on Moore, a second before the ball crossed the line.

'There is no doubt about it — the fact that the referee did not play the advantage rule was a huge setback for us, just when we were oncoming with great zest', says Eamonn Cregan.

Richie Bennis put the free over the bar to level the scores. It seemed small consolation to the Limerick side. This was one occasion when a goal made all the difference not just on the scoreboard but in the minds of players.

Tipperary were then awarded a free and Len Gaynor came up to take it. Despite the rain and the now-wet ball he sent it over the bar to regain the lead for Tipperary.

Pell Mell Finish

This was the time that umbrellas were cast aside, the rain forgotten about, as the two sides, with the clock nearing the 80 minute mark, threw every ounce of energy and will into the match. Every ball was a small game in itself, with ferocious body-clashes, teeth-grinding races for the ball. It was a lung-searing few minutes for men who had used up all their power.

The battle of the rain-soaked gladiators went on without a score for two minutes but to followers it seemed a lot longer. Then Limerick were awarded a free from far out. Richie Bennis, whose calm temperament served him well on such occasions, struck it over the bar with deadly accuracy to bring the sides level with time almost up.

Flanagan's Point

From the puck out there was a tremendous scramble in the midfield area for the ball. It eventually landed up in the hands of John Flanagan, about 40 yards out.

'He took a few shoulders and was actually shouldered into the clear where he had room to hit the ball', says Cregan.

Flanagan's shot sailed over the bar to put Tipperary ahead. Jim O'Brien rushed to take the puck out and there were desperate attempts by Limerick to get the ball upfield for an equalising score but Frank Murphy, who had had a good game overall, blew the long whistle.

Scenes of Joy and Heartbreak

Ecstatic hordes of Tipperary followers, waving flags, coats and hats, raced onto the sodden field. They roared and shouted, almost unable to express their delight and admiration for their men. The Tipp players, beaming with joy, were surrounded by jostling groups of people who shook their hands, slapped them on the back.

This was one of Tipperary's greatest victories by a team that had been outplayed by a fine Limerick side for the first half yet had the resilience and the game experience to come back in and take the Munster title.

The Limerick players were utterly stunned. Some knelt on the wet grass, head in hands, and wept unashamedly, their frustration and disappointment too much to bear. Others shuffled off the field, dragging their hurleys behind them, heads drooping with dismay.

Their followers were drained by the drama, the excitement and the great disappointment after hopes being raised so high.

The buzz of animated conversation in the Tipperary dressing-room went on for a long time after the players and officials had come in from the presentation of the Munster cup. This was to become one of the county's most cherished and well-remembered victories because it had been largely brought about by spirit and great grit under difficult circumstances.

The Limerick side were utterly depressed. There was a great deal of searching about for what had happened to a side so totally superior in the first half. They seemed to have become over-confident, lost a crucial fraction of their edge and will to win and allowed a team that had a fighting tradition to come back in and take the game from them.

Eamonn Cregan, when he got dressed, wandered alone to a park. The rain had now eased off and was only falling lightly. He found a seat and sat there for a long time, dazed and dumb. For such an ambitious competitor being second best did not come easy.

It was no consolation to Limerick to be told that this great game had restored the fading reputation of the Munster final as a sporting occasion of great hurling and excitement.

Victors Win All-Ireland

For all the talk that the best team had lost in Killarney, Tipperary went on to prove themselves the best team in the country. In the All-Ireland final they met one of the greatest sides ever put out by Kilkenny and beat them in a pulsating game. The very exacting Tipperary followers considered this no more than the county was due. To go six years without an All-Ireland title was considered a serious deprivation at that time.

Limerick recovered from the trauma of defeat and once again began their preparations to take the top prize. They contested the league with great determination and reached the final, played in the spring of 1972. They lost their title to a Cork side that played great hurling in the first half and were able to hold off the second-half challenge of the Shannonsiders.

Many hurling lovers were hoping for a rematch between Limerick and Tipperary in 1972. It seemed very likely at the start of the championship that year. Yet there are no certainties in sport as in life. Limerick, hot favourites to trounce Clare at Ennis, were instead beaten there. Tipperary, the All-Ireland champions, were held to a draw by Cork and beaten in the replay.

Then in 1973 the two sides renewed their rivalry in the National League. They met in the semi final in Kilkenny. For forty minutes Limerick were on top but did not translate their superiority into scores. Tipperary came back and went in front and seemed to have the game won — some Tipperary supporters were already on their way to their cars to avoid the traffic jam when Limerick came back to score two goals to draw the game. One of them was struck in by a man of small stature but tigerish attitude, Liam O'Donoghue of Mungret. A star of that game was Seamus Horgan, who now held the goalkeeping position. The Tournafulla player was to prove his agility in the months ahead.

Tipperary, by this time, had also a new goalkeeper, a young player of great promise, the fair haired Tadhg Murphy. Another young newcomer to the team was Jimmy Crampton of Roscrea, a very gifted ball player who was outstanding for his club.

The league semi-final replay was at Birr. Once again the sides battled it out, minute by minute. This time it seemed that Tipperary would win, as they were in front coming up to the final whistle. Yet Eamonn Cregan put the sides level just as full time was called. Extra time was played. At one stage Tipperary went five points ahead but Limerick hauled them back and then passed them out in a great surge of power hurling in the last ten minutes.

New Trainer

This match certainly whetted the appetite for a championship encounter between the two sides. But before that a number of important factors were to have an impact on the Limerick side. The outspoken Joe

McGrath fell foul of officialdom in Limerick for some of his comments and was dropped as trainer. Some of the players were disgruntled at the dismissal of a man who had added organisation and zest to the team training. But the good of the team prevailed and a new trainer, Mick Cregan, who had retired from the county team, was appointed.

New Full Forward

The other factor was the league final against Wexford. Limerick were favourites but defensive lapses let the Slaneysiders in for a number of goals and the game went away from Limerick. This served to prompt Jackie Power and the chairman of the selectors, Dr Dick Stokes, to reassess their resources to meet the needs of the championship.

They needed a strong, bustling player at full forward, someone who could disrupt play and break the ball for players like Cregan and a small, razor-sharp ball striker, Frankie Nolan, who was now in the full forward line.

Ned Rea, who played hurling with Faughs in Dublin, hated the full back berth in which he had played in the league final. He had been blamed for some of the defensive errors that lost the game for Limerick. So he accepted his new role with enthusiasm. It was to prove a key decision on the part of the Limerick mentors.

Limerick overcame Clare, rather luckily, in their first championship outing and qualified for the provincial final. Tipperary, on the other hand, had the hard side of the draw. They found themselves up against the Cork side that had played the previous year in one of the great All-Ireland finals. It looked for most of the game that Tipperary would be demolished and time was beginning to run out when, against all expectations and against the run of play, Tipperary scored goal after goal — four in all — to stun and defeat the Munster champions. Roger Ryan, the burly full forward, was the architect of this victory.

Thurles the Venue

All was now set for the final. This time Limerick agreed to toss for home venue. Tipperary won. The game was to be in Thurles, where Limerick had not beaten Tipperary in a Munster final since way back in 1936, when all the great Shannonside stars were at their best: Timmie Ryan, Paddy Clohessy, Paddy Scanlon, Mick Kennedy and Jackie Power himself.

There was a feeling that the wide open spaces of Semple Stadium might not at all suit Limerick's tearaway style, that they might burn themselves out before the 80-minute game was over. In Killarney two years before Tipperary had paced themselves better and used their big-time experience to advantage.

The prospect of another great game between the sides drew a huge crowd to Thurles on this hot, sun-filled day. The crowd of 41,000 was the biggest for ten years. It was testimony to the attractiveness of the pairing and a renewed faith in the Munster final to provide a thrilling encounter.

Crowds Pour In

On the roads into the town were long rows of cars, their roofs glinting in the hot sunshine, windows down to let fresh air in. Trains drew into the railway station to disgorge floods of people who crowded the streets of the town. This is always a time of happy greeting, of suppressed excitement, of great expectation of a blood-stirring encounter.

Once the clock on the cathedral tower strikes half past twelve the movement towards the stadium, up the long road over the railway bridge, becomes hurried. Half an hour later the people walking along the roadway are impatient, have to overcome a desire to run. After that an air of urgency takes hold of the crowd, haunted by the prospect of being locked out, of missing the game of the year.

Shirts and light summer frocks were bright in the sunshine as the teams emerged onto the field to tumultuous cheering from the rival supporters.

There was no need for the players to introduce themselves to one another. They had spent the spring playing against one another. But Tipperary had Mick Roche and Michael Keating, who had been absent for the league semi-finals, back on their side. Roche was now at centre forward and there was some speculation that a man of his hurling style, who had been so accomplished as a centre back, might be out of place at centre forward. It remained to be seen.

Compared to the sides which met two years before in Killarney, there were new faces as well as positional changes on both sides. Tipperary had newcomers to this occasion in Murphy in goal, Jim Fogarty at right corner back, and Crampton at right half back. On the Limerick side, going into provincial final battle for the first time were Horgan in goal, Nolan, O'Donoghue and a bustling centre forward in Mossie Dowling.

In Memory of Jimmy Maher

Before the ball was thrown in there was a minute's silence in memory of a small man with a red, weather-beaten face. He had played in goal for Tipperary the last time the same two teams met in Thurles in a Munster final. Jimmy Maher of Boherlahan, who had died a few days before, had played well that day in 1945 and most especially in the final against Kilkenny in September. The hurling community has a strong tradition of revering and remembering its heroes.

Early Goals for Limerick

Tipperary were playing into the town goal, against a warm breeze, in the first half. When the ball was thrown in, it was Limerick who got off to a whirlwind start. They whipped the ball along the dry, lively sod at great speed and shortly after the start got a sideline cut from the left corner of

The teams as they lined out were:

TIPPERARY

Tadhg Murphy
(Roscrea)

Jim Fogarty	John Kelly	John Gleeson
(Moyne)	(Kilruane)	(Moneygall)

Jimmy Crampton	Tadhg O'Connor	Len Gaynor
(Roscrea)	(Roscrea)	(Kilruane)

P.J. Ryan   Seamus Hogan
(Carrick Davins)   (Kiladangan)

Francis Loughnane, capt	Mick Roche	Noel O'Dwyer
(Roscrea)	(Carrick Davins)	(Borrisoleigh)

John Flanagan	Roger Ryan	Michael Keating
(Moycarkey)	(Roscrea)	(Ballybacon)

Substitutes/panel: Jack Ryan (Moneygall); Dinny Ryan (Sean Treacy's); Paul Byrne (Sarsfields); Seamus Shinnors (Newport); Jimmy Doyle (Sarsfields); Martin Esmonde (Moyne); Jim Keogh (Silvermines); Paddy Williams (Kilruane). *Coach*: Donie Nealon. *Mentors/selectors*: Sean Ryan (Toomevara); Jimmy Hennessy (Dundrum). *Masseur*: Ossie Bennett. *Team assistant*: Gerry Doyle. *Medical officer*: Dr Paddy Moloney.

LIMERICK

Seamus Horgan
(Tournafulla)

Willie Moore	Pat Hartigan	Jim O'Brien
(Doon)	(South Liberties)	(Bruree)

Phil Bennis	Jim O'Donnell	Sean Foley
(Patrickswell)	(Doon)	(Patrickswell)

Richie Bennis   Eamonn Grimes
(Patrickswell)   (South Liberties)

Liam O'Donoghue	Mossie Dowling	Bernie Hartigan
(Mungret)	(Kilmallock)	(Old Christians)

Frankie Nolan	Ned Rea	Eamonn Cregan
(Patrickswell)	(Faughs)	(Claughaun)

Substitutes: Tom Ryan (Ballybrown); Jim Hogan (Claughaun); Andy Dunworth (Claughan); Paudie Fitzmaurice (Kileedy); both Mick Graham (Claughaun) and Jack O'Dwyer (Pallas Green) figured in earlier games that year but were off the panel through injury. *Coach*: Jackie Power. *Trainer*: Mick Cregan. *Mentors/selectors*: Dick Stokes (Pallas Green); Sean Cunningham (Doon); Denis Barrett (Bruff); Jim Quaid (Feohanagh). *Masseur*: Vincent O'Connor.

The referee was Mick Slattery of Clare.

their attack, at the Killinan end of the field. Their sideline-cut expert, Eamonn Grimes, came up to take it. He clipped a fast ball well over head height into the Tipperary square. With Ned Rea showing how difficult his bustling presence was going to be, backs and forwards went for it. Frankie Nolan pulled on it overhead on his left side, met the incoming ball perfectly and sent it into the net. It was a tonic start for Limerick. A huge cheer went up from the green and white supporters.

From the puck out there were great scrambles as players came to terms with one another as the ball came their way. Moore and Pat Hartigan cleared away the ball in a few thrilling clashes with Keating and Ryan. Roche hit a few good balls goalward but the Limerick backs were on top at this early stage and Bernie Hartigan sent a good drive into the Tipperary goalmouth. Limerick were awarded a 21-yard free. Richie Bennis came up to take it. He bent and then took a wide swing on the ball, leaning into it. The ball sped like a bullet but went a few inches wide, to the cheers of the Tipperary followers and the groans of those from Limerick.

Bennis made amends shortly afterwards when another 21-yard free was awarded. He drove it with all his might, an unstoppable shot that billowed the netting. He followed this with a point immediately afterwards. Limerick were racing all over the field in control and were now 2–1 to no score for Tippearary. In those first 15 minutes Tipperary seemed to be gasping for breath.

Tipp Come Into Game

Then Tipperary began to play themselves into the game. Mick Roche, master of ball play, left or right, in air or on ground, got the measure of his own game and began to send in low balls to the forwards or deft passes out to the wings. Jim O'Donnell had his hands full trying to limit the damage the Carrick Davins man might do.

The fair haired Grimes and Bennis had been on top at midfield during the first quarter but now Ryan and Hogan found their feet, and challenged for every ball. The play began to break even in the centre, with hurleys swinging on every high ball, and the stinging clash of ash on ash as the four players fought for supremacy. The Tipperary men began to get a slight edge.

The Tipperary forward line attacked again and again. The Limerick backs gave away frees and scores. Loughnane, the captain, with his crouching style, hard to dispossess when he had the ball, sent over a point. He took the frees with unerring accuracy — a great boost to the Tipperary side which saw the disastrous start being hauled back on the scoreboard. Michael Keating, though closely marked by Willie Moore, ran onto a ball and hit it as he met it to sent it over for an angled point.

In front of goals was the battle of the old adversaries Hartigan and Ryan. Both over six foot and fourteen stone in weight, they jostled and collided with bone-thudding impacts. Hartigan kept his opponent out of the goal but Ryan was more than a heavyweight bustler and sent out passes to incoming colleagues and scored a point himself.

Horgan Holding Fort

It was in this period that Seamus Horgan showed his mettle. Noel O'Dwyer, the big red haired Borrisoleigh player, sent in a cannonball of a shot which seemed like a goal until Horgan, hair falling over eyes stopped it, controlled it and cleared it. He got a great round of applause from the spectators for this feat. It was one of a number of goal saves he was to make during the course of the game. At this stage Flanagan and Loughnane had swopped positions and both were playing better.

Limerick were now fighting to stop themselves being pushed out of the game. They put all they had into their efforts. Foley was playing well on the wing of the half back line and Willie Moore made several interceptions to keep the ball away from Keating.

The Power of Rea

The bustling, hard running Mossie Dowling was now proving difficult to curb. Eamonn Grimes got the ball at midfield and sent a long delivery into the Tipp goal area. Once again Rea was the centre of attention as he went for the ball. He was big and tall and very strong and John Kelly found himself at a great physical disadvantage, peering over the Faughs' man's shoulder as the ball came in. On this occasion the confusion caused by Rea left Dowling free to propel the ball on into the net for Limerick's third goal in the 24th minute.

Tipp Respond

Dowling's goal roused Limerick and they began to play better, doing all they could to stay ahead. Then Roche, so capable of sending in pinpoint balls to land two feet in front of running forwards, flighted in a centre. Roger Ryan got it. Hartigan was on his back but the big Roscrea man flicked the ball out to the captain, Loughnane, who was running forward. He shot hard and Horgan could do nothing about it.

Keating, who had great confidence in hitting difficult balls from out near the sideline, got his second point of the half. The scores were now level at 1–8 to 3–2.

The ball went from end to end. The cheering of the crowd, delighted with this great display of competitive skill and courage, went on and on. The jerseys of the players became darkened with sweat. The temperature on the field was in the mid-seventies. The first half had not ended yet and even the spectators were feeling exhausted by the thrills and the heat.

Loughnane Goal

From midfield, in the 37th minute, the thick-haired P.J. Ryan fought for the ball, got it and sent it in towards the Limerick goal. Loughnane, the great opportunist who was full of drive and determination, risked his body to get onto it and tap it into the net. Things were looking good for Tipperary with this kind of play. They attacked again. Once again Limerick gave away a free and once again Loughnane took it and sent it over the bar. Tipperary were now four points ahead as the half-time whistle went.

The gale of appreciative handclapping from the enthralled attendance lasted until the last player had left the field, with the familiar figures of Jackie Power and Donie Nealon accompanying them in.

At this stage many were predicting a win for Tipperary. They had absorbed the expected Limerick onslaught and had then taken over to go ahead. They seemed to have a better sense of pace, the kind of sense that comes from big-time experience, a virtue that might be badly needed in the lung-searing heat in the second half. And one of their stars, Mick Roche, had adapted extremely well to his unaccustomed role in the forward line. Cregan, the Limerick danger man, had been well marked by Fogarty and had come out the field for part of the second quarter but had not yet made any impact.

When the teams came out again and lined out it was seen that Limerick had made changes. They had moved Bernie Hartigan to midfield, a position he was well used to and in which he had played consistently well during the league. Eamonn Grimes went to left half forward. Sean Foley had taken over from Jim O'Donnell at centre back while Tom Ryan from the Ballybrown club went in at right half back.

Tipp Go Six Up

When the ball was thrown in to a resounding roar it seemed as if these changes would have little effect on the pattern of play. In the very first minute Tipperary were awarded a free and Loughnane sent over another point at the Killinan end to send out signals that Tipperary meant to take this game. This was reinforced when Seamus Hogan, playing very well, sent a point soaring over the bar from a long-distance free to put his side six points ahead.

Limerick Surge Back

This was the time when Tipperary supporters began to relax, to enjoy the game that was clearly going their way. Yet this was precisely the time that Limerick came back in. Foley had begun to curb the clever play of Roche, fighting to be first to meet the ball and on several occasions belting it way down the field. Limerick went on the attack and forced a 70. Foley took it and flighted into the square. There was a flurry of hurleys to meet it but one of the fine first-timers on the Limerick side, Nolan, whipped it to the net.

Thousands of Limerick voices shouted and roared encouragement, wishing their team to take back the command they had lost for so long.

Tipperary replied by a fine point by Keating, whose way of striking the ball rapidly, close to his body, made him difficult to hook. But Limerick were now in full flight and they went on the attack again and again. The dust rose in the Tipperary square where Rea challenged and harried, using his weight to wear down the full back line, sending out passes to the forwards.

Cregan was now operating in the left half forward position but was often out at midfield. This wily player, reading the play with great intensity, loping about, waiting to pounce, was difficult for a newcomer like Jimmy Crampton to watch. In another attack Rea got a pass out to Cregan. The Claughaun man had tremendous confidence in his own ability and struck the ball without a second's hesitation into the Tipperary net.

Powerless Coach

On the sideline Donic Nealon found what a frustration it could be to be a coach, knowing better than most the form and the ability of each player, but not having the power of a selector. He begged the mentors to bring Noel O'Dwyer back to mark Cregan but they took no decision.

Four minutes later came one of the best scores of the game. Rea ran out of the square, gathered the ball, turned and send a waist high hard shot across the goalmouth. Cregan, going at full speed, lunged forward in front of his marker and pulled hard on the incoming ball. It went so fast into the net many people did not see it. Cregan, to hold his balance, kept running, ending out near the sideline. Many spectators thought that he had the ball. A guttural Limerick voice roared at him, 'Get rid of the ball, Blondie, for God's sake.'

By that time the umpire was starting to wave the green flag for Limerick's sixth goal. This had Limerick ahead on a scoreline of 6–3 to 2–13.

The tempo of this torrid but sporting duel in the sun rose yet another degree and so did the sound from the crowd, now almost continuous as the battle swayed from end to end. This was a testing time for the players.

Munster Final Temperament

'You want great temperament for a Munster final. Some players can lift their game, playing in front of a huge crowd. They enjoy the occasion. They can turn it on. They have the spirit and the character. They won't allow themselves to be upset by their markers. They are determined to impose their will and not to yield', explained Donie Nealon. 'These qualities are essential for any inter-county player and even then it can take time to develop them. So a green, unseasoned player, no matter how good he is, can be at a disadvantage in the cauldron of a Munster final.'

At midfield the powerful playing of Bernie Hartigan was telling as he pulled well on moving balls, caught others, challenged his opponents relentlessly. He sent in good balls that kept the Limerick forwards on the move. The full back line now played with flair and confidence. Willie Moore effectively curbed Michael Keating, the architect of Limerick's defeat in 1971. Pat Hartigan and Jim O'Brien hurled back the Tipperary attacks while Foley played a great inspirational game at centre back, striking some great long balls out of defence that roused the crowd and his own side.

Bennis went for a goal from a 21 yard free. It was a mistake at this crucial time. The shot was saved, the clearance sent down the field and Loughnane scored a point and followed it with another.

The Tipperary selectors eventually acted on Nealon's advice and brought Noel O'Dwyer back to mark Cregan. Crampton, playing in his first Munster final, was taken off. Jack Ryan came on and went into the forward line.

Tipperary came roaring back. Seamus Hogan sent a hard ball into the goalmouth but Horgan got to it and saved. John Flanagan, one of the dangermen of the Tipperary attack, pulled hard on a ball from 20 yards that went like a rocket. Once again Horgan saved. This was inspired goalkeeping; later he pounced on a hazardous rebound that was on its way over the line.

Level Again

Despite these frustrations Tipperary kept coming back and their efforts resulted in two frees being given away. Loughnane, always workmanlike in his approach to placed balls, sent both of them over the bar. The last one raised an enormous cheer from the Tipperary supporters — the teams were now level in the 34th minute and Tipperary were used to pulling it off in the last minutes of a tight game. At this time the quick-running Dinny Ryan came in for Jack Ryan.

The tension on the field and on the terraces and stands became almost unbearable as both sides fought to gain even the smallest advantage. Hurleys clashed, some splintered, lungs gasped, knuckles were barked, as every ball evoked a fierce contest in a few square yards of ground before the ball went away and another group clashed fiercely, trying to get the pull in first, or block or baulk the opponent.

See-Saw Scoring

Tipperary went ahead when Loughnane was again the marksman but Limerick kept attacking and a free was given away. The imperturbable Bennis took it and sent it over to level the score again. Then he took another while the crowd held its breath and many looked at their watches. Limerick were now in the lead with little more than two minutes to go.

Almost from the puck out the fair-haired John Flanagan, who had moved to the half forward line, got the ball 70 yards out. The man whose point had decided the issue in Killarney two years before now struck a great ball that went sailing between the uprights to the ecstasy of the Tipperary supporters.

Controversial 70

It seemed that this great contest was going to end in a draw. But Limerick went into a last attack, with Rea again upsetting the backs by his challenging and harrassing. Now came a controversial incident. Amid the melee of hurleys, legs and boots, the ball seemed to go over the end line, out of play. In his anxiety to get it for a quick puck out Tadhg Murphy stopped it with his hurley. The umpire judged that he had touched the ball just before it had crossed the line and he gave a 70 to Limerick, much to the chagrin of the Tipperary players in the vicinity.

Ice Cool Under Blazing Sun

Now, in a game full of incident and drama, came the climax. When the ball was pucked out to the 70 yard line everyone in the crowd saw Mick Slattery look at his watch, look at Richie Bennis and beckon to him that this was the last puck of the game. He would have to score direct.

The crowd held their collective breath as Bennis came forward. In the stand was his mother and other members of his family. In the crowd was half the populace of Patrickswell, his home place. He looked at the uprights. For Limerick supporters they seemed so far away. Bennis shifted his feet a little, getting the balance right. Very few players would relish this kind of pressure, with the outcome of the game hanging on a single puck.

This is when his ice cool nerves stood him so well. He lifted the ball with the point of the hurley, seemed as usual to readjust his grip as he swung and hit the ball soaring goalwards. At first it seemed destined to go over the centre of the crossbar but near the end of its flight it began to tail off to one side and went over near the top of the right hand upright.

To a tumultuous cheer from the Limerick crowd and most of the neutrals in the crowd the umpire put up the white flag as the referee blew the full-time whistle. Limerick had won their first Munster final since 1955.

A Near Thing

There was controversy whether this ball, high in the air, over the tip of the upright had actually been a point. Some of the Tipperary players had waved it wide. And in the animated discussions that took place for weeks on end in pubs and gathering-places there were those who claimed to have been behind the goals and watched the ball carefully. But there was no unanimity in their conclusions.

'It was a point for certain', says Donie Nealon. 'I ran down behind our goal and had Bennis in line of sight with the uprights. The ball veered away near the end but it went over.'

Moment of Rare Triumph

One minute after the final whistle there were thousands of people on the pitch at Semple Stadium. Most of them were Limerick supporters, shouting and laughing with delight and relief. Some of the players who had wept with anguish two years before now wept for joy. This moment of rare triumph was a time of great emotion for Limerick people.

Two hours later as the grounds were being closed there were three or four groups of Limerick people still standing on the grass, gesticulating, going over all that had happened. It was as if they were reluctant to leave the scene of this great victory, to savour every moment of the afterglow of that great occasion and lovely summer evening.

That game lifted a burden of tension and inhibition from the Limerick side. This allowed them the freedom to concentrate on getting themselves back into physical and mental shape for the All-Ireland. In the final against Kilkenny they opened their shoulders and played with great abandon to win the county's first title for thirty-three years.

'Never mind — we'll come again', said the Tipperary supporters as they shuffled along the crowded roads from Semple Stadium. It was a phrase based on past realities. Tipperary were never long out of the honours list. Few could have realised that this county and its hurling-lovers was in for a long period of disappointment. They would be beaten year after year, often by Limerick, in the Munster championship, and would not even reach a final until 1984. They would not win a provincial final again until 1987 nor an All-Ireland until 1989 — a long eighteen years since their victory in 1971.

By that time, like Limerick in 1973, they too would have to fight against the inhibitions and anxieties bred by years of defeat and disappointment so that they could be free to open their shoulders and hurl at their best.

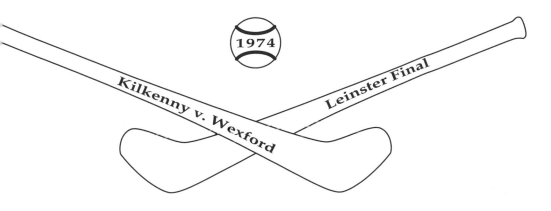

1974

Kilkenny v. Wexford

Leinster Final

DAY OF TRIUMPH AND TRAGEDY

It was an unbelievably nail-biting finish. There had been 44 scores — goals and points — and sides were level almost at the end of 80 minutes. Then, to the anguish of the Wexford team and supporters, Kilkenny were awarded a free.

Eddie Keher, ace marksman, walked over to take it. It was near the sideline under the Hogan Stand. He would have to hit the ball into a wind blowing from the Canal end across the pitch. People looked at their watches as Keher, a compact player who wore a black helmet, reached the ball.

The spectators, exhausted by the endless thrills of a pulsating game, waited for him to line up the posts with his stance and hit the ball. But Keher knelt down and calmly began to tighten and tie one of his bootlaces. This brought howls of derision and impatience from the frustrated Wexford followers who had just seen their depleted team's lead of a point cancelled out a minute before. With less than a minute to go Keher was taking his time.

'No — I was not wasting time. Anyone who knows how I took frees can tell you that when I stood over a ball everything had to be right', says Keher. 'An open bootlace would have been a distraction in my mind — a small distraction but enough to put me off.'

Then, his preparations complete, this ice-cool player ignored the angry yells from some of the Wexford followers who felt they were being cheated of victory. With his left hand well down the shaft of the hurley he lifted the ball carefully and struck it firmly. It shot away, rising and breasting the breeze. Keher, who had taken ten thousand frees in practice in all wind conditions at that stage of his career, had allowed for the deflection of the breeze and the ball went between the uprights.

It raised an exultant cheer from the black-and-amber flag wavers, who only a few minutes before were shaking their heads in acceptance of defeat. The Wexford goalkeeper, Pat Nolan, hurried to take the puck out, full of urgency as he belted the ball well past the centre of the field.

It seemed that there might still be enough time for Wexford to score a wind-assisted point and bring the scores level again. The way scores had come from both sides, one after another all through the game, this was a distinct possibility. There were still some 20 seconds to go to full time. Then, to the surprise of those with stopwatches in the press box, and the utter dismay and anger of the Wexford followers, the referee blew the long whistle for full time.

Sorry for Wexford

That such a marvellous game, acknowledged to be one of the best provincial finals between the sides, should end in such an unsatisfactory way added to the controversy which had already enlivened this game.

Most of the neutral spectators felt very sorry for Wexford, who had laboured under a major disability for the 40 minute second half — playing with fourteen men — and yet had almost snatched victory. At the very least it should have been a draw, people felt as they walked out of Croke Park into the dusty sunlight of the street outside.

However, when these two sides met in the '70s, drama, last minute scores, neck and neck races to the line were not uncommon. They reflected a race for provincial supremacy that had been going on for at least two decades.

Rivalry of Neighbours

The rivalry between Wexford and Kilkenny was so intense, the sides so intent on besting one another in meeting after meeting that the games between them were often the best matches by far in the championship.

Some of their clashes in the '50s, '60s and '70s were far more thrilling and exhilarating than the All-Irelands or the Munster finals.

Only the rivalry of Cork and Tipperary, reaching peaks in the period 1949–54 and renewed from the mid-eighties onwards, can compare with that of the neighbours of southeast Leinster, the hurlers from town, farm and pasture-land separated by the rivers Nore and Barrow.

This tradition of a do-or-die competitiveness began at the end of the 1940s as a team of big men from hurling areas of Wexford like Rathnure, Cloughbawn, Horeswood, New Ross and Enniscorthy emerged on the scene. The game had lain dormant in some of these districts, over-shadowed by Gaelic football or indifferently played while the traditonal heartland of hurling was on the eastern side of the Slaney and its wide estuary — Castlebridge and Shelmalier and other areas 'across the water'.

Nick Rackard

An increasingly absorbing and vibrant county championship threw up players of exceptional merit and ability and they formed a team that began to harbour ambitions. They were jauntily led by one of the great personalities of Wexford hurling, Nick Rackard. He had attended one of the nurseries of Kilkenny hurling, St Kieran's College, and had seen and absorbed something about management of teams, of motivation, of training, of developing skills.

Nobody knew better than Rackard how adept Kilkenny teams were making the best of their resources. He played against some of their best men and when he was picked for Leinster in the Railway Cup competition in 1943 and 1948 he played with them.

When Wexford began to challenge seriously in the Leinster championship they saw Kilkenny as the chief obstacle to their winning the provincial crown. Billy Rackard recalls many of the team gathered in his home in Killane, at the foot of the Blackstairs Mountains, discussing their hopes and expectations and laying plans.

'Nick had just returned from watching Kilkenny playing and he was asked how they had played. There was complete silence as he considered the question. Then in a quiet, determined voice he said "We can beat that side." We were all fired with a fierce resolve to put Wexford hurling at the top', he says.

In 1949 Kilkenny beat Wexford easily. By the following year it was becoming clear that Wexford, with a side of tall, strong, resolute men, were no longer championship fodder. The sides met in a Leinster final that drew a record attendance of 36,484 people to Nowlan Park in Kilkenny. Kilkenny won by a goal but the excitement, the thrills and the quality of play had reached a new level in the province.

Rivalry of the '50s

In 1951 the elimination of Kilkenny by a good Laois side helped Wexford win their first Leinster title for an age and go on to unsuccessfully contest the final against Tipperary. But Wexford now bestrode the Leinster scene like a colossus and the following year brought their first championship win in modern times against Kilkenny. It was a close run thing in an exciting game but Wexford came out on top by three points.

When they met again in 1953 a crowd of 37,533 turned up in Croke Park to see the traditional kingpins of the province, Kilkenny, take on the cheery newcomers. It was a thrilling match. The battle between Nicky Rackard and Pat 'Diamond' Haydon on the edge of the Kilkenny square went into legend. In the end Kilkenny won by two points in a game which was by far the best of the All-Ireland championship,

The year 1954 saw something which could not have been predicted even five years before — the defeat of Kilkenny by Wexford on a scoreline of 5–11 to 0–7. Rarely had any team in Leinster or elsewhere inflicted this kind of defeat on the Noresiders. The following year Kilkenny's determination to avenge such an unaccustomed humiliation drew a crowd of 41,226 to Croke Park. Wexford survived by a goal in another neck-and-neck race and went on to win the county's first All-Ireland in 45 years.

52,077 at Game

The days of holding Kilkenny-Wexford games anywhere but the spacious Croke Park were long over. No less than 52,077 watched them battle it out in the Leinster final of 1956. This was an epic game — the speed of play, the flashes of brilliant hurling, the closeness of the scores made it one of the memorable games of the decade. Wexford again just got by and were now Leinster champions for the third year in a row. They went on to retain their All-Ireland crown as well.

The games of that era set the tone for subsequent matches between the sides. There was a clash of traditions, the long-established kings of Leinster being challenged by the fresh-faced princes. There was a clash of styles — the clever, economical, wristy play of Kilkenny against the power and zest of their adversaries. The Kilkenny men were expert at flicking the ball quickly, to a colleague or to the net; the Wexford side had developed an expertise at catching the high ball and they had the strength to break out to hit the ball hard.

As the members of the great Wexford side of the mid-'50s gradually retired Kilkenny began to reassert their supremacy. Yet the sides met in four successive finals from 1965 to 1968 with each side victorious on two occasions. Wexford won by a single point in 1965 and 1968 but the final of 1967 produced some of the best hurling ever seen in Croke Park.

By that time their battle for supremacy in Leinster had become one of the most talked-about aspects of the championship and for that reason the GAA authorities had a seeded draw to keep them apart in the preliminary games. As a result the two sides contested each final from 1970 until 1979.

Ten Successive Finals

These ten Leinster finals produced some of the most unforgettable games between the two sides. One or two were considered among the best games of the decade. They were usually far better than the highly vaunted Munster finals, with a few exceptions. They became one of the sporting events of the year. Kilkenny were victors on seven of the ten occasions.

These finals were invariably good not just because of the fierce rivalry that had now developed between them. Kilkenny had put together one of the great teams of all time that contested five All-Irelands in a row from 1971 to 1975, winning three of them. Wexford, hungry for new success since their All-Ireland triumph of 1968, strove with might and main to dislodge the talented Kilkenny side and did so in '70, '76 and '77. Unfortunately for them, on those occasions when they beat their Noreside rivals and reached the All-Ireland they came up against powerful Cork teams.

Wexford's first real challenge each year was to get out of Leinster and to do that they had to meet and to beat Kilkenny in the final.

In 1972 the sides drew on a score of 6–13 each — an indication of the scoring power of the forwards, the great scrambles in defence and the skill it took to survive. Kilkenny won the replay and went on to beat Cork in one of the best All-Ireland finals of all time.

The Meeting of 1974

It was in 1974 that one of the truly great Leinster finals took place. It was a game that had everything — high drama, anguish, tension, courage and a nerve shattering finish. It was a game of controversy, of criticism of the referee, and of sadness for one of the heroes of the Wexford side. A great Kilkenny team came out on top but one of the memorable features of the game was Wexford's courage and extraordinary zest in the face of adversity and disadvantage.

The Leinster final of that year epitomised just how difficult it was for even the most determined side to beat Kilkenny. The Noresiders used all their hurling artistry, all their playing guile, all their game experience to wrest the match from opponents many thought deserved to win. But the game has gone into hurling lore as one of the most remarkable played between these adversaries.

Kilkenny Stung by Defeat

At the start of the year Kilkenny were determined to be back in Croke Park on All-Ireland day. The previous year they had lost their title to a rampant Limerick side on a grey day of continuous rain. There were many arguments about whether they might have won the game were it not for the fact that some of their best players were out of contention due to injury or illness — Eddie Keher, Jim Treacy, Kieran Purcell.

Both Kilkenny and Wexford had dismal showings in the 1973/74 National League but they were primarily concerned with the championship and were only using the league to try out some of the new players now shouldering for places on the panel if not on the team itself.

Kilkenny started off the championship with a great flourish, beating Offaly by 4–14 to 2–6. By and large, they had a settled team of players who were used to one another's play and had perfected a flexible and effective pattern of teamwork.

Kilkenny Team

Kilkenny were bidding for their 46th provincial title and for something they had hitherto never achieved — four titles in a row. They had in goal a man who was integral to their side, Noel Skehan. His performances had inspired great confidence in all the backs who had played in front of them. On this occasion he had to his right a player who had made the corner his own, Fan Larkin. Larkin was a small, tenacious marker who was an experienced reader of the game, sensed what opponents were going to do and where the ball was likely to go.

In the centre was a rugged full back, Nicky Orr of Johnstown Fenians, who kept guard in the square and ensured no forward got free shots at goal. He was also captain of the side. The left corner was filled by one of the veterans of the side, Jim Treacy. Though stocky and strong he was known as a hurling corner back, who moved to the ball and cleared it away.

The Half Back Line

Right half back on the Kilkenny team for the Leinster final was a small, dark haired man from Bennettsbridge, Pat Lalor. He had a great understanding with Larkin and with Pat Henderson and was always around to move into space to collect a pass. Because of this he seemed to get more unimpeded strokes of the ball than most other players.

In the centre was the commanding Pat Henderson. By this time he had established himself as one of the best that Kilkenny ever had in that position. He was the leader of the defence, tall and strong. As Phil Wilson of Wexford said of him, 'When that man burst out of the square he could take all six forwards on his back and then shake them off to clear the ball away down to the other goal.'

His brother Ger was on the left wing that day. This was his first Leinster final and he was to play in many more during his illustrious career.

Midfield and Forwards

Frank Cummins, by this stage of his career recognised as one of the great midfielders of the era, had a newcomer as his midfield partner, Billy Harte, one of the power-houses of the emergent Galmoy club. His normal partner, Liam 'Chunky' O'Brien, had been posted in the half forward line, on the right. Centre of that line was the redoubtable Paddy Delaney, the strong, durable ball carrier from Johnstown. His marker Mick Jacob would have to try to stop him grabbing the ball and turning his muscular shoulder to begin charges towards goal. On the left was the lanky Mick Crotty, a player who criss-crossed the field during a game, snapping up the ball and sending over points or the occasional opportune goal.

The Kilkenny full forward line had between them a store of great goals and innumerable points. Mick 'Cloney' Brennan from Castlecomer ran at defences with the ball. He took a lot of buffeting and bruising as he came in along the right side of the end line. He had a very accurate stroke off his left side so the position suited him.

Full forward was a man who combined strength and skill, Kieran Purcell from Windgap. One of his great attributes was his capacity to hold his position under the dropping ball, protect his catching hand with the hurley and grab the ball among swinging hurleys and thumping elbows. He frequently exchanged places with Delaney and from the 40 fired over points like rifle shots.

In the left corner was the most outstanding hurler of that era, Eddie Keher. He was now in his fifteenth year playing senior. His accuracy, his capacity to see an opening and race into it, his sense of team work and his ball control were all exceptional. Despite his demeanour he was tough; he had to be because his ability to win games off his own stick was a matter of record.

The Wexford Side

In the Leinster final Keher would be marked by a small, fast, agile man, one of the new breed of hurling corner backs, Teddie O'Connor of Rathnure. He knew Keher's form and how much he needed minding.

The Wexford full back was a product of St Peter's College, Wexford, Enda Murphy. He was on the side that won the All-Ireland colleges title and on the minor team that took the trophy to Wexford for the second time in 1966. In the other corner was the fair-haired Willie Murphy, one of the heroes of the 1968 final. This hard tackling, swift striking player had played at wing back that year but had since adapted well to the corner.

In front of O'Connor was Vincie Staples, another of the stalwarts of the 1968 win. He was small in stature but fast to the ball, a sharp tackler and blocker who had made the position his own. At centre back was the gingery-haired Mick Jacob from Oulart. Jacob had started out as a goal-keeper and had the sharp reflexes of the net-minder. He was a fine catcher of the ball and his nimbleness enabled him to make room to clear it well down the field.

Wexford's left wing was manned by the tough-tackling Colm Doran who was a fast, tidy hurler who belted balls away with a flourish which endeared him to the fans. He had immense courage, tearing in to block down balls. He was one of the many brave hurlers whose front teeth had been knocked out long since.

Midfield and Scorers

At centrefield was the tall Martin Quigley, one of the famous hurling family from Rathnure. He was a tall strong player who held the hurley in the right-hand-under grip. He was not a stylist but he was deter-mined and wholehearted and an inspirational figure on the team. His partner was another right-hand-under player, Martin Casey from Buffer's Alley. He was strong and forceful and had plenty of stamina. Among the Wexford followers there was some criticism of the selectors for not balancing the midfield with a neat sticksman to partner one or other of these two earnest players.

The right half forward position was allotted to one of the most experi-enced players on the side, Phil Wilson. He was in the veteran stage but he was supremely fit, a dedicated hurler whose displays in the All-Irelands of 1962 and 1968 were already part of hurling lore. At centre forward was the tall Christy Keogh from the Raparees club. He was a good sticksman, often described as a pure hurler, well able to take the ball on his stick and race down the middle. On the left wing was Sean Kinsella, a fast neat player who had had many good games with the team but had also been plagued by injuries.

Quigley, Doran and Byrne

All the commentators agreed that the Wexford full forward line was one of the best on the side. In the right corner was the stocky figure of John Quigley. He had great skill and ball control, and he raced through gaps to hit the ball left or right. But it was his drive and enthusiasm that fired his team-mates. The spectators liked this cheeky, daring player from Rathnure.

At full forward was one of the strong men of the side, Tony Doran. Every full back and every full back line in the country had tried to stop him catching the ball and bursting his way towards goal to palm or strike the ball into the net. He launched his fourteen stones into the air to reach up a brawny arm and catch the ball at the very last second. Then the only thing to do was to hold him. No game went by without him being given frequent frees.

In the other corner was a tall, black haired player, Tom Byrne, who had been captain of the All-Ireland winning minor side in 1966. He was strong and, like Doran, was good under the high dropping ball.

Last Link with '56

In the Wexford goal was a man whose career spanned the great days of Wexford hurling and was a link with the past. Pat Nolan had been a sub in 1956 and when Art Foley emigrated he took over the goalkeeping duties, playing in four finals and being on the winning side in two. He was the epitome of reliability.

Kilkenny Tipped

There was no question about who the favourites were. Kilkenny, because of their power, experience and the several star-quality hurlers on their side, had to be given the verdict. Much the same sides had met the previous three years and Kilkenny had won on each occasion. The previous year saw the Noresiders at their most awesome. They were like a well-oiled machine, doing everything right, beautiful stickwork, strength down the middle, players finding one another in a fine display of precision teamwork.

Hurling lovers were now coming to watch Kilkenny play rather than to see a good even game. At the weekend of the Leinster final there was no huge influx of people into the capital. Many in Kilkenny saw it as a foregone conclusion. Many in Wexford had the same opinion and while the core of faithful followers still travelled, mostly coming up by car, bus or special train on the Sunday, there was not the same numbers as in other years. As a result only 20,742 were there to see what was, by a mile, the best game of the whole championship.

Wilson's View

'We knew what we were up against', said Phil Wilson, who was assistant trainer for the Wexford side. 'Kilkenny were the best team in the country — so consistently good, match after match, month after month, year after year. And every one of their six forwards was a match-winner on his own.'

Nobody more than Wilson knew about the deft, clever way Kilkenny had of making use of their resources. He recalled one of his first games against them when he was playing in the half back line. He rose the ball twice and on each occasion a Kilkenny player tipped it off his stick. The full back Nick O'Donnell came running out and told him to clear the ball away on the ground, quickly. 'If you take your time about hitting it your marker will hit it for you', O'Donnell said.

'Kilkenny always believed that they were the best and that conviction gave them great confidence in themselves', declared Wilson. 'As well as that they had this mental cuteness in their heads all the time, knew what moves to make, knew how to win games at the last minute. We were not afraid of them but we knew they would be hard to beat that day.'

Kilkenny Mentors

Part of the tradition that teams like Wexford were up against was the astuteness of the mentors. The Kilkenny sideline men were always keen-eyed readers of the game, knew where weak points were emerging, on their own or in their opponents' ranks, and were quick to make effective switches.

One of the most respected former hurlers and mentors, Bob Aylward, had died that week; the flags were at half mast and the Kilkenny players wore black armbands in his memory.

The afternoon of Sunday 21 July was sunny and warm, but with a breeze blowing from the Canal end, not directly down the field but into the Hill 16 corner.

Hurling Lovers

There was one thing to be said about the relatively small crowd. These were the true hurling lovers, those who would not miss such a match on any account, the men of scarred knuckles, camogie players who knew the game , the young who hoped to emulate the skills and deeds of the seniors. There was a buzz and an excitement that was powerful because it came from the knowing rather than the diluted attendance one gets on All-Ireland day.

The teams as they lined out were:

KILKENNY

Noel Skehan
(Bennettsbridge)

Fan Larkin   Nicky Orr, capt   Jim Treacy
(James Stephens)   (Fenians)   (Bennettsbridge)

Pat Lalor   Pat Henderson   Ger Henderson
(Bennettsbridge)   (Fenians)   (Fenians)

Frank Cummins   Billy Harte
(Blackrock)   (Galmoy)

Liam O'Brien   Pat Delaney   Mick Crotty
(James Stephens)   (Fenians)   (James Stephens)

Mick Brennan   Kieran Purcell   Eddie Keher
(Castlecomer)   (Windgap)   (Rower Inistioge)

Substitutes: Nicky Brennan (Conahy Shamrocks); Billy Fitzpatrick (Fenians); P.J. Ryan
(Fenians); Martin Fitzpatrick (Fenians); Jim Murphy (Rower-Inistioge); Tony Teehan
(Coon); Dick McNamara (St Senan's); Tom Barry (Windgap). *Coach*: Fr Tommy Maher.
Trainer: Mick Lanigan. *Selectors/mentors*: Paul Skehan (Fenians); Sean 'Georgie' Leahy
(James Stephens); Mick O'Neill (St Senan's). *Team doctor*: Dr Kieran Cuddihy.

WEXFORD

Pat Nolan
(Oylegate)

Teddie O'Connor   Enda Murphy   Willie Murphy
(Rathnure)   (Ferns)   (Faythe Harriers)

Vincie Staples   Mick Jacob   Colm Doran
(St Martin's)   (Oulart)   (Buffer's Alley)

Martin Quigley   Martin Casey
(Rathnure)   (Buffer's Alley)

Phil Wilson   Christy Keogh   Sean Kinsella
(Raparees)   (Raparees)   (Gorey)

John Quigley   Tony Doran   Tom Byrne
(Rathnure)   (Buffer's Alley)   (Oulart)

Substitutes: Jimmy Prendergast (Oulart); Rory Kinsella (Naomh Eanna, Gorey); Jim
Furlong (Adamstown); John Nolan (Geraldine O'Hanrahans); John Tobin (Askamore);
Jim Kehoe (Cloughbawn); Paddy Kehoe (Oulart); Jim Quigley (Rathnure); David Lawlor
(Adamstown); Johnny Murphy (Crossabeg-Ballymurn). *Team manager*: Fr John Doyle.
Assistant coach: Phil Wilson. *Team doctor*: Dr Bob Bowe.

The referee was Mick Spain of Offaly.

Kilkenny had eight subs and Wexford eleven subs. Substitutions had become increasingly important because the 80-minute game was a sore trial of the stamina of amateur players.

The First Half

A harsh competitive roar erupted from the crowd as the referee looked at his watch and prepared to throw the ball in, with Wexford to play into the Canal end. There had been handshakes as the players had taken their places but from now on the body contact was intensely competitive, even intimidating, as men tried to establish control over their section of green grass before the ball came their way. There was preliminary shouldering and some glowering glances.

The ball went in to the sound of smacking ash on ash as the mid-fielders pulled for all they were worth. Whenever the ball came between two players they scrambled for it together, shouldering and sometimes elbowing, jaws tight with determination. They pulled hard on the ball, wherever it was.

There were unwritten rules for these encounters and others like them. A player would not deliberately hit another with the hurley but once the ball was there then it did not matter if shins, legs or hands were in the way. Within a minute of this game getting under way there were skinned knuckles and weals on legs.

Ball in Net

In all the striving to establish mastery in the midfield areas Kilkenny gave a free away. Mick Jacob took it from the half way line. He had the warm breeze in his face as he raised the ball. He had a neat and controlled swing on the ball and it sailed off and landed right in the Kilkenny goal area. The tall Tom Byrne, shouldering his marker aside, grabbed the ball and palmed it to the net.

The burst of Wexford cheering was choked off when the referee called back play for a Kilkenny foul. He had already blown the whistle when the goal was scored. 'What about the advantage rule, ref?' shouted some Wexford followers from behind the goal. Byrne took the free. He was the cool headed Wexford marksman and he sent it over the bar.

No Easy Strokes

There was a great clash of bodies and hurleys when the first ball came sailing into the Wexford goal area. This was shoulder to shoulder stuff with the two Murphys and O'Connor not giving Keher, Purcell and Brennan any room to swing the hurley or to run. The ball went back out with the full backs exchanging encouraging grimaces.

Jacob had to use all his anticipatory powers and speed to keep the ball away from Delaney and managed to do so the few times the ball came near them. But, on a dry sod, the ball was going so fast up and down the field that few players got a hold of it for a clean stroke. One of the exceptions was Wilson who used his speed and experience to get the better of the newcomer Ger Henderson. He set off some attacks, sending in low balls to John Quigley, who was beginning a battle of speed and brawn with Jim Treacy, who had been playing in the left corner of the defence since 1966.

In the seventh minute Wilson was fouled. He took the free, from near the sideline under the Cusack stand. It was 60 yards out, against the breeze, but he had a good stroke of the ball and he sent it over.

Ten minutes had elapsed and the vaunted Kilkenny forward line had not yet scored. Part of the reason was that Martin Quigley and Martin Casey were playing powerfully at midfield and there was a shortage of good forward ball going into the Kilkenny goal area. Colm Doran and Vincie Staples were also making it difficult for Chunky O'Brien and Mick Crotty to get any kind of clean possession.

Kilkenny did get an attack going and forced a 70. It was taken by Pat Henderson. His reliability with the long-distance frees was one of his strengths. He stood tall over the ball, bent his knees, scooped up the ball and hit it with a careful swing. It went over the bar for Kilkenny's first score.

Skehan Saves

Right from the puck out Wexford went on the assault. Tony Doran bustled his way towards the ball, grabbed it in his large right hand, turned and slapped the ball hard with his palm from short range. Skehan somehow got in front of it to make a miraculous save that heartened his side.

To try to loosen the grip of the Wexford backs the Kilkenny mentors changed Crotty and Brennan. The latter managed to get the ball in his new position and sent it over the bar. It was to be his last score because although he made a good contribution to forward play the wily Vincie Staples stopped him getting clean pucks of the ball.

When the ball came near the Kilkenny 40-yard line John Quigley ran out to it fast, side-stepped Jim Treacy, and ran through. Orr and Larkin were tight against Doran and Byrne and Quigley decided to send it over the bar. It was clear at this stage that the most fruitful Wexford attacks were down the right wing where Wilson and Quigley were on top.

A minute later Wilson found himself alone with the ball on the 40 and he hit it hard and made allowance for the breeze and it went over for another Wexford point.

In the Wexford full forward line Byrne and Doran found that possession was difficult to capitalise on — the marking was too tight. The next time the ball came in, Doran, red hair waving in the wind, raced to meet it 30 yards out, turned and with a wide well-directed swing, sent it over the bar. This made the score 0–5 to 0–2 in Wexford's favour.

The feeling among spectators was that Wexford should have been further ahead at this stage with the kind of possession they were getting.

The disallowed goal and Skehan's great save kept them from building up a score that reflected their temporary superiority.

First Goal

It was Kilkenny that got the first goal of the game. The lanky, ever-foraging Crotty, always looking for openings and opportunities, got behind the defence and collected a ball that came via Delaney. He raced long-legged into the goal and handpassed a goal that Nolan was unable to stop.

Wexford came charging back and a move between Quigley, Tom Byrne and Martin Casey ended up with a pile-driver towards the Kilkenny goal. Unfortunately for Wexford it cracked off the woodwork and rebounded to safety.

However the next Wexford assault resulted in a point from a free by Tom Byrne when Jim Treacy fouled the ebullient John Quigley. Jacob and Delaney were cancelling one another out but the Fenians' man managed to tip on a ball that Crotty once again grabbed.

O'Brien to Midfield

It was at this stage that Kilkenny decided to put Billy Harte into the forwards and take O'Brien out to midfield. O'Brien had an immediate impact and the Kilkenny forwards began to see a lot more of the ball.

Crotty got hold of the ball again. There was no way that Willie Murphy was going to allow him a free run in for another handpassed goal so he pulled him down.

This was Keher's first free. Despite the fact that he practised endlessly, putting the first free over was important to him for confidence and composure. He did it without difficulty. It levelled the score. A minute later he was called upon to take a semi-penalty.

There was a buzz about the stands and terraces as it became clear that he intended to go for a goal. This was one of the thrilling set-pieces of the Keher era. He loped forward, lifted the ball and swung hard on it. This 100 mph missile billowed the back of the net.

Keher was being well policed by the fiery and gritty O'Connor but it was impossible to mark him out of any game. The battle of wits between Christy Keogh and Pat Henderson went on as well, with the score about even. Just the same Henderson managed to get in one of his long clearances. As it fell to the ground Keher raced across from the left, gathered the ball, and back-pedalling athletically to keep clear of his marker, shot a typical Keher point.

Delaney and Purcell Switching

To try to unsettle the Wexford backs Delaney and Purcell were roving about so that their markers were not sure if they had changed positions, as they so frequently did. After these two strong hurlers had combined in an attack the ball ended up in the large hand of Delaney. He was not far out and he smashed the ball past Nolan for another goal.

The breeze was strong enough to affect the bouncing ball and when the Kilkenny backs misjudged one such bounce, Doran was on hand, well out of goal to gather and send over a point. Shortly afterwards he got the ball in the square. Rather than allow him pass Nicky Orr fouled him. It was a 21-yard free. Someone from the crowd roared out, 'Come on Byrne — send it into the net.' Byrne was taking no chances at this stage of the game and sent it over the bar; but some felt that if such a chance had fallen to Keher he would have gone for goal.

With 32 minutes gone the ball came lobbing into the Wexford goal-mouth. Purcell had now come back to full forward and he got hold of the ball. The doughty Enda Murphy dogged him but Purcell had great ball control and he managed to flick it over the bar.

Frustrated Mentors

By this time, with the score 3–6 to 0–8 the Wexford mentors began to shift forwards all over the place. There was frustration creeping in because the side were playing very good hurling without it being reflected on the scoreboard. The changes made little appreciable difference except to lead to some confusion among the players themselves and indeed some spectators.

Martin Casey was moved to right corner forward, John Quigley appeared in the centre forward position, Christy Keogh went to right half forward and Phil Wilson to midfield.

Martin Quigley, earnest and urgent in his play at midfield, kept trying to set up attacks and sometimes joined them. In one of these he was running in towards goal when he was obstructed by Frank Cummins. Tom Byrne took the free to the left of the posts. His swing missed the ball but he atoned by cutting the ball off the ground to send it over the bar. Shortly afterwards Keher pointed a free.

Frank Cummins, having a hard battle to keep his side in the picture at midfield, cut a long ball across to Keher's corner. Keher came running out and sent it over the bar despite a fierce block by a defender which smashed the Inistioge man's hurley. He signalled to the sideline for one of his meticulously weighted and carefully honed hurleys which for him were an extension of his hands and arms.

Intense Entertainment

At centre back for Wexford Jacob had to deal alternatively with Delaney and Purcell but he knew the style of both and he held his own. Players all over the pitch sometimes never got more than a pull or a flick or a touch of the ball in the frantic tussles. These teams were so well matched that players found it difficult to make space for a long carefully directed shot. Yet there was brilliant stickwork, marvellous skill, thundering physical impacts on view. It was enthralling stuff, bringing a froth of excitement to all who witnessed it, so that sedate souls shouted and yelled, strangers plucked one another's sleeves, bonded by the thrill of this epic encounter.

Just coming up to half time, John Quigley, now at midfield, ran into an opening as Mick Jacob took a free, grabbed the ball and sent it over the bar to leave the score 3–8 to 0–10 in favour of Kilkenny. It was an unsatisfactory situation for Wexford who had hurled so well yet were seven points in arrears. This scoreline seemed to underline the fact that in the battle of wits and strategy, of timing and opportunism, Kilkenny were very hard to match. Mediocre Kilkenny sides had often beaten good sides simply because they were game-wise.

Yet Wexford followers were hopeful. If they could hurl as well in the second half they would be in there with a great chance. And they would have the breeze behind them.

Tragic Incident

Then came one of the most dramatic and tragic incidents in this incident-spiked game. Keogh and Henderson, tussling hard all during the half went for a high ball together. It broke behind them, not far from the side-line on the Cusack Stand side, and hopped on the ground. Wilson came running over and put down his left hand for the ball at the same time as Pat Lalor pulled on it. Wilson grabbed the ball but Lalor's hurley swung up and caught the Wexford man a hard blow on the bridge of the nose. He went down, pole-axed.

The Wexford mentors and the St John's Ambulance team crowded round the stunned player. Both his nose and his hand had been injured. Seven stitches were going to be required for the facial injury and several more on his hand.

After a minute he came round and was helped to his feet. He looked dazed and was being led off the field when Lalor came over as if to make a sympathetic gesture. The blow was not intentional but, like much of the pulling, was uncaring. Suddenly Wilson gave his adversary an admonitory slap on the head with the flat of the hurley. It was not a hard blow but it looked bad and brought a gasp from the crowd. The referee was standing right beside both players. He ordered Wilson off the field. The Wexford mentors told him that the injured player was already on his way off, to be replaced by a substitute but the referee insisted that Wilson was being sent off for striking on the field of play and that he could not be replaced.

This was a great blow to Wexford. The long-striding, long-hitting Wilson was having a very good game. He could have been expected to go all out in the second half because for a man so dedicated to physical fitness the 80-minute game was well within the range of his energies. This was a personal tragedy for this player who had played memorably in the county's last All-Ireland victory in '68. This incident shadowed the remainder of his long hurling career.

After this unhappy incident Mick Spain blew the whistle for half- time. It seemed like half the people on terraces and stands hurried below, not so much to go to the toilets and refreshment counters as to urgently discuss the game. Red-faced men gathered in groups, all talking loudly at the same time. People shook their heads, talked so quickly so that only those used to the accent could be sure of what opinion was being offered. These animated conversations only ended when they heard the band leaving the field to make way for a renewal of battle.

A Handshake

When the two teams came out of the tunnel, Wilson and Lalor shook hands on the sideline. It was a healing gesture but it was of little real value to the Slaneysiders. Forty minutes with the disadvantage of a man short was a high mountain for Wexford to have to climb. Many another side would have been dismayed at the prospect, especially when they were seven points in arrears. But this was when the Slaneysiders drew on their great tradition of facing adversity with grit and courage. They reappeared on the field full of fire and zest to take on the provincial champions for the second half.

The mentors had decided that the best place for the vacancy was the right corner forward position. This would leave Jim Treacy the freedom to control that area but it was their intention not to allow many balls to go there.

The Wexford side went into attack straight from the throw in. Martin Casey, full of drive, got the ball and belted it over the bar. This was a defiant start by the underdogs. Now they powered into the game all over the field and set up wave after wave of assault on the Kilkenny goals. Doran and Byrne were the target men, both with Orr and Larkin right at their sides as each ball came in. There was a great deal of jostling and buffeting as the Wexford half forwards came piling in as well.

It was in this period that Noel Skehan saved his side from a deluge of goals. He parried and blocked on the goal-line like a champion fencer. He stopped balls in the air and on the ground, put his hurley in front of some, his body in front of others. 'He can't keep that up forever, surely', spectators said.

In the end Tom Byrne did manage to get a goal through after a great tussle on the line. This evoked a loud cheer from the heartened Slaneyside supporters. This score reduced Kilkenny's lead to three points. But it had taken a great deal of effort and energy.

Kilkenny Hit Back

Not long afterwards, however, Kilkenny showed how resilient and how dangerous they could be. Purcell and Jacob battled for a ball on the 40.

This time the square-shouldered Windgap player caught it and sent a lobbing ball into the square. Crotty, vigilant as a hungry heron, tapped the incoming ball over to Keher who had slipped into space in front of goal. Keher held the ball on his stick to avoid the charges of the Wexford backs and then, although his arms were virtually pinioned, calmly palmed the ball into the net. Some of the Wexford backs had hesitated momentarily, convinced that their efforts to stop Keher would result in a free, but the referee played the advantage rule.

Wexford Put On Pressure

The score now stood at 4–8 to 1–11 in favour of the provincial champions. After all their efforts Wexford still had virtually the same mountain to climb. But they began straight away. The hard-driving, ever-running John Quigley gathered near the midfield and, running forward, sent over a point. Nicky Orr kept harrassing Tony Doran and they bumped and bored in front of the goals, gasping and grunting. It was hard for the Kilkenny captain to stop his opponent catching high incoming balls. 'That man has a hand like a potato basket', shouted a Wexford voice when Doran's big right hand grabbed the ball once more. Orr would not allow him to pass but Doran suddenly moved out and found room to strike a point.

Kilkenny attacks on the wings were being repulsed by O'Connor and Staples and on the other side of the field the teak-tough Colm Doran shouldered opponents out of the way, twisted and weaved with the ball and then swung hard, close to his body, left or right. Willie Murphy, whose wholehearted play resulted in an injury, was replaced by Jimmy Prendergast.

In the tenth minute the dark haired, red-faced Casey, moving all over the forward line, shouldered his way to the ball, lifted it and swung on it and scored another point for Wexford. He kept proving the point that lack of delicate skills can be effectively countered by power and resolve.

Sean Kinsella, whose even battle with Pat Lalor was one of the best personal duels of the game, had moved into the corner in an exchange with Tom Byrne. When he got the ball on the left, about 14 yards out, he sent over an angled shot.

This was now four points in a row for Wexford in a great spell of dominance. They were only two points behind. Their numerical disadvantage did not seem to be affecting their game. Jim Treacy was a hurling corner back, not the highly mobile rover that might have given Kilkenny more advantage. The Kilkenny mentors saw this and they replaced Treacy with a young under-21 team player, Nicky Brennan.

O'Brien Starring

There was one player that was now making all the difference to Kilkenny. Chunky O'Brien was running all over the midfield area. He deftly intercepted balls, cheekily cut off passes, and he went on jinking runs with the ball motionless on his weaving hurley. He was always fast enough to make space and, when he had done so, often pulled up to steady himself and measure the distance to the goalposts.

He did just that in the 13th minute when he scored a point to put an end to the scoring sequence of the opposition and to bring his side's lead back to three points.

Shortly afterwards came one of the best scores of the game. Kieran Purcell raced out and reached up to catch a high ball. Then he came racing in along the Hogan Stand side. He struck the ball with great force and accuracy, sending it across the face of the goal and in to the far corner of the net for a fine goal. This kind of shot was always a goal-keeper's nightmare but there were some who said that the Pat Nolan of five years before would not have let it in.

As if to emphasise their capacity to confound the backs and pick off neat scores Crotty and Delaney combined in an attack. It began from a good clearance from Pat Henderson, now coming into his own at centre back. The movement ended with Delaney sending the ball over the bar. The score now stood at 5–10 to 1–15.

Another foul by Orr on Doran saw Byrne send over a Wexford point. Two minutes later came a disastrous event for Wexford. Crotty, from 30 yards out whipped hard on the ball on the ground. It was a dangerous ground ball. It struck Pat Nolan's hurley and spun into the goal.

Nine Points Behind

It seemed as if Wexford, despite matching their opponents around the pitch, were never going to get level on the scoreboard. They were now nine points behind. Yet this was the time that Wexford dug deep into their reserves and developed another great surge of hurling power.

Rory Kinsella, who had replaced the exhausted Martin Casey, used his speed and fresh energy to outpace the Kilkenny defence after taking a pass from John Quigley. He came racing in from the right to the Kilkenny goal at the Railway end. From 20 yards out he sent in a shot that went sizzling through backs and forwards locked in combat and into the net past the unsighted Noel Skehan. Not long afterwards the same player sent over another point. It raised the question of why this live wire had not been brought on earlier.

Wexford kept up the pressure. A ball came into the corner. Sean Kinsella got it and was trying to go flying along the endline when Fan Larkin stopped him illegally. The referee whistled up for a free. Tom Byrne, totally reliable, put it over the bar.

The two low-sized dynamos around the middle of the field, John Quigley and Liam O'Brien, now and then clashed. In one of these encounters the Wexford man neatly took the ball from his opponent and sent a long shot over the bar to further reduce Kilkenny's lead.

Back to Two Points

The next Wexford attack ended up for a 70. Teddie O'Connor ran out to take it. This was a key moment. At such a time in a game any hard won frees must not be missed. The low-sized O'Connor lifted it well and struck it well and it went between the uprights to leave two points between the sides.

Enda Murphy cleared the ball out of the Wexford goal area several times in succession; Colm Doran latched on to two of these and sent his side into the attack. The Kilkenny backs, under severe pressure, were now having to give away frees to stop forwards racing in with the ball or Doran or Byrne palming into the goal. From one of these frees Tom Byrne pointed again. Two minutes later, in yet another attack, Doran raced out to 30 yards to catch the ball, swerved to deceive Nicky Orr and send the ball over the bar.

Wexford Level and Go Ahead

This was the equaliser. The Wexford followers were ecstatic. With 11 minutes to go their side, against all the odds, were back on level terms. But those Kilkenny supporters who had come to Croke Park that Sunday were joyful too. They loved hurling, revelled in the ferocious competition these sides engendered, delighted in the skills and the artistry that was on display every moment of this game. This was an occasion so full of incident, of battles all over the field that it was impossible to see them all, to store them for discussion when the game was long over.

It was John Quigley, running himself into sheer exhaustion, who got the point that put his side into the lead with ten minutes remaining. He had got the ball but had been shouldered to the ground. Up he rose, face red with effort, fair hair dark with perspiration, and with a great effort struck the ball from far out. It sailed over the bar. The purple and gold flags waved all over the stadium.

Level Again

This was the kind of pell-mell finish in which Kilkenny teams always thrived. Billy Fitzpatrick from Johnstown Fenians, who had replaced the injured Billy Harte, came racing in and sent out a neat pass to Keher. The ace marksman hit it with great certainty over the bar.

Four minutes to go. The sides level again. Every muscle of every player on the field was strained to the very utmost. Every ball was crucial, every tussle frenzied in its urgency. At this stage many of the spectators in the stands could not remain seated and stood up, heedless of the annoyed shouts of those behind them. Before the end most people would be on their feet with those in the back rows standing on the seats.

Wexford A Point Ahead

With four minutes to go, the red headed Doran, who had taken a lot of shouldering and bumping during the game, came foraging desperately out 60 yards from the Kilkenny goal. He won a ball and came thundering in. As he was being challenged, he passed it to Tom Byrne who sent it over the bar. Wexford were ahead again.

Fresh Player Equalises

With two minutes to go Kilkenny mounted an attack. There was tremendous pulling and blocking in the goal area. By now, in the warmth of the afternoon players were visibly flagging after 80 minutes of intense effort. The ball came out from the Wexford goal to one of the freshest players on the field, the alert Nicky Brennan of Conahy, who had replaced Jim Treacy. He hit the ball smartly over the bar for the equaliser.

It was right on the 40th minute that in a desperate scuffle near the Hogan Stand side the tireless Delaney came out and collected the ball. It was a hopeless scoring position but he held the ball, juggling it about as if inviting defenders to dispossess him. In such a nerve-wracking climax it was hard for defenders to avoid fouling the burly Fenians player. They did so and from this Keher put over the winning point.

When the referee finally blew the whistle, players from both sides sank to their knees, totally drained by the effort. Their heads were soaked in sweat, their chests heaved. Some rubbed their legs to relieve the pains of cramp. The Kilkenny side were overjoyed. It was as if they realised that they would have no greater challenge than that of their near neighbours and most dogged opponents.

It was not just a question of creating a record by winning four provincial titles in a row but being well on stream for the All-Ireland title. They went on to beat Limerick, rather easily, in a game that could not come anywhere near this game against Wexford for quality of play, or excitement or sheer drama.

As the referee was leaving the field there was some booing and verbal abuse from frustrated Wexford supporters at his blowing the final whistle with some seconds remaining. He could not be blamed; with 80 minutes to play, with scores coming at either end in rapid succession, with the ball flying from one end to the other, with clashes and incidents tumbling upon one another every minute, no one person could be expected to be perfect.

Indeed for a time during the game the scoreboard keepers at either end were at variance with one another, such was the fast flow of scores at either end.

The following year that great Kilkenny side would hold on to their provincial title after another rousing joust with Wexford. Again they would win the All-Ireland title — against Galway — after a match not anywhere on a par with the Leinster final.

Wexford people were entitled to feel that if their team had beaten Kilkenny in '74 and '75 they would have won the All-Ireland as well. It was 1976 before they finally got the better of their old rivals in a one-sided game that spelt the beginning of the end for the great Kilkenny side but which did not lead to Wexford winning the All-Ireland crown for which they yearned.

The rivalry between the counties still remains. But it has faded as the power of Wexford hurling had faded. Yet the memory of their great battles in the 1970's is still fresh in the memory of many and no more so than the epic encounter of 1974.

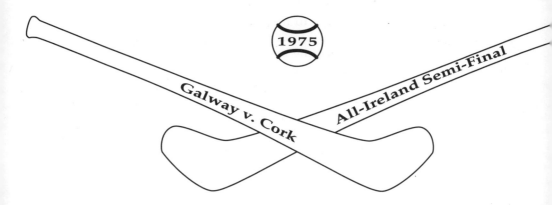

THE END OF A 'MERE FORMALITY'

When the Galway team came running out on to the green sward of Croke Park on a warm, sunny day in August 1975 to play Cork in the All-Ireland semi-final it marked the end of one era and the beginning of another for the Westerners.

In retrospect it is easy to say that they looked exceptionally fit, had a vibrant spring in their step as they pucked the ball about in the pre-match warm-up before a crowd of 27,000 spectators, at least 15,000 of whom had travelled from the West that morning.

Most of the media commentators, hidebound by tradition and old certainties, had predicted that Cork would win. They did make reference to the power the Galway team had shown in winning the National League. But this was the real thing, the championship, and Galway could not realistically be expected to beat a very talented Cork side, from a county which had won twenty-one All-Irelands to Galway's single victory.

Most of the neutral observers felt the same. Galway, ploughing their lone furrow in the province of Connacht, came forward year after year to meet the Munster or Leinster champions in the semi-finals. Invariably they were hammered, often humiliated. Only three years before, in assessing the progress of the Kilkenny team to the All-Ireland, the *Kilkenny People* referred to the semi-final with Galway in a single dismissive sentence: 'The game against Galway was a mere formality.'

The only occasion that they had won a semi-final was in 1953 when a very fine side, which had been narrowly beaten in championship encounters the previous years, beat Kilkenny. That team, powered by players of the calibre of Joe Salmon, Inky Flaherty and Josie Gallagher, had been defeated in the final by Cork in a tense, tough, close encounter. They had never beaten Cork before or since in a championship game.

Galway Decline

Despite producing several great individual players, Galway went into yet another long decline. Due to a bad administrative decision, they got a bye into the All-Ireland of 1958 when they were comprehensively beaten by Tipperary.

After that drubbing Galway decided it might help if they moved in with Munster and got competitive games in that provincial championship. They were there for ten years and hardly won a single game, being beaten ritually each year by the other counties.

Galway's lack of success in the championship was one of the enigmas of the hurling world, frustrating to their followers and the many lovers of the game who wanted to see new colours and counties at the top of the championship scene.

The game had a strong tradition in the southern part of the county. A team from Meelick-Eyrecourt contested the first All-Ireland in 1887. Hurling was played with great passion and pride in an area roughly south of the railway line from Dublin and the long stretch of scrubby, boggy land that ran parallel to it, with the exception of places like Castlegar and Turloughmore.

Damaging Club Rivalry

Part of the reason why Galway found it difficult to translate that intense feeling for the game to All-Ireland level was because the county championship had, for periods of time, been both imbued and soured by a ferocious rivalry between the clubs. There were rough encounters that became legendary for their wild pulling, where players eventually lost their tempers and matches degenerated into rows in which mentors, spectators and even umbrella-brandishing parish clergy joined in. This undisciplined parochial competitiveness bred dislike and a disinclination to come together for the sake of a serious effort to win an All-Ireland.

This happened in other counties also but in Cork, Kilkenny and Tipperary there emerged strong, self-willed administrators who wielded enough authority to submerge such divisiveness in the effort to win All-Irelands. These counties also bred a line of self-assured and astute trainers — the precursors of today's team managers — who knew how to weld diverse club elements into a good county team, who were not afraid to replace players no matter what club they came from, who were masters in the dressing-room, and who brooked no arguments about changes or tactics.

These men could be genial and affable, like Paddy Leahy of Tipperary or Jim Barry of Cork, but no one was in any doubt about who was in charge of the team.

Galway and indeed counties like Offaly, Clare and Wexford often lacked such iron-willed trainers, men seemingly impervious to criticism at club and county level or in the local newpapers.

Inky Flaherty

What now gave added hope to Galway followers was that one such person had come on the scene, the soft-spoken, good-natured but determined M.J. Flaherty, known endearingly by his nickname 'Inky'. His hurling career reflected the heartbreak and frustration of Galway hurling at championship level.

A strong, skilful player, he had been in many championship battles in the '40s and '50s in which, agonisingly, Galway had let the game slip away from them in the last ten minutes, when the very prospect of winning at long last seemed to paralyse players who had been full of running for fifty minutes of the game.

He had played for the outstanding Galway side that emerged at the end of the 1940s, which won the Railway Cup in a memorable final against Munster in 1949, was narrowly beaten by Cork in the All-Ireland semi-final in 1952 and were again beaten by them in the final of 1953.

When, in 1974, he took charge of the team at the start of the league campaign he declared that they were going to make a real effort to win an All-Ireland. Because of his prowess on the field of play and his quietly persuasive personality he had the respect of all the players. Flaherty emphasised that the players needed to engender a strong self-belief in themselves, a will to win and the mental and physical strength to keep going right to the end of the game.

Moment of Resolve

Joe McDonagh, the right half back on the team, recalls a moment of significance as the team sat on the Belfast-Dublin train, one Sunday evening, homeward bound after playing and beating Antrim. 'We were in the second division of the National League in 1974/75 and it was looking like we were going to make the quarter final. P.J. Qualter, one of the veterans of the side and something of a father figure, called us all together. It was the first real team talk we ever had, with every player having his say. We became fired by a great resolve to go into every game full of determination and with a belief that we could win.'

Galway faced Cork in the quarter-final at the Gaelic Grounds at Limerick. There was a small crowd. Cork were not taking the league too seriously, much more concerned about preparing a team of marvellous ability for the championship. But they were expected to beat the Division Two champions without much bother.

Instead of that the fine Cork forward line was well held by the Galway backs. Sean Silke dominated at centre back and Cork's talented Jimmy Barry Murphy had a poor outing on him and was replaced at half-time.

The Westerners won by 4–9 to 4–6. But they had struck many wides and had made hard work of winning.

League Victories

They met Kilkenny in the league semi-final at Thurles. Kilkenny were also expected to win. They were the All-Ireland champions, with players like Keher, Delaney, Cummins, Purcell and Henderson who had added lustre to the game of hurling during the late '60s and early '70s. They had returned from a tour of America and it was said they were tired. Galway won an exciting game by 1–9 to 1–6.

The final was against the third of the dominant Brahmins of the hurling scene, Tipperary. This was a thundering game at Limerick. The Tipperary side included players who had won All-Ireland medals four years before and saw the league as a stepping stone back on to the All-Ireland scene. One of the Galway players who made his mark in that rousing encounter was Frank Burke of Turloughmore, big, strong and fast, who ran with the ball on his hurley, elbows outspread to protect it, spearheading the Galway attacks.

It was neck and neck all the way until the last few minutes when Tipperary edged ahead by two points. Galway, no longer folding up under pressure as the clock ran out, made a great burst for their opponents' goal. It ended in a penalty. The captain, John Connolly, powerful and accurate, struck the ball hard. It bounced off a defender's hurley but the inrushing Qualter whipped it to the net to give Galway their first National League title in 24 years. The score was 2–7 to 2–4 in their favour.

As the crowd of 32,000 dispersed many of the Galway faithful were filled with hope that this might be a team to end the endless story of failures, of being beaten by teams that were not better but were able to outfox the Westerners at crucial moments in a game.

Euphoria

There was great euphoria in Co. Galway after this heartening win. Starved of a win of any kind for so long, there were celebrations all over the hurling area of the county. The cup was taken in triumph along the stone-walled roadways of the flat, sheep-cropped countryside round Castlegar and Turloughmore, over the winding byways towards Ballinderreen and Kinvara by the seaweedy shores of Galway bay, down to the hedgy farmlands about Gort and Kilbeacanty. There was singing late at night in little pubs in towns and crossroads. At last the county had something to celebrate.

'Now for the Double' said the *Connacht Tribune*, meaning that the team could add the All-Ireland title to the National League. The team itself made a great effort to put an end to their own involvement in celebrations, to get over the euphoria and to get back down to hard training.

Promising Cork Team

The reason that most of the media commentators and many hurling followers favoured Cork to put an end to the league-induced ecstacy of the Westerners was because a team of great promise was being readied by the banks of the Lee. There were experienced players who had won All-Irelands and in doing so established themselves as among the best sticksmen ever to come out of Cork — Gerald McCarthy, Charlie McCarthy, Con Roche and Ray Cummins. Added to them were players who had been blooded in the great final of 1972 against Kilkenny and wanted so much to be on the winning side on All-Ireland day. These included Brian Murphy, Denis Coughlan and Sean O'Leary. Added to that were players of exceptional ability like Jimmy Barry Murphy and Pat Moylan.

All these players emerged from the test of skill and stamina that is the Cork club championship. With thousands playing at senior level only the most accomplished could hope to be selected on a senior club team. Standards of skill were exacting and the spectators highly critical of any lack of will or ability. The three city teams of that era, St Finnbar's, Glen Rovers and Blackrock, had substitutes who would have been selected on the county teams of some of the less prominent hurling counties.

Cork had this fierce pride, a grinding determination to win and a great facility in being able to use the stick to best effect.

It made players like Gerald McCarthy practise endlessly until he could pull hard on a ball coming towards him at fifty miles an hour and send it back up the field — or pull with it and send it flying forward, usually directed with uncanny skill towards Charlie McCarthy, waiting for the fast ball in the corner.

On their way through the Munster campaign they had first beaten Waterford by 4–15 to 0–6, showing much of the awesome forward power that was to make this team one of the greatest of the modern era. In the semi-final they came up against a very good Clare team who held them until well into the second half. Cork went on to win 3–14 to 1–9. Limerick, who had been Munster champions for the past two years, were their opposition in the Munster final, holding them for 45 minutes but then succumbing to the firepower of Cummins, O'Leary and Barry Murphy.

Galway's only game was against the 'B' champions, Westmeath, when they won on a score of 6–14 to 1–8. This was not considered a real test of their mettle. Only the championship game against Cork would reveal their real worth.

Midfield

Certainly many hurling followers were looking forward to mettle-testing at midfield where John Connolly and Sean Murphy would be pitched against Gerald McCarthy and Pat Hegarty. Hegarty had been moved from the right half back position to partner the St Finbarr's man, in a move to strengthen the midfield. Connolly, the great Castlegar player, was in top form. For a long time his well-honed skills as a natural hurler, good on the ground or in the air, had been expressed in isolation. Often he was the lone star of the West, the only man the opposition feared, the one to be marked out of a game. He would be marking Gerald McCarthy, the powerhouse of the Cork team, who played with such strength and competitiveness that he roused the whole team.

The Galway half back line of Joe McDonagh, Sean Silke and Iggy Clarke were emerging as the best on the hurling scene but they would be put to the test in this match. Clarke, brother of full back Joe, would have to mind the most elusive and elegant stick artist in Barry Murphy, who could fade away and suddenly reappear in front of goal to flick in an unexpected goal. Silke, of Meelick-Eyrecourt, and Willie Walsh of Youghal were both sturdily build men, with Walsh a great bustler and distributor of the ball. Galway's right half back McDonagh would have to cope with the versatile Dinny Allen, who, like Barry Murphy was a first class footballer as well.

Lethal Full Forward Line

Many readers of the game felt that it would eventually hinge on whether the most lethal full forward line in the business, Charlie McCarthy, Ray Cummins and Sean O'Leary, could be held. McCarthy, small and compact, had supreme control of any ball that came his way. He was one of the very few players with enough skill and confidence to hit a hopping ball on the half-volley, whipping it on the split second that it left the ground. Paddy Lally was going to have to stick by this lightning fast ball-striker from start to finish. But Lally had played very soundly in the league and was growing as a player with each game.

Ray Cummins was to prove himself one of the best full forwards of all time. Tall and angular, standing over six feet, he had great anticipation for the incoming ball, could rise like a bird of prey to grab it, turn and flick or palm it towards the net. Once he got the ball in his hand it only took two strides of his long legs to be on the goal line to hand-pass it into the net. The soft spoken, undemonstrative Father Joe Clarke had the job of minding this danger man. He had not only to prevent him scoring himself but to try to stop him sending out pin-point passes to McCarthy, O'Leary and other incoming forwards.

O'Leary often looked deceptively overweight. The reality was that he was the fastest sprinter on the Cork team. And he had the weight to knock his man off the ball. With his thick legs and heavy body he was difficult to dispossess, knew where to lie in wait for one single half chance. His marker was the tall Niall McInerney, of the tousled russet hair. There was something fiercely determined about him. He cleared the ball with great swinging strokes that lifted the spirits of the team and the followers. More than anyone else, this Clareman epitomised the hard steel that had begun to enter the soul of the Galway team.

Galway Forwards

Most commentators said that the Galway forwards could not quite match the Corkmen in terms of skill and experience and that seventh sense called 'cuteness'. They had two strong tall men in the middle, the hard-running Frank Burke on the forty and the vastly experienced P.J. Qualter waiting about the edge of the square for any loose balls. Centre back for Cork was the very able Martin O'Doherty while behind him Pat McDonnell had been keeping a good space in front of goal during the Munster campaign. He had emerged as a fine full back several years before and had been Hurler of the Year.

Gerry Coone and Marty Barrett made up the right wing. They were up against two outstanding players of the era, Con Roche and Brian Murphy, battle hardened warriors who were great to get possession of the ball and clear it away without fuss. But the two Galway men had speed and a zest for winning that would give them additional energy on a blazing day.

P.J. Molloy had to try to evade the attentions of Teddie O'Brien, one of the stars of Cork last All-Ireland win in 1970. The Athenry man, stocky but fast, held the hurley in the awkward-looking right hand under grip, but he was an endless forager for the ball and he had scored and made scores in the league campaign. Galway's left corner forward that day was Padraig Fahy, noted for his speed off the mark and endline running. He was up against a veteran in Tony Maher, who had marked some of the best forwards out of the game, including Eddie Keher in the 1972 final until the Kilkenny sharpshooter was moved away from him out to the half forward position.

Martin Coleman had taken over in goal from Paddy Barry and was to prove one of the great net-minders in this team of all the talents. In short, this Cork side was now the best source of hurling entertainment in the country, as the great Kilkenny team of the early '70s began to fade away.

Ready to Go

What was the attitude of the players themselves towards the game before them? Gerald McCarthy recalls, 'Well of course Justin McCarthy, who was in charge of the team, warned us that this was a hungry Galway side, as hungry as we ourselves had been in 1966. But we had been made favourites by the newspapers and by our followers and it was hard to avoid feeling confident if not complacent. There may have been a feeling at the back of our minds that Galway teams did not win important games like this. They might keep pace for three-quarters of the game but then they might fold. And we had come through a hard Munster championship and had a great belief in ourselves and our capacity to win. So we were fairly confident.'

Joe McDonagh remembers the feelings that vibrated amongst the Galway players as they togged out in the dressing-room beneath the

The teams as they lined out were:

GALWAY

Michael Conneely
(Sarsfields)

Niall McInerney	Joe Clarke	Paddy Lally
(Liam Mellowes)	(Mullagh)	(St Brigid's)

Joe McDonagh	Sean Silke	Iggy Clarke
(Ballinderreen)	(Meelick-Eyrecourt)	(Mullagh)

John Connolly, capt   Sean Murphy
(Castlegar)   (Carnmore)

Gerry Coone	Frank Burke	P.J. Molloy
(St Brigid's)	(Turloughmore)	(Athenry)

Marty Barrett	P.J. Qualter	Padraig Fahy
(Padraig Pearse's)	(Turloughmore)	Carnmore

Substitutes: Michael Hanniffy (Oranmore-Maree); Michael Connolly (Castlegar); Ted Murphy (Castlegar); Larry Bohan (Moycullen); Seamus Grealish (Carnmore); Vincent Mullins (Ardrahan). *Trainer/coach*: M.J. Flaherty (Liam Mellowes). *Selectors/mentors*: Frank Fahy (Turloughmore); Pat Robinson (Tynagh); Tom Fahy (Craughwell); Kevin Shaughnessy (Castlegar); Sean Conroy (Padraig Pearse's). *Team doctor*: Dr Mary McInerney. *Masseur*: Fred Smyth.

CORK

Martin Coleman
(Ballinhassig)

Tony Maher	Pat McDonnell	Brian Murphy
(St Finbarr's)	(Inniscarra)	(Nemo Rangers)

Teddie O'Brien	Martin O'Doherty	Con Roche
(Glen Rovers)	(Glen Rovers)	(St Finbarr's)

Gerald McCarthy, capt   Pat Hegarty
(St Finbarr's)   (Youghal)

Jimmy Barry Murphy	Willie Walsh	Denis Allen
(St Finbarr's)	(Youghal)	(Nemo Rangers)

Charlie McCarthy	Ray Cummins	Sean O'Leary
(St Finbarr's)	(Blackrock)	(Youghal)

Substitutes: Denis Burns (St Finbarr's); John Horgan (Blackrock); Eamonn O'Donoghue (Blackrock); Sean Lucey (Mayfield); John Fenton (Midleton); Frank O'Sullivan (Glen Rovers). *Coach*: Justin McCarthy (Passage). *Selectors*: Fr Bertie Troy (Newtownshandrum); Dan O'Mahony (Passage); Paddy Fitzgerald (Midleton); Jack Barrett (Kinsale); Michael Murphy (St Finbarr's). *Masseur*: John 'Kid' Cronin (Glen Rovers).

The referee was Mick Spain of Offaly.

Hogan Stand. 'Inky kept telling us that we could do it. He kept hammering at the theme of self-belief and self-confidence in our capacity to win. We felt great. We were superbly fit. We felt that Cork might be writing us off in their own minds — the Galway teams of other years satisfied to make a reasonable showing for most of the match. We were determined to give it all we had.'

Hurricane From West

Not even the most expectant Galway supporter was prepared for what happened after the throw in. The Western side, playing into the Canal end against a breeze, took off like so many greyhounds out of the traps. Cork had to concede a free which was taken by the neat-striking Iggy Clarke. His puck from 70 yards out on Galway's left touchline went just wide of the uprights at the Canal end. There was a great battle for Coleman's long puck out but the ball came flying over to Coone who went racing up the touchline, hotly pursued by Con Roche. Qualter, who had begun his roving tactics, took Coone's pass. Pat McDonnell was on to him, but Qualter, back-pedalling furiously, hit a great point to open the scoring.

Galway Goal

The ball had hardly been pucked out when there was a fierce scramble near midfield. Then the ball came into the Galway goal area. McInerney, sticking close to O'Leary wherever he ran, found himself blocking and shouldering two Cork players out of his way. The ball eventually went down the field to Padraig Fahy, one of the fastest men on the pitch. Eluding Tony Maher, he passed the ball to Frank Burke who was already starting a diagonal run. The hard-striding Turloughmore man went twenty yards with the ball on his stick. His speed took him far away from his pursuers to allow him to take his powerful wide swing with his heavy hurley. The sound of ash on leather could be heard all over the stadium followed by a huge roar from the Galway followers who saw the umpire raise the green flag. Many had not seen even the blur of the bullet shot and Coleman could not be blamed at all.

This score seemed to sound a hunting horn that Galway were now in full flight and going all out. They won individual battles all over the field, were faster to the ball, gave their more vaunted opponents no time to settle. P.J. Molloy came running onto a ball which Gerry Coone sent his way and he steadied himself to hit it over the bar.

Near Thing for O'Leary

But it was not all Galway. Gerald McCarthy, having what was to be a neck and neck battle with John Connolly, pulled accurately on a head-high ball, sending it into O'Leary's corner. Suddenly accelerating, the deceptive Youghal man broke through the Galway defence. Michael

Conneely, with his wide-bossed hurley, came forward. O'Leary hit the ball while being buffetted. Conneely stopped it but only pushed it back to O'Leary. It glanced off the forward's body and went wide. A great sigh of relief — and some uneasy head-shaking — went up from the Galway supporters after this near shave.

'Steady up, Conneely', someone shouted urgently from among a host of maroon and white flags.

John Connolly's Fine Goal

Galway kept in control by speed and skill and in the eighth minute John Connolly joined the attack. He raced out to the right wing, lifted the ball effortlessly and went running in, always elegant even in full flight. Qualter, scheming and varying his tactics, had ghosted into a free position in front of goal. A pass seemed on but Connolly kept going, side-stepping two defenders before spinning round in a deceptive full turn to send the ball crashing into the net from ten yards out. The Galway crowd went wild. This was their hero, man of all the skills, at long last part of a good team instead of trying to do it all on his own.

With only eight minutes gone Galway were ahead, 2–2 to no score. Then Barry Murphy, who had an uncanny facility to collect a ball from frantic play, struck over a point for Cork's first score. It raised a small cheer from the weak Cork contingent. However, from the puck out the ball came flying into the Cork danger area. Qualter was pursued out to the left wing by the speedy McDonnell who leapt up and grabbed the high dropping ball. Before he could clear it he was harrassed and let it fall. Fahy pounced and swept away at speed along the flank. At the last minute before being tackled he hit the ball out to the in-rushing Qualter who pulled on it to score the best goal of the day.

Scoreboard Reflecting Play

Nine minutes gone and Galway had got three goals. Only in wild fantasy could their followers have imagined such a whirlwind start. Not alone were they making the running but, most important, it was reflected on the scoreboard unlike many times past.

Cork were unsettled by this onslaught and had not really got into the game. A sign of this was when Cork were awarded a free from 45 yards out. Charlie McCarthy sent it in hard at knee height. It was a dangerous ball but it went wide.

Just afterwards McCarthy sent a 21 yard free over the bar. But Cork's anxiety to get back into the game led them to seek goals when points were there for the asking through most of the play to follow.

The midfield contest between Connolly and McCarthy, the two hard-ened battlers, was one of the great highlights of the game. Both played well, but they often cancelled one another out. But Galway achieved the upper hand here by the great play of Sean Murphy, a natural midfielder pitted against Pat Hegarty, who many felt was out of position. Murphy started to win more of the ball on either side of the pitch and send in sharp ground balls to the corner forwards.

Cork Strike Back

With jerseys darkened by perspiration in a 75° temperature, the Cork team were trying desperately to get going. A quick ball came in to O'Leary. Trying to shoulder aside the attentions of McInerney, he thundered along the end line goalwards and put the ball into the net. But Mick Spain, not playing the advantage rule, had whistled for a penalty. The Galway guardians, with Conneely and his wide-bossed hurley in the middle, crouched as the ball came flying in. Conneely got his board-like stick to it and the ball skittered away a short distance. Here Dinny Allen gathered it and sent a pin-point pass straight at Barry Murphy who had appeared alone and unmarked in front of goal, as he was wont to do. He crashed the ball to the net with great style.

Just on 15 minutes Coone came out to take a free from 65 yards. At this stage, with Cork now settling down to business, such frees were important. He sent it unerringly between the posts.

The pace all over the field had not slackened, despite the heat. The marking was close but just the same there was great stickwork, great ball-control to be seen, first-time striking even under the hardest tackling. Cork went into the attack more often. Allen snapped up a sideline cut on the run and struck it straight over the bar. Not long afterwards Willie Walsh, although handicapped by a heavily bandaged left arm, for once escaped the attentions of Silke, whose agility and ball play was superb. The Youghal player, thundering goalwards, hit the ball first time on the run and it screamed over the bar.

Burke A Powerhouse

On the other 40 yards mark, Martin O'Doherty was having a difficult time trying to watch the rampant Frank Burke. The Turloughmore man was not a sylish hurler, holding the stick in the right-hand-under grip. But he trained hard and tried hard and ran hard. And when he was on song, as he was that day and in the National League final, he was the ideal centre forward. He put his hand up for the aerial ball, protecting it with the hurley held across it. When he got the ball he shouldered his way clear and then ran or passed.

On one of his rampaging runs with the ball he was fouled. Coone sent the free over the bar from 30 yards. A minute later Burke came pounding down the right wing. The veteran Con Roche tackled him on the run and had almost dispossessed him when Burke spotted Molloy loose over on the left. He sent a perfect ground ball straight as a die across the field and Molloy struck it quickly over the bar.

This point for point scoring was essential for Galway morale. It showed they could still score after the surprising opening whirlwind had ended.

Cummins A Danger

The Galway half back line was clearing away a lot of ball but on those occasions when it came into the Galway square there were gasps of anxiety from the Galway followers when the tall figure of Ray Cummins reared up to reach for the high ball or crouched to strike or control a ground ball. His first touch of the ball was so sure and accurate that he was lethal in any kind of scramble in front of goal.

Joe Clarke kept doggedly after him, behind him all the time to stop him turning, contesting every ball. He tried to fulfil this difficult role without fouling his opponent. But this happened now and from the resultant free Charlie McCarthy, with his neat, controlled swing, put it over the bar.

The score now stood at 3–5 to 1–5.

The play was sweeping from end to end. There were soaring clearances from both sets of backs but there were scrambling tussles all round the field, with the ball bobbing and spinning beneath flailing hurleys and legs. Con Roche, slowed by the weight of old injuries suffered during his years of service to Cork, still made some of his great clearances. This was the last time he would grace the scene at Croke Park in a championship match.

On Galway's left wing Molloy and Fahy were foraging and running constantly, difficult to mark; the next score came from a passing movement between them, with the broad-shouldered Molloy sending over a point.

Conneelly Saves

Coming near the end of the first half, with the Cork mentors yelling encouragement from the sideline, the Leeside players were straining to come to terms with their ebullient opponents. The forwards, finding it hard to outrun and outfox their competent markers, were unable to mount serious attacks. Yet a ball came bouncing into the Galway goalmouth and Michael Conneely, though saving it, fouled the ball on his line. A penalty was awarded. Once again the Sarsfields goalkeeper got his broad-bossed hurley to the ball that came zipping in and made amends for his error.

It seemed that there were going to be no easy goals or scores of any kind for the highly-rated Cork forwards. Salt was rubbed in the wound when the clearance went all the way down the field to the 40 yards line and the elusive Qualter, racing out from the full forward position, got possession and hit it over the bar.

There was another significant event shortly afterwards. Jimmy Barry Murphy got hold of the incoming ball and had let fly goalwards when McInerney jumped in the path of the ball and stopped it with his body. As it bounced away and was cleared upfield the corner back got a rousing cheer for his courage and hardiness.

Almost on the call of half time Gerald McCarthy snapped up a ball at midfield and tore away on a run, dodging and jinking, his moustachioed face hard with never-say-die determination. Once again the staunch McInerney came out to meet him from the corner. McCarthy tried to palm the ball to the net but he was bundled away. The umpire awarded a 70.

Con Roche, who always rose the ball beautifully and hit it with the dead centre of the boss, did so once again and the ball took off and went high between the uprights for the last score of the half.

As the teams, faces red with exertion, jerseys soaked with perspiration, left the field there was a huge ovation for the great value they had given to the 27,000 present. With the score now at 3–7 to 1–6 the Galway followers were jubilant that their men had shown such skill and spirit and opportunism. Nobody had any illusions however, that this Cork team would simply fade away. Cork teams did not do that. Nor could it be expected that their talented players could be held for the full seventy minutes.

The Dressing-Rooms

In the Cork dressing-room the mentors plotted tactics for the second half. Teddie O'Brien, not having the kind of game of which he was capable, was replaced by the experienced Denis Burns at half back. There was going to be a flexible attack with Ray Cummins and Willie Walsh exchanging places at a pivotal point in the game. Sean O'Leary was told that he might be asked to go in full forward for a while. Cork intended to break the grip the Westerners had on the run of the play and to make a big surge in the second half.

Inky Flaherty in the Galway dressing-room said firmly that they were to keep playing with confidence and dash, to do everything to maintain the rhythm of their play — and to expect a powerful Cork effort. Marty Barrett, whose tussles with Brian Murphy in the corner were so close that neither player was seen to good effect, had picked up a hand injury. He was replaced by Michael Connolly. His brother John reappeared on the field with a bandage round his head.

Good Start by Cork

The game resumed uneasily for the Westerners. Sean Murphy, the outstanding player at midfield, was bested by Pat Hegarty who struck the ball downfield where O'Leary sprinted on to it, scooped it up easily, pivoted like a plump ballet dancer and struck over a great point. It brougth a cheer of encouragement from the small Cork contingent.

Seconds later Willie Walsh caught the Galway defence on the wrong foot and sent the ball only inches wide. Not long after, John Connolly was wide with a 55-yard free and then Fahy, having collected a ball sent in from midfield and eluded the veteran Tony Maher, sent it wide also. It seemed as if there was going to be a change of control in the game.

A great cheer went up when John Horgan of the long blond hair, who had played many great games in Croke Park as minor and senior, came on to replace Martin O'Doherty. The centre back had gone down after a clash of bodies with Frank Burke. Horgan, fresh on a day of energy-sapping heat, was shortly to swap places with Brian Murphy and both of them played exceptionally well. Burke would not be as dominant from now on.

In the fifth minute Gerald McCarthy fought tigerishly for a ball ricochetting among legs and hurleys, shouldered his way out into the open and sent over a point from 30 yards out.

Points by Michael Connolly

As if to answer him Michael Connolly neatly trapped a ball 45 yards out, struck it deftly and sent it over the bar. A minute later, from almost the same spot, he did exactly the same thing. These were heartening scores when Cork seemed about to mount a real onslaught. They kept Galway in control, despite the fact that the reliable Roche hit over another 70 not long after.

Now came the most crucial score of this exciting game. Gerald McCarthy, in recalling it, said that every team needs to have its share of good fortune to balance the bad luck that inevitably comes to rest on the shoulders of any team. Perhaps it was that in the past Galway had a share of bad luck at key moments and that now the Fates had decided to redress the balance.

Mis-Hit Goal

P.J. Qualter, moving and backpedalling constantly, got the ball about 30 yards out and ducked and swerved goalwards. He had Martin Coleman alone to beat when he was fouled 23 yards out. Gerry Coone came up to take the free. His intention was to strike it hard and high between the uprights. Backs and forwards and umpires awaited the point. He swung on the ball, mis-hit it and it flew unexpectedly goalwards at head height. A back instinctively raised a hurley and the ball was deflected into the back of the net to leave the score 4–9 to 1–9.

This was a disastrous bit of bad luck for Cork. It seemed that the game was really out of their reach at this stage. Martin Coleman, who cold not be blamed for the goal, gritted his teeth and sent yet another huge puck down the field despite the breeze in his face. From this puck out Cork attacked, hitting the ball first time goalwards, so that it flew along on the sun-hardened ground. Galway conceded a free. O'Leary lifted in with simple style and clipped it quietly over the bar.

Cummins on 40

The next time the ball came into the Galway half the tall Cummins tapped it into his hand, feinted away from Silke and sent it over the bar.

The Blackrock man had now moved out and Silke's dominance at the centre of the line was significantly diminished. Cummins towered over him and the forward's hand seemed like a magnet to which high balls sped. Silke soldiered on, blocking and harrassing his opponent, limiting his effectiveness. With his helmet and black beard, Silke looked like a tough Roman centurion guarding the pass.

In the 17th minute of the second half Padraig Fahy, running and twisting like a hare, outpaced Tony Maher and sent over a point.

At the other end Charlie McCarthy also left his marker Pat Lally behind and came running in along the end line to send the ball across the goalmouth. All it needed was a touch to go to the net but no hurley reached it before it skimmed wide. The tension and excitement of the spectators began to rise even higher. There was a strong feeling that a Cork fightback was not far off.

Cork's Time of Dominance

However, when Fahy got his second point after a pass from Frank Burke it seemed that Galway were going to match their opponents point for point until the final whistle. But Cork's moment of regeneration had arrived. It was fueled by a goodly dollop of good fortune. Under pressure of a flailing attack, Joe Clarke had no option but to give away a 70.

Backs and forwards tensed and shouldered as Con Roche stood over the ball. He knew that this one should be dropped into the square. A goal was needed to fire the team, to change the tenor of the game, to put Galway under pressure for a change. The St Finbarr's player lifted the ball, weighted his stroke carefully and sent it high into the air. To a great gasp of expectation from the spectators, it came dropping down right in front of the goal. Conneely seemed to have it covered but the ball bounced off the upper part of his stick and hopped across the line. As the umpire raised the green flag for this fortuitous goal there was a sustained burst of applause and encouragement from the small Cork contingent.

Hell for Leather

With Cork now six points behind and thundering into the game the excitement went up another notch and the sound of the constant applause went up a decibel as the two sides battled for supremacy. Every ball was contested with bone-shaking clashes. The speed of the game was intense under the sun and at this stage the game became a blur of incidents and scores for many spectators.

Padraig Fahy got the third of his points but to a roar of 'Come on, Gerald boy' from the terraces, McCarthy burst forward and put over another point. Galway came back on the attack and from 70 yards out Michael Connolly struck one of the best points of a great scoring game.

Now, with 55 minutes of the game gone, Cork made the supreme effort to get on top. Many of their players began to find their full form.

The ball began to come towards the Galway end again and again, where the Western backs had to block and tackle and try to clear without respite. Connolly and Murphy had their hands full with McCarthy and Hegarty and could not help out.

Six Points in a Row

Galway conceded a free at midfield. The perspiring Roche came up and sent it straight and true between the posts. It was to be the first of six points in a row from the Corkmen. Eamon O'Donoghue, who had come in for Willie Walsh in the 58th minute, snapped up a ball in the middle of a tussle and worked his way clear. The lanky Glen Rovers man hit it over the heads and hurleys of the relentlessly pursuing Galway backs. Cork were now five points behind.

Then Sean O'Leary shook off McInerney and came charging into the goal area to unleash a cannonball shot. Conneely faced it and made a heroic attempt to stop it and succeeded to a great roar from the hoarse Galway supporters. But in the ensuing scramble, with Connolly on his knees and backs and forwards swinging and toppling, the ball finished up in the net. Referee Spain did not allow the goal but awarded a 21-yard free. The Galway backs expected O'Leary to put all his weight into a piledriver and crouched intently. Instead O'Leary snapped it over the bar. Four points in the difference now and about seven minutes to go.

Calm Under Pressure

Once again the ball came flying towards the Galway goalmouth. There the unobtrusive but calm presence of Joe Clarke seemed to epitomise the new Galway. In bygone years Galway teams often panicked under such pressure, belting the ball anywhere, crowding and getting in one another's way, making foolish mistakes. This time it was different.

In the outer line of defence McDonagh, Silke and Iggy Clarke were cool and methodical even under the most desperate pressure as the ball began to run well for their opponents. Inside McInerney, Lally and the full back were now being buffetted about by the endless charging of forwards, having to block and tackle and hook again and again. They managed to contain forwards of the calibre of Charlie McCarthy, O'Leary and Barry Murphy who could win matches off their own sticks on the merest chance. But no back was going to make huge clearances from this maelstrom of bodies and hurleys. It took them all their time to keep the ball from being flicked or handpassed into the net.

Four Minutes to Go

In another Cork onslaught Joe Clarke gave away a 70. Con Roche bent, lifted and struck the ball and sent it soaring over the bar. Only a goal now separated the sides with four minutes to go to full time. O'Leary almost got it when he grabbed the ball from a whirling tussle of arms and sticks and tried to turn goalwards.

Joe Clarke was judged to have held him and a penalty was given.

On the terraces and stands people craned their necks or raised themselves from their seats to watch the drama. The backs lined the goalmouth for this duel in the sun. The stocky O'Leary stood over the ball. 'Come on Seanie, put it in the net', a man roared from the stands. Instead, much to the surprise of the Galway backs, O'Leary sent it over the bar. 'They were going for goals when they should have been going for points and going for points when they should have been going for goals', complained one of the Cork followers.

But many felt that O'Leary was right. Cork were piling on the pressure and there was still time enough to draw if not win. There were now only two points separating the sides. The Cork forwards, with great first-time striking, sent the ball across the field, passing deftly to one another. Gerald McCarthy joined them and finding himself with room hit over a point to leave his side only one point behind. This comeback from such a disastrous start was one of the best ever seen in Croke Park and indeed it presaged a similar effort by Cork the following year in the All-Ireland final against Wexford.

Coup De Grace Expected

Now, with time running out, there was an expectation that Cork would deliver a *coup de grace* to a side representing a county who had never beaten them in a championship match. But this time it was a different Galway team on show. They pulled out the stops in a great final effort and came charging back. Burke, Fahy, Connolly, Coone, Qualter and Molloy raced for the ball, prevented it being cleared if they could not get possession, clipped it onwards even if only a few yards. This was desperation play but the ball went goalwards. Coleman, who had made many excellent saves, fell on his knees and was adjudged to have fouled the ball.

Before Gerry Coone took the free he had a brief consultation with his captain Connolly. Then from 21 yards, right in front of goal he took an easy point. This put Galway two points ahead.

The excitement of this game reached its highest level in the next minute when the Cork side threw everything they had into an effort to get a winning goal. People in the stands rose to their feet. Followers shouted and yelled without pause. Most neutrals were for the Western underdogs and they too clapped and bellowed as the great contest reached its climax. Ray Cummins, who had an uncanny first touch on the ball, got control of it and sent it goalwards but it went wide. From the puck out Cork attacked again and the ball came in low and hard and rocketed about among legs and sticks before going out of play after a defender had touched it.

For the last time Con Roche came up to the 70 yard line. The Galway backs and midfielders pressed into the backs of the waiting forwards as he bent over the ball. 'In around the house, Roche' a Cork-accented voice yelled. Roche hit it well and it soared goalwards. It began to drop from its height 20 yards out, slowed by the breeze. But it went over the bar, to the great relief of the Galway team and supporters.

Injury Time

Conneely ran up with the puck out, putting all his weight and strength behind the wide swing of his hurley. The clock had gone over the 35 minutes but there were two minutes of stoppage time to be added on. This was the most vital ball of all to drop out of the sky. As it came down from on high, a cone of entwined arms and hurleys rose up to meet it. The breaking ball fell at the feet of a Galway player who struck it fast along the ground. Qualter and McDonnell scrambled together for it, shouldering hard while the other forwards and backs bumped and bored and, when the ball came their way, flailed frantically at it. But it was impossibe for any one player to get in any kind of stroke. It went over the line off a Cork back and a 70 was given.

When John Connolly went to the line to place the ball and settle his feet on the ground the whistles from the terraces and stands were signalling that time was up. The big man from Castlegar took his time, seeming to savour the last moment of victory for his success-starved county. Then, with great composure, he lifted the ball, hit it perfectly and it went in a great sailing trajectory between the gleaming white uprights. Galway were two points ahead at the call of time.

Martin Coleman's puck out was still high in the air over the sun-drenched scene when Mick Spain blew a long, shrill whistle to signal the end of one of the greatest and most exciting semi-finals of the modern era. It could be compared with the famous Tipperary-Kilkenny semi- final of 1958. Nothing quite like it would be seen at semi-final stage for another twelve years until Tipperary and Galway met on another day of heat and sunshine.

Western Delight

There was ecstasy among the Galway players and supporters on the boot-scarred field of play. This was the county's greatest hour for years and years. Middle aged and elderly men, some who had hurled for the county during the long era of disappointment and disillusion, walked about in stunned aimlessness, not knowing how to express their joy. Many had been travelling to support the team for years and had never seen them win a championship game.

In the dressing room there was euphoria. Inky Flaherty beamed. The players who came in from the field, their backs smarting from the endless slaps of congratulation, sat on the benches, chests heaving, oblivious to bloodied knuckles and weals on legs and arms. They laughed and joked. All the physical and mental and collective effort had borne fruit and, unlike 1958, had brought them on merit to an All-Ireland final.

It was no consolation to the Cork players to tell them that they had provided one of the most thrilling and entertaining games of hurling in many a long day. Their skill and determination and the indomitable will that had made them fight back against great odds would remain and serve them well in the years ahead.

Cork Benefit from Defeat

That defeat by Galway might be said to have helped Cork to regroup in a way which was to create one of the finest teams of the modern era. When the dust had settled after this enthralling contest some of the fine veterans of the side bowed out: Con Roche, Tony Maher, Teddie O'Brien, Pat Hegarty, Willie Walsh. Denis Allen was to concentrate on football and go on to win an All-Ireland medal when he too had reached the veteran stage. Very accomplished players like Denis Coughlan, Johnny Crowley, Pat Moylan and others were to take their places and become part of an unbeatable combination. Beginning the following year they would win three All-Irelands in a row. They were to reign supreme until 1979 when in the semi-final they once again met the team that had just beaten them — Galway.

Galway Fail in Final

For the victorious Galway side of 1975 there was to be no All-Ireland victory. Though they trained hard and tried hard, they found themselves up against the All-Ireland champions, Kilkenny, in the final. This Kilkenny team had been one of the best ever to emerge from the county, powered by players like Keher, Delaney, Henderson, Purcell. It was now breaking up slowly but 1975 was its triumphant last hurrah. Galway's speed and drive proved no match for the game-wise Kilkenny men, whose vast repository of All-Ireland experience was drawn on to out-play the newcomers from the West.

For Galway, however, merely to contest the All-Ireland was a significant achievement in itself. They were in no way demoralised by the defeat. It only renewed their determination to achieve for their county the prominence and rewards its love of hurling deserved. The following year they met conquerers of Kilkenny, Wexford, in the semi-final at Pairc Ui Caoimh beside the river Lee in Cork. A pulsating game ended in a draw. The replay at the same venue was equally exciting, with the sides neck and neck almost to the end, until a disputed goal by John Quigley tipped the balance for the Wexfordmen.

In 1979 the Westerners defeated the reigning champions Cork in the semi-final. It was an unexpected victory though not quite as unexpected as 1975. The men in maroon were achieving stature and respect in the hurling world. That year they again met Kilkenny in the final. This time they matched their opponents in all but sideline acumen and threw away a game they could have won. However, the following year they won their way to the final once again where they met and beat Limerick to bring the McCarthy Cup across the Shannon for the first time since 1923. Playing with great consistency and a new sense of self-belief, they became the leading team of the 1980s, reaching the All-Ireland final in 1981, '85, '86, '87 and '88. They were to be victorious in '87 and '88 and were only narrowly beaten in '81.

The team of 1975 put pride and belief into Galway sides and nobody who knew anything about the game of hurling was ever dismissive of them again. Their semi-final victory on that hot August afternoon put an end to the notion that playing them could be regarded as a 'mere formality'.

INDEX

(*p*) indicates that the subject appears in a photograph in this book.

Allen, Dinny, 177, 179, 182, 190
Allis, Jim, 133
Antrim, 174
Aylward, Bob, 159

Barrett, Denis, 143
Barrett, Jack, 9, 179, (*p*)
Barrett, Marty, 178, 179, 184, (*p*)
Barron, John, 23, 26, 27, 36, (*p*)
Barron, Seamus, 95
Barry, Jim 'Tough', 5, 9, 11, 76–7, 80, 87,
    89, 173, (*p*)
Barry, Paddy, 178
    Cork v. Kilkenny 1966, 77, 80, 82, 84,
        88, (*p*)
    Kilkenny v. Cork 1972, 108, 110,
        115–16, 118, 122, 124
    Wexford v. Cork 1956, 2, 7, 9, 12, 13,
        15, (*p*)
Barry, Seanie, 74, 78, 80, 82–6, 88, (*p*)
Barry, Tom, 160
Bennett, Jim, 80
Bennett, John, 75, 78, 80, 82, 88, (*p*)
Bennett, Ossie, 45, 60, 95, 133, 143
Bennis, Phil, 129, 133, 143
Bennis, Richie, 129, 131, 133, 138, 143–4,
    148–9
Bergin, Martin, 60
Bernie, Dave, 95, 96, 98, 101, 104
Berry, Jack, 91, 94–5, 97–102, 104
Bohan, Dominic, 44
Bohan, Larry, 179
Bohan, Mick, 40, 44, 50, (*p*)
Bolger, Ted, 8, 9
Boothman, Achill, 40, 44, 46, 47, 49, 51, (*p*)
Boothman, Bernard, 40, 44, 46–9, (*p*)
Bourke, Davy, 133
Bowe, Dr Bob, 95, 160
Brennan, Mick 'Cloney', 156, 160–62
Brennan, Nicky, 160, 167, 170
Brohan, Jimmy, 2, 7, 9, 15, 75
Brophy, Mick, 25, 27, 28, 32
Browne, Mick, 95

Browne, Sean, 5, 9
Buckley, Jimmy, 9
Buckley, Sean, 73, 80, 84, 85, 86
Buggy, Ned, 95
Buggy, Paddy, 19–20, 25, 27, 30–31, 34
Burke, Frank, 175, 178–80, 182, 185–6,
    188, (*p*)
Burns, Denis, 179, 184
Burns, Mick
    Tipperary v. Dublin 1961, 42, 45, 46, 50
    Tipperary v. Wexford 1962, 58, 60,
        65, (*p*)
    Wexford v. Tipperary 1968, 92, 94–5,
        97, 99, 104
Byrne, Martin, 3
Byrne, Mickey 'Rattler', 137
Byrne, Ned, 107–8, 110, 114, 118, 120, (*p*)
Byrne, Paul, 133, 137, 143
Byrne, Tom, 158, 160–64, 166–70

Campbell, Christy, 127–8, 133, 135
Cardiff, Nick, 95
Carey, Kieran, 91, 92, 133
    Tipperary v. Dublin 1961, 42, 43, 45,
        50, (*p*)
    Tipperary v. Wexford 1962, 58,
        60–64, 66, (*p*)
Carroll, Dick, 25, 27, 30, 32, 33–4
Carroll, Pat, 80, 84–5, 87
Carroll, Ted, 72, 80
Casey, Martin, 157, 160, 162–4, 166, 167,
    168
Casey, Paudie, 27, (*p*)
Casey, Sean, 89
Cashman, Mick, 8, 9, 11, 13
Cheasty, Tom, 21–3, 25, 27, 29, 31–2, 35,
    (*p*)
Clare, 69, 74, 92, 108, 127, 128, 131, 140,
    141, 174, 176
Clarke, Iggy, 177, 179, 180, 187, (*p*)
Clarke, Joe, 177, 179, 183, 186–8, (*p*)
Cleere, Liam, 27
Cleere, Seamus, 72, 78, 80, 82, 84, 86–7

Clifford, Johnny, 2, 4
Clohessy, Paddy, 141
Clohosey, Sean, 22–4, 26–8, 30–31, 34, 39
Coady, Joe, 27, (p)
Coakley, Fr Donal, 109, 110
Codd, Martin, 7, 9–12, 15, (p)
Coffey, Tom, 27
Coleman, Martin, 110, 178–80, 185, 188–9
Colfer, Ned, 54, 59, 60, 63, (p)
    Wexford v. Tipperary 1968, 95, 97,
        100, 102–3, (p)
Collins, Donal, 110
Collins, Paddy 'Fox', 9
Condon, Jackie, 25, 27, 29, 34, (p)
Conneely, Michael, 179–83, 186–7, 189, (p)
Connolly, John, 175–7, 179–81, 184,
    188–9, (p)
Connolly, Liam, 60, 65, (p)
Connolly, Michael, 179, 184, 186–7
Connolly, Ned, 80
Connolly, Tony, 74, 77–8, 80, 84, (p)
Conroy, Sean, 179
Coogan, Martin, 72, 78, 80, 82, 85–7, 110,
    121, 124, (p)
Cooke, Senan, 110
Coone, Gerry, 178–9, 180, 182, 185,
    188, (p)
Cork, 20, 24, 38, 41, 55, 92, 93, 105, 127,
    128, 131, 140, 141, 152, 155
    v. Galway 1975, 172–91
    v. Kilkenny 1966, 69–89
    v. Kilkenny 1972, 106–25
    v. Wexford 1956, 1–17
Costigan, John, 93, 95, 101
Coughlan, Dan, 80
Coughlan, Denis, 110, 113, 117, 123, 176,
    190
Coughlan, Eudie, 79, 110
Crampton, Jimmy, 140, 142, 143, 148
Cregan, Eamonn, 74, 78, 127–8
    Limerick v. Tipperary 1971–3, 133–5,
        137–40, 143, 146–8
Cregan, Mick, 133, 141, 143
Croke, Paddy, 38, 40, 44, 46, (p)
Cronin, John 'Kid', 179
Cronin, Pat, 74
Crotty, Mick
    Kilkenny v. Cork 1972, 107–8, 110,
        115–16, 120, (p)

Kilkenny v. Wexford 1974, 156, 160,
    162–3, 167–8
Crowley, Johnny, 190
Crowley, Paddy, 110
Cuddihy, Dr Kieran, 27, 80, 110, 160, (p)
Cummins, Frank, 175
    Kilkenny v. Cork 1972, 109–10, 113,
        123–4, (p)
    Kilkenny v. Wexford 1974, 156, 160,
        164
Cummins, Ray
    Galway v. Cork 1975, 176–7, 179,
        183–6, 188
    Kilkenny v. Cork 1972, 107–8,
        110–11, 116–19, 121–2, 124
Cunningham, Sean, 143
Cunningham, Tom, 27, 31, (p)

Dalton, Terry, 27
Daly, Jackie, 8, 9
Daly, Dr Pat, 9, 60
Daly, Willie John, 3, 7, 9–12, 14
de Valera, Eamon, 81, 116
Delahunty, Pat, 80
Delaney, Paddy
    Kilkenny v. Wexford 1974, 156–7,
        160–61, 163–4, 168, 170
Delaney, Pat, 175, 190
    Kilkenny v. Cork 1972, 105, 107, 110,
        113–14, 118–20, 122–5, (p)
Devaney, Liam
    Tipperary v. Dublin 1961, 42, 45–7,
        50–51
    Tipperary v. Wexford 1962, 53–4, 57,
        60, 63–4, 66, (p)
    Wexford v. Tipperary 1968, 92, 94–5,
        97–9, 100, 102–3
Dillon, Pa, 77, 80, 83, 85, 110–11, 116,
    118–19, 121–2, (p)
Dixon, Tom, 2, 7, 9, 11, 13, 15, (p)
Donohoe, Tom, 95
Doolan, Peter, 75, 77, 80, 83, 84, 86–7, (p)
Doran, Colm, 157, 160, 162, 167, 169
Doran, Tony
    Kilkenny v. Wexford 1974, 158, 160,
        162, 166–8, 170, (p)
    Wexford v. Tipperary 1968, 93–5,
        97–8, 101–4
Dowling, John, 60, 62, 67, 95, 96, 103, 105

Dowling, Mossie, 142, 143, 145
Dowling, Pat, 7, 9, 11, 15
Down, 129
Downey, Paddy, 67
Doyle, Gerry, 45, 60, 95, 133, 143
Doyle, Harry, 60
Doyle, Jimmy, 45, 47–9, 51, 93, 100, 143
    Limerick v. Tipperary 1971, 130,
      133–5
    Tipperary v. Wexford 1962, 53–5,
      59–62, 64–7, (p)
    Wexford v. Tipperary 1968, 92, 94–9,
      100, 103
Doyle, John, 91
    Tipperary v. Dublin 1961, 40–43,
      45–6, 49–50
    Tipperary v. Wexford 1962, 53, 58,
      60, 63, 65, (p)
Doyle, Fr John, 160
Drumgoole, Noel, 39, 44, 47, 48, 51, (p)
Dublin, 20, 24, 93
    v. Tipperary 1961, 37–52
Dunne, Claus, 76, 80, 83, 86, 88
Dunphy, Dick, 80
Dunphy, Joe, 76–7, 80, 84, 86
Dunworth, Andy, 143
Dwyer, Billy, 22–3, 26–7, 29–30, 32–3
Dwyer, Philly, 45, 60

English, Jim, 2, 7, 9, 11, 12, 16, 59–61,
    65, (p)
English, Joe, 60
English, Theo, 91, 133
    Tipperary v. Dublin 1961, 42, 45, 47
    Tipperary v. Wexford 1962, 53, 57,
      60, 62, (p)
Enright, Leonard, 133
Esmonde, Billy, 9
Esmonde, Martin, 143

Fahy, Frank, 179
Fahy, Padraig, 178–81, 183–4, 186, 188, (p)
Fahy, Tom, 179
Fanning, Pat, 27
Fenton, John, 179
Ferguson, Dessie 'Snitchie', 39, 44, 46–7,
    50, (p)
Ferguson, Liam, 39–40, 44, 48–9, (p)
Fitzgerald, Gerry, 27, 28, 44, 51

Fitzgerald, Paddy, 74–5, 78, 80, 83, 86,
    179, (p)
Fitzmaurice, Paudie, 143
Fitzpatrick, Billy, 160, 169
Fitzpatrick, Martin, 160
Flaherty, M.J. 'Inky', 172, 174, 179, 180,
    184, 189
Flanagan, John, 92
    Limerick v. Tipperary 1971–3, 130, 133,
      135, 137, 139, 143, 145, 148–9
Flannelly, Mick, 21, 27, 34, 35, (p)
Fleming, Mick, 25, 27, 30, 34
Flood, Tim, 7, 9–13, 15, 39, (p)
    Tipperary v. Wexford 1962, 53, 58,
      60, 63, 65, 66, (p)
Flynn, Austin, 23, 26, 27, 29, 30, 36, (p)
Flynn, Donal, 133, 134, 138
Fogarty, Jim, 142, 143, 146
Foley, Artie, 1, 2, 8, 9, 11, 13–15, 158, (p)
Foley, Des, 39, 40, 44, 46–9, 51, (p)
Foley, Lar, 39, 44–5, 47, 50, (p)
Foley, Sean, 127–9, 133–4, 143, 145–6, 148
Fouhy, Matt, 7, 9, 11, 14
Fripps, Mick, 80
Furlong, Jack, 27
Furlong, Jim, 95, 160

Gallagher, Josie, 172
Galway, 4, 23, 28, 69, 108, 170
    v. Cork 1975, 172–91
Gavin, Ignatius, 60
Gaynor, Len, 92, 94–5, 97, 104, 133, 136,
    138, 143
Gleeson, John, 93, 95, 102, 133, 143
Goode, Declan, 27
Gough, Oliver, 8, 9
Goulding, Eamon, 7, 9, 11, 13–15
Grace, Paddy, 40
Graham, Mick, 130, 133, 134, 143
Gray, Jimmy, 37–9, 40, 44, 45, 50–52, (p)
Grealish, Seamus, 179
Grimes, Eamonn, 127–8, 133, 138, 143–6
Grimes, Paul, 28, 32
Grimes, Phil, 21, 23, 25, 27, (p)
Guinan, Larry, 22, 25, 27–8, 30, 33–4, (p)

Hanlon, Mick, 8, 9, 95
Hanniffy, Michael, 179
Harney, Joe, 23, 26–7, 35–6, (p)

Harte, Billy, 156, 160, 163, 169
Hartigan, Bernie, 128, 133–5, 143–4, 146–8
Hartigan, Christy, 60, (p)
Hartigan, Pat, 127–8, 133, 138, 143–5, 148
Hartnett, Josie, 6–7, 9, 10, 12, 13
Hassett, Matt, 42, 45, 48, 50, 60, (p)
Hatton, Jimmy, 80, 88
Haydon, Pat 'Diamond', 153
Hayes, Christy, 40, 44, 48–9, (p)
Healy, Sgt Denis, 9
Healy, Pat, 8, 9
Hearne, Seamus, 7, 9, 10, 11, 15, (p)
Heaslip, Denis, 22, 25, 27, 29, 30, 34, 59
Heath, Edward, 116
Hegarty, Pat, 108–10, 112–13, 118, 190
    Galway v. Cork 1975, 176–7, 179, 182,
        184, 187
Henderson, Ger, 156, 160, 162
Henderson, Pat, 175, 190
    Cork v. Kilkenny 1966, 76, 80, 82, 88
    Kilkenny v. Cork 1972, 107, 110, 112,
        116–21, 123–4, (p)
    Kilkenny v. Wexford 1974, 156, 160,
        162–3, 165, 168
Hennessy, Jim, 27
Hennessy, Jimmy, 95, 133, 143
Hickey, Dan, 133
Hickey, John D., 67
Hickey, Mick, 20
Hogan, Jim, 133, 135, 136, 143, 144
Hogan, Seamus, 133, 134, 143, 146, 148
Hogan, Tom, 27
Horgan, John, 179, 185
Horgan, Seamus, 140, 142, 143, 145, 148
Hough, John, 45, 49
Hurley, Denis, 80

Jackson, Billy, 40, 44, 46, 48, 50, (p)
Jacob, Christy, 93, 95, 97, 99, 101
Jacob, Mick, 95
    Kilkenny v. Wexford 1974, 156–7,
        160–61, 163–7
Jones, Michael, 133

Keane, John, 20, 21, 23, 27, 31
Keating, Michael 'Babs', 129–30, 132–7
    Limerick v. Tipperary 1973, 142–5,
        147–8
    Wexford v. Tipperary 1968, 90, 92,
        94–9, 101–2, 104, 105, (p)

Keher, Eddie, 27, 36, 155, 175, 178, 190
    Cork v. Kilkenny 1966, 70, 73, 78, 80,
        82–8
    Kilkenny v. Cork 1972, 107, 109–10,
        114, 117–25, (p)
    Kilkenny v. Wexford 1974, 151, 157,
        160–61, 163–4, 167, 169–70
Kehoe, Jim, 160
Kehoe, Paddy, 8, 9, 160
Kehoe, Padge, 7, 9, 10–11, 15, 39, (p)
    Tipperary v. Wexford 1962, 53, 57,
        60–65, 66, (p)
    Wexford v. Tipperary 1968, 93, 95,
        99–100
Kelly, Dermot, 127
Kelly, Eddie, 95, 96–7, 100, 102, (p)
Kelly, John, 133, 143, 145
Kelly, Mickey, 23, 27
Kelly, Paddy, 25, 27, 31–3
Kelly, Terry, 7, 9, 11–13
Kelly, Timmie, 27, 31
Kennedy, Dan, 80
Kennedy, John, 60
Kennedy, Martin, 45, 60, 95
Kennedy, Mick, 141, (p)
Kenny, Brian, 95
Kenny, Mick, 23
Kenny, Paddy, 60
Kenny, P.J., 95
Keogh, Christy, 158, 160, 163, 164, 165
Keogh, Jim, 143
Kiely, John, 23, 24, 27, 29, 30, 31, (p)
Kildare, 131
Kilkenny, 3, 5, 17, 39, 55, 91–3, 105, 131,
        140, 150, 172–3, 175, 178, 189–91
    v. Cork 1966, 69–89
    v. Cork 1972, 106–25
    v. Waterford 1959, 18–36
    v. Wexford 1974, 151–71
Kinane, Archbishop Jeremiah, 10
King, Liam, 133, 135
Kinsella, John, 107, 110, 115, 116, 119, (p)
Kinsella, Mick, 95
Kinsella, Rory, 160, 168
Kinsella, Sean, 158, 160, 167, 168

Lacey, Mick, 25, 27, (p)
Lally, Pat, 177, 179, 186, 187, (p)
Lalor, Pat, 110, 112–13, 118, 123, 156,
        160, 165–7, (p)

Lane, Noel, 133, 134, 135
Lanigan, Jim, 133
Lanigan, Mick, 109, 110, 160
Laois, 56
Larkin, Fan, 109–11, 117–19, 121, 156, (p)
   Kilkenny v. Wexford 1974, 160, 162,
      166, 168, (p)
Lawlor, David, 160
Leahy, Mick, 44
Leahy, Nick 'Chew', 80
Leahy, Paddy, 41, 45, 56, 60, 173
Leahy, Sean 'Georgie', 160
Leahy, Terry, 81
Lemass, Sean, 81
Lenihan, Joe, 44, (p)
Limerick, 4, 5, 20, 56, 69, 74, 91, 108, 170,
   176, 191
   v. Tipperary 1971, 126–39
   v. Tipperary 1973, 140–50
Looney, Seamus, 110, 113, 118, 119, 123
Loughnane, Francis
   Limerick v. Tipperary 1971–3, 133,
      136–7, 143–6, 148
   Wexford v. Tipperary 1968, 95, 103–5
Lowry, Phil, 95
Lucey, Sean, 179
Lynch, Jack, 116
Lynch, Jim, 77, 80, 81, 86
Lynch, Paul, 58, 60, 62, 66, (p)
   Wexford v. Tipperary 1968, 93–7,
      100–101, 103–4
Lynch, Shay, 40, 44, 45, 49, (p)
Lyng, Martin, 56, 60, 61, 63, 65, (p)
Lyons, Eddie, 95
Lyons, John, 2, 6, 9, 11

McCarthy, Charlie, 74, 78, 80, 82, 85,
   86, (p)
   Galway v. Cork 1975, 176, 177, 179,
      181, 183, 186–7
   Kilkenny v. Cork 1972, 107–8,
      110–11, 118–20, 124, (p)
McCarthy, Gerald
   Cork v. Kilkenny 1966, 70, 74–6, 78,
      80–82, 84–7, 89, (p)
   Galway v. Cork 1975, 176–80, 184–5,
      188, (p)
   Kilkenny v. Cork 1972, 108, 110, 112,
      118, 121, 125

McCarthy, Justin, 178, 179
   Cork v. Kilkenny 1966, 74, 78, 80,
      82–3, 88, (p)
   Kilkenny v. Cork 1972, 108, 110, 113,
      116–17, 119
McDonagh, Joe, 174, 177–80, 187, (p)
McDonald, Wattie, 80
McDonnell, Pat, 110, 114, 118, 125,
   178–81, 189
McGovern, Johnny, 25, 27, 31, 39
McGrath, Joe, 129, 133, 140–41
McGrath, Nicky, 78, 80
McGrath, Oliver 'Hopper', 58, 60–62,
   66, (p)
McInerney, Dr Mary, 179
McInerney, Niall, 177, 179–80, 182–4,
   187, (p)
McKenna, John 'Mackey', 95, 96–7, 102
   Tipperary v. Dublin 1961, 43, 45, 49
   Tipperary v. Wexford 1962, 57, 60,
      61, 65–6, (p)
Mackey, Mick, 126, 127, 135
McLoughlin, John, 60
McLoughlin, Sean, 45, 50
   Tipperary v. Wexford 1962, 55, 59,
      63–4, 67, (p)
   Wexford v. Tipperary 1968, 94–8,
      102–4, (p)
McNamara, Dick, 160
Maher, Jimmy, 142
Maher, John, 24, 27, 28, 29
Maher, Michael, 92
   Tipperary v. Dublin 1961, 42, 45,
      50
   Tipperary v. Wexford 1962, 53–4,
      58, 60–63, 65–6, (p)
Maher, Fr Tommy, 27, 78, 80, 109, 110,
   121, 160
Maher, Tony, 108, 110, 114, 117, 119–22,
   178–80, 184, 190
Malone, Eamonn, 44, 50, (p)
Malone, Mick, 110, 112, 119, 121
Meagher, Lory, 40, 79, 110
Meyler, Paddy, 60
Mitchell, John, 60
Molloy, P.J., 178, 179, 180, 182, 183,
   188, (p)
Moloney, Dr Paddy, 45, 60, 133, 143
Moloughney, Billy, 43, 45

Moloughney, Tom
    Tipperary v. Dublin 1961, 43, 45–6,
        48, 51
    Tipperary v. Wexford 1962, 54–5, 58,
        60, (*p*)
Moore, Willie, 130, 133, 138, 143–5, 148
Moran, Paddy, 76, 78, 80, 83, 87, 110
Morris, Brendan, 60
Morrissey, Eamon, 107, 110, 112, 118,
    121, 123, (*p*)
Morrissey, Jim, 7, 9, 12, (*p*)
Morrissey, Martin Og, 23, 25, 27, 29, 33,
    34, (*p*)
Morrissey, Mick, 7, 9, 11–12, (*p*)
Morrissey, Ted, 8, 9
Mounsey, Roger, 45, 60, (*p*)
Moylan, Christy, 20
Moylan, Pat, 176, 190
Mullins, Vincent, 179
Murphy, Billy 'Long Puck', 80
Murphy, Brian, 110, 114–15, 118,
    125, (*p*)
    Galway v. Cork 1975, 176, 178, 179,
        184–5
Murphy, Denis, 77, 80, 84, (*p*)
Murphy, Dinny Barry, 9
Murphy, Enda, 157, 160, 161, 164, 169
Murphy, Frank, 110, 133, 139
Murphy, Gerry, 8, 9
Murphy, Jim, 160
Murphy, Jimmy Barry, 174
    Galway v. Cork 1975, 176, 177, 179,
        181–3, 187, (*p*)
Murphy, Johnny, 160
Murphy, Michael, 60, 179, (*p*)
Murphy, Mossie, 120, 125
Murphy, Mossy, 110
Murphy, Sean, 176, 179, 181–2, 184,
    187, (*p*)
Murphy, Sean Og, 9
Murphy, Tadhg, 140, 142, 143, 149
Murphy, Ted, 179
Murphy, Tommy, 80, 85, 86
Murphy, Wattie, 110
Murphy, Willie, 93, 95, 97, 101–4, 157,
    160, 163, 167

Nealon, Donie, 130, 132–3, 135–6, 143,
    145, 147–9

    Tipperary v. Dublin 1961, 42–3, 45–8,
        50–52
    Tipperary v. Wexford 1962, 53–4,
        59–63, 64, 66, (*p*)
    Wexford v. Tipperary 1968, 90, 92,
        94–6, 98–9, 102, 103
Neville, Tom, 59–61, 63, (*p*)
    Wexford v. Tipperary 1968, 95, 96,
        98–9, 100, 102
Nolan, Frankie, 133, 141–4, 146
Nolan, John, 54, 59–62, 64–5, 160, (*p*)
    Wexford v. Tipperary 1968, 95, 96,
        98, 100, 102, 104–5
Nolan, Pat, 8, 9, 95, 104
    Kilkenny v. Wexford 1974, 152, 158,
        160, 163–4, 168
    Tipperary v. Wexford 1962, 54–5,
        59–60, 63, 65–6, (*p*)
Nolan, Tom, 80
Norberg, Frank, 109–10, 115–16, 117,
    119–20

O'Brien, Donie
    Tipperary v. Dublin 1961, 41–2, 45,
        47, 50, (*p*)
    Tipperary v. Wexford 1962, 59–62,
        65–6, (*p*)
O'Brien, Freddie, 27, (*p*)
O'Brien, Jim, 130, 133–4, 139, 143, 148
O'Brien, Jimmy, 58, 60, 63–5, 95, 100,
    102–4, (*p*)
O'Brien, Liam 'Chunky'
    Kilkenny v. Cork 1972, 110, 113,
        115–17, 119–21, 123, (*p*)
    Kilkenny v. Wexford 1974, 156, 160,
        162–3, 167–8
O'Brien, Teddie, 110, 120, 178, 179, 184,
    190
O'Brien, Tony, 130, 133, 134, 136, 137
O'Connell, Tommy, 26–7, 29, 32–3, 35–6,
    80
O'Connor, Michael, 27, (*p*)
O'Connor, Tadhg, 133, 136, 143
O'Connor, Teddie, 95, 157, 160–61, 163,
    167, 169
O'Connor, Vincent, 143
O'Doherty, Martin, 178, 179, 182, 185
O'Donnell, Jim, 133, 137, 143, 144,
    146

O'Donnell, Nick, 39, 159
   Tipperary v. Wexford 1962, 53, 54–5,
      58, 60, 63, 65, (*p*)
   Wexford v. Cork 1956, 1, 2, 4, 7, 9, 12,
      15–16, (*p*)
O'Donoghue, Eamonn, 179, 187
O'Donoghue, John, 95, 99, 102, 103, 133
O'Donoghue, Liam, 140, 142, 143
O'Donoghue, Tom, 77, 80, 83, 85, (*p*)
O'Driscoll, Christy, 44
O'Dwyer, Jack, 143
O'Dwyer, Noel, 130, 133–4, 137, 143,
   145, 147–8
Offaly, 24, 69, 76, 174
O'Gara, Matt
   Tipperary v. Dublin 1961, 42, 45–8, 49
   Tipperary v. Wexford 1962, 54, 58,
      60, 65, (*p*)
O'Gorman, Noel, 95, 101
O'Halloran, John, 78, 80, 84, 87, (*p*)
O'Hehir, Michael, 10, 81
O'Leary, Ger, 80, (*p*)
O'Leary, Pat, 110, 117, 118
O'Leary, Sean, 107, 110, 111, 121, 122, (*p*)
   Galway v. Cork 1975, 176–7, 179–81,
      182, 184–5, 187–8
O'Mahony, Dan, 110, 179
O'Mahony, Teddy, 80
O'Neill, Finbarr, 80, (*p*)
O'Neill, Mick, 160
O'Regan, Jim, 77, 80, 87, 108–9, 110
O'Regan, Mick, 7, 9, 11–13
O Riain, Seamus, 105
O'Riordan, Denis, 75, 77
Orr, Nicky, 110, 156, 160, 162, 164,
   166–9, (*p*)
O'Shaughnessy, Tony, 7, 9–13, 80
O'Shea, Christy, 7, 9, 12, 13
O'Sullivan, Frank, 179
O'Sullivan, Gerry, 80, 83, 84, 86, (*p*)
O'Sullivan, Jerry, 75, 77
O'Sullivan, Paddy Joe, 27
O'Sullivan, Peter, 133, 135
O'Sullivan, Tom, 8, 9

Phelan, Paddy, 72
Philpott, Paddy, 7, 9, 10, 11, 14
Power, Jackie, 42, 126, 129, 133, 141, 143,
   145

Power, Ned, 24, 27, 29, 33, 91, 93, (*p*)
Power, Seamus, 19–21, 25, 27, 29–30,
   33–5, (*p*)
Prendergast, Jimmy, 160, 167
Prenderville, Eddie, 133
Purcell, Kieran, 155, 175, 190
   Kilkenny v. Cork 1972, 107–8, 110,
      114, 118, 120, 122, 125, (*p*)
   Kilkenny v. Wexford 1974, 156–7,
      160–61, 163–4, 167–8
Purcell, Nicky, 27, 80

Quaid, Jim, 143
Qualter, P.J., 174–5, 178–81, 183, 185,
   188–9, (*p*)
Quigley, Dan, 76, 93, 95, 97–8, 100,
   102–5, 104, (*p*)
Quigley, Jim, 160
Quigley, John, 95, 100–102, 104, 190
   Kilkenny v. Wexford 1974, 158, 160,
      162–5, 167–9
Quigley, Martin, 157, 160, 162–4

Rackard, Billy, 6, 9, 10, 12–14, 39, 153, (*p*)
   Tipperary v. Wexford 1962, 53, 57,
      60–61, 63, 65–6, (*p*)
Rackard, Bobby
   Wexford v. Cork 1956, 4–7, 9, 12, 14,
      15, (*p*)
Rackard, Nick, 55, 56, 60, 95, 99, 153
   Wexford v. Cork 1956, 2, 3, 6, 9, 11,
      13–15, 17, (*p*)
Randall, John, 14
Rea, Ned, 141, 143–5, 147, 149
Ring, Christy, 70–71, 75, 127
   Wexford v. Cork 1956, 1, 2, 4–6, 7, 9,
      12–17, (*p*)
Robinson, Pat, 179
Roche, Con, 80, 106, 108, 110, 115, 119,
   122–5, 190
   Galway v. Cork 1975, 176, 178–80,
      182–7, 189
Roche, Mick
   Limerick v. Tipperary 1971–3,
      129–30, 132–4, 136, 142–6
   Wexford v. Tipperary 1968, 90–92,
      94–5, 97–8, 100–101, 105
Roland, Patsy, 95
Rothwell, John, 110

Ryan, Dinny, 133, 134, 137, 143, 148
Ryan, Jack, 133, 143, 148
Ryan, Jimmy, 93, 95, 98, 102
Ryan, J.P., 133
Ryan, Paddy 'Sweeper', 95
Ryan, Pat, 45
Ryan, P.J., 95–8, 104, 160
  Limerick v. Tipperary 1971–3, 133–5,
    137, 143–5
Ryan, Roger, 133, 135, 141, 143, 145
Ryan, Sean, 45, 60, 133, 143
Ryan, Timmie, 141
Ryan, Tom (Ballybrown), 143, 146
Ryan, Tom (Killenaule), 66, (p)
Ryan, Tom (Toomevara), 45, 49–50,
    59–61, 65, (p)
Ryan, Tom (Wexford), 2, 7, 9, 11, 13,
    14, (p)

Salmon, Joe, 172
Scanlon, Paddy, 141
Scannell, Andy, 9
Shanahan, Con, 133
Shannon, Larry, 40, 44, 46, 48, 49, 50,
    51, (p)
Shaughnessy, Kevin, 179
Sheehan, Colm, 78, 80, 84, 86, 87, (p)
Sheehan, Donal, 80, (p)
Sheehan, Kevin, 5, 9
Sheehan, Sean, 86
Shelley, Dr Milo, 27
Shinnors, Seamus, 95, 143
Silke, Sean, 174, 177, 179, 182, 185–7, (p)
Skehan, Noel, 155–6
  Kilkenny v. Cork 1972, 108, 110,
    115–16, 118–19, 121–2, 125, (p)
  Kilkenny v. Wexford 1974, 160,
    162–3, 166, 168
Skehan, Paul, 160
Slattery, Mick, 143, 149
Slevin, Ronnie, 60, (p)
Smyth, Fred, 179
Spain, Mick, 110, 116, 125, 160, 165, 179,
    182, 187, 189
Staples, Vincie, 93, 95, 97, 103
  Kilkenny v. Wexford 1974, 157, 160,
    162, 167
Stapleton, Jim, 45, 60
Stapleton, Matt, 95

Stokes, Dr Dick, 141, 143
Sutton, John, 27, 34

Teehan, John, 76, 78, 80, 82, 83, 86
Teehan, Tony, 160
Thorpe, Wilkie, 3
Tipperary, 3–5, 16, 20, 23, 28, 69, 71–2,
    73, 74, 107–8, 114, 152–3, 173, 175,
    189
  v. Dublin 1961, 37–52
  v. Limerick 1971, 126–39
  v. Limerick 1973, 140–50
  v. Wexford 1962, 53–68
  v. Wexford 1968, 90–105
Tobin, John, 160
Treacy, Jim, 155–6
  Cork v. Kilkenny 1966, 76, 80, 82, 86
  Kilkenny v. Cork 1972, 110–11,
    117–19, 124, (p)
  Kilkenny v. Wexford 1974, 160,
    162–3, 166–7, 170, (p)
Treacy, Martin, 27
Troy, Fr Bertie, 110, 179
Twomey, Vincent, 2, 8, 9, 12

Wall, Tony, 91
  Tipperary v. Dublin 1961, 42–3, 45–6,
    49–50
  Tipperary v. Wexford 1962, 57, 60,
    62–5, 67, (p)
Walsh, Frankie, 21–2, 24, 27–9, 30–31,
    33–4, (p)
Walsh, John 'Link', 27, 29, 35
Walsh, Mick, 25, 27, 31, 33
Walsh, Ollie, 19, 23–4, 27–32, 35, 108,
    110, 115, 118, (p)
  Cork v. Kilkenny 1966, 72, 80, 82–3,
    86–7
Walsh, Tom, 24, 27, 29, 31, 72–3, 76–7,
    80, 82, 84–6, 88, (p)
Walsh, Willie, 8, 9, 177, 179, 182, 184,
    187, 190
Walton, Sim, 79
Ware, Charlie, 23, 24, 27, 29, 31, (p)
Ware, Jim, 27
Waterford, 16, 56, 69, 71, 127, 176
  v. Kilkenny 1959, 18–36
Waters, Mick, 78, 80, 83, (p)
Westmeath, 176

Wexford, 24, 39, 41, 107, 108, 111–13,
    115, 127, 131, 141, 174, 188, 190
  v. Cork 1956, 1–17
  v. Kilkenny 1974, 151–71
  v. Tipperary 1962, 53–68
  v. Tipperary 1968, 90–105
Wheeler, Ned, 3–4, 6, 7, 9–14, 39, (*p*)
  Tipperary v. Wexford 1962, 53, 54,
    58, 60–67, (*p*)

Whelan, Donal, 24, 27, 29, (*p*)
Whelan, Fran, 40, 44, 47–9, (*p*)
Whelan, Seamus 'Shanks', 95, 97, 100
Williams, Paddy, 143
Wilson, Phil, 56, 60–61, 64, 93–8, 101–4,
    156, (*p*)
  Kilkenny v. Wexford 1974, 158–61,
    164–6
Wolstenholme, Kenneth, 26